Total Quality

Total Quality

A User's Guide for Implementation

Dan Ciampa
President and
Chief Executive Officer
Rath & Strong, Inc.

ADDISON-WESLEY PUBLISHING COMPANY
Reading, Massachusetts • Menlo Park, California • New York
Don Mills, Ontario • Wokingham, England • Amsterdam • Bonn
Sydney • Singapore • Tokyo • Madrid • San Juan • Milan • Paris

Library of Congress Cataloging-in-Publication Data

Ciampa, Dan.
    Total quality—a user's guide for implementation / Dan Ciampa.
        p.   cm.
    Includes bibliographical references.
    ISBN 0-201-54992-1
    1. Production management—Quality control.   2. Quality Control.
I. Title.
TS156.C56   1991   91-16302
658.5'62—dc20   CIP

This book is in the Addison-Wesley Series on Organization Development.
Editors: Edgar H. Schein, Richard Beckhard

ISBN 0-201-54992-1
1 2 3 4 5 6 7 8 9 10 BA 959439291

Dedication

This book is for Devon, the right balance of innocence, determination, joie de vivre, *and charm. She will, no doubt, have her own definition of Total Quality as she develops her own future.*

Other Titles in the Organization Development Series

Parallel Learning Structures: Increasing Innovation in Bureaucracies

Gervase R. Bushe and A.B. Shani

1991 (52427)

Parallel learning structures are technostructural interventions that promote system-wide change in bureaucracies while retaining the advantages of bureaucratic design. This text serves as a resource of models and theories built around five cases of parallel learning structures that can help those who create and maintain them be more effective and successful. For those new to parallel learning structures, the text provides practical advice as to when and how to use them.

Managing in the New Team Environment: Skills, Tools, and Methods

Larry Hirschhorn

1991 (52503)

This text is designed to help manage the tensions and complexities that arise for managers seeking to guide employees in a team environment. Based on an interactive video course developed at IBM, the text takes managers step by step through the process of building a team and authorizing it to act while they learn to step back and delegate. Specific issues addressed are how to give a team structure, how to facilitate its basic processes, and how to acknowledge differences in relationships among team members and between the manager and individual team members.

Leading Business Teams: How Teams Can Use Technology and Group Process Tools to Enhance Performance

Robert Johansen, David Sibbett, Suzyn Benson, Alexia Martin, Robert Mittman, and Paul Saffo

1991 (52829)

What technology or tools should organization development people or team leaders have at their command, now and in the future? This text explores the intersection of technology and business teams, a new and largely uncharted area that goes by several labels, including "groupware," a term that encompasses both electronic and nonelectronic tools for teams. This is the first book of its kind from the field describing what works for business teams and what does not.

The Conflict-Positive Organization: Stimulate Diversity and Create Unity

Dean Tjosvold

1991 (51485)

This book describes how managers and employees can use conflict to find common ground, solve problems, and strengthen morale and relationships. By showing how well-managed conflict invigorates and empowers teams and organizations, the text demonstrates how conflict is vital for a company's continuous improvement and increased competitive advantage.

Change by Design

Robert R. Blake, Jane Srygley Mouton, and Anne Adams McCanse

1989 (50748)

This book develops a systematic approach to organization development and provides readers with rich illustrations of coherent planned change. The book involves testing, examining, revising, and strengthening conceptual foundations in order to create sharper corporate focus and increased predictability of successful organization development.

Organization Development in Health Care

R. Wayne Boss

1989 (18364)

This is the first book to discuss the intricacies of the health care industry. The book explains the impact of OD in creating healthy and viable organizations in the health care sector. Through unique and innovative techniques, hospitals are able to reduce nursing turnover, thereby resolving the nursing shortage problem. The text also addresses how OD can improve such bottom-line variables as cash flow and net profits.

Self-Designing Organizations: Learning How to Create High Performance

Susan Albers Mohrman and Thomas G. Cummings

1989 (14603)

This book looks beyond traditional approaches to organizational transition, offering a strategy for developing organizations that enables them to learn not only how to adjust to the dynamic environment in which they exist, but also how to achieve a higher level of performance. This strategy assumes that change is a learning process: the goal is continually refined as organizational members learn how to function more effectively and respond to dynamic conditions in their environment.

Power and Organization Development: Mobilizing Power to Implement Change
Larry E. Greiner and Virginia E. Schein

1988 (12185)

This book forges an important collaborative approach between two opposing and often contradictory approaches to management: OD practitioners who espouse a "more humane" workplace without understanding the political realities of getting things done, and practicing managers who feel comfortable with power but overlook the role of human potential in contributing to positive results.

Designing Organizations for High Performance
David P. Hanna

1988 (12693)

This book is the first to give insight into the actual processes you can use to translate organizational concepts into bottom-line improvements. Hanna's "how-to" approach shows not only the successful methods of intervention, but also the plans behind them and the corresponding results.

Process Consultation, Volume 1: Its Role in Organization Development, Second Edition
Edgar H. Schein

1988 (06736)

How can a situation be influenced in the workplace without the direct use of power or formal authority? This book presents the core theoretical foundations and basic prescriptions for effective management.

Organizational Transitions: Managing Complex Change, Second Edition
Richard Beckhard and Reuben T. Harris

1987 (10887)

This book discusses the choices involved in developing a management system appropriate to the "transition state." It also discusses commitment to change, organizational culture, and increasing and maintaining productivity, creativity, and innovation.

Organization Development: A Normative View
W. Warner Burke

1987 (10697)

This book concisely describes and defines the theories and practices of organization development and also looks at organization development as change in an organization's culture. It is a useful guide to the field of organization development and is invaluable to managers, executives, practitioners, and anyone desiring an excellent overview of this multi-faceted field.

Team Building: Issues and Alternatives, Second Edition

William G. Dyer

1987 (18037)

Through the use of the techniques and procedures described in this book, managers and consultants can effectively prepare, apply, and follow up on the human processes affecting the productive functioning of teams.

The Technology Connection: Strategy and Change in the Information Age

Marc S. Gerstein

1987 (12188)

This is a book that guides managers and consultants through crucial decisions about the use of technology for increasing effectiveness and competitive advantage. It provides a useful way to think about the relationship between information technology, business strategy, and the process of change in organizations.

Stream Analysis: A Powerful Way to Diagnose and Manage Organizational Change

Jerry I. Porras

1987 (05693)

Drawing on a conceptual framework that helps the reader to better understand organizations, this book shows how to diagnose failings in organizational functioning and how to plan a comprehensive set of actions needed to change the organization into a more effective system.

Process Consultation, Volume II: Lessons for Managers and Consultants

Edgar H. Schein

1987 (06744)

This book shows the viability of the process consultation model for working with human systems. Like Schein's first volume on process consultation, the second volume focuses on the moment-to-moment behavior of the manager or consultant rather than on the design of the OD program.

Managing Conflict: Interpersonal Dialogue and Third-Party Roles, Second Edition

Richard E. Walton

1987 (08859)

This book shows how to implement a dialogue approach to conflict management. It presents a framework for diagnosing recurring conflicts and suggests several basic options for controlling or resolving them.

Pay and Organization Development

Edward E. Lawler

1981 (03990)

This book examines the important role that reward systems play in organization development efforts. By combining examples and specific recommendations with conceptual material, it organizes the various topics and puts them into a total systems perspective. Specific pay approaches such as gainsharing, skill-based pay, and flexible benefits are discussed and their impact on productivity and the quality of work life is analyzed.

Work Redesign

J. Richard Hackman and Greg R. Oldham

1980 (02779)

This book is a comprehensive, clearly written study of work design as a strategy for personal and organizational change. Linking theory and practical technologies, it develops traditional and alternative approaches to work design that can benefit both individuals and organizations.

Organizational Dynamics: Diagnosis and Intervention

John P. Kotter

1978 (03890)

This book offers managers and OD specialists a powerful method of diagnosing organizational problems and of deciding when, where, and how to use (or not use) the diverse and growing number of organizational improvement tools that are available today. Comprehensive and fully integrated, the book includes many different concepts, research findings, and competing philosophies and provides specific examples of how to use the information to improve organizational functioning.

Career Dynamics: Matching Individual and Organizational Needs

Edgar H. Schein

1978 (06834)

This book studies the complexities of career development from both an individual and an organizational perspective. Changing needs throughout the adult life cycle, interaction of work and family, and integration of individual and organizational goals through human resource planning and development are all thoroughly explored.

Matrix

Stanley M. Davis and Paul Lawrence

1977 (01115)

This book defines and describes the matrix organization, a significant departure from the traditional "one man-one boss" management system. The author notes that the tension between the need for independence (fostering innovation) and order (fostering efficiency) drives organizations to consider a matrix system. Among the issues addressed are reasons for using a matrix, methods for establishing one, the impact of the system on individuals, its hazards, and what types of organizations can use a matrix system.

Feedback and Organization Development: Using Data-Based Methods

David A. Nadler

1977 (05006)

This book addresses the use of data as a tool for organizational change. It attempts to bring together some of what is known from experience and research and to translate that knowledge into useful insights for those who are thinking about using data-based methods in organizations. The broad approach of the text is to treat a whole range of questions and issues considering the various uses of data as an organizational change tool.

Designing Complex Organizations

Jay Galbraith

1973 (02559)

This book attempts to present an analytical framework of the design of organizations, particularly of types of organizations that apply lateral decision processes or matrix forms. These forms have become pervasive in all types of organizations, yet there is little systematic public knowledge about them. This book helps fill this gap.

Organization Development: Strategies and Models

Richard Beckhard

1969 (00448)

This book is written for managers, specialists, and students of management who are concerned with the planning of organization development programs to resolve the dilemmas brought about by a rapidly changing environment. Practiced teams of interdependent people must spend real time improving their methods of working, decision making, and communicating, and a planned, managed change is the first step toward effecting and maintaining these improvements.

Organization Development: Its Nature, Origins, and Prospects
Warren G. Bennis
1969 (00523)

This primer on OD is written with an eye toward the people in organizations who are interested in learning more about this educational strategy as well as for those practitioners and students of OD who may want a basic statement both to learn from and to argue with. The author treats the subject with a minimum of academic jargon and a maximum of concrete examples drawn from his own and others' experience.

Developing Organizations: Diagnosis and Action
Paul R. Lawrence and Jay W. Lorsch
1969 (04204)

This book is a personal statement of the authors' evolving experience, through research and consulting, in the work of developing organizations. The text presents the authors' overview of organization development, then proceeds to examine issues at each of three critical interfaces: the organization-environment interface, the group-group interface, and the individual-organization interface, including brief examples of work on each. The text concludes by pulling the themes together in a set of conclusions about organizational development issues as they present themselves to practicing managers.

About the Author

Dan Ciampa is President and Chief Executive Officer of Rath & Strong, Inc., a management consulting firm in Lexington, Massachusetts. He has consulted in the people-side of problem solving and in making companywide improvement work effectively and has helped leaders better manage organization cultures, implement new business strategies, and introduce new technology. His projects have improved production flexibility, product quality and customer service, information systems, and new product introduction, as well as the organization climate and teamwork.

Foreword

The Addison-Wesley Series on Organization Development originated in the late 1960s when a number of us recognized that the rapidly growing field of "OD" was not well understood or well defined. We also recognized that there was no one OD philosophy, and hence one could not at that time write a textbook on the theory and practice of OD, but one could make clear what various practitioners were doing under that label. So the original six books launched what has since become a continuing enterprise, the essence of which was to allow different authors to speak for themselves instead of trying to summarize under one umbrella what was obviously a rapidly growing and highly diverse field.

By the early 1980s the series included nineteen titles. OD was growing by leaps and bounds, and it was expanding into all kinds of organizational areas and technologies of intervention. By this time, many textbooks existed as well that tried to capture the core concepts of the field, but we felt that diversity and innovation were still the more salient aspects of OD.

Now as we move into the 1990s our series includes twenty-eight titles, and we are beginning to see some real convergence in the underlying assumptions of OD. As we observe how different professionals working in different kinds of organizations and occupational communities make their case, we see we are still far from having a single "theory" of organization development. Yet, a set of common assumptions is surfacing. We are beginning to see patterns in what works and what does not work, and we are becoming more articulate about these patterns. We are also seeing the field connecting to broader themes in the organizational sciences, and new theories and theories of practice are being presented in such areas as conflict resolution, group dynamics, and the process of change in relationship to culture. The new titles in the series address current themes directly: Ciampa's *Total Quality,* for example, addresses the challenge of creating a climate where employees continuously improve their ability to provide products and services that customers will find of particular value; Johansen et al.'s *Leading Business Teams* draws the link between OD skills and emerging electronic tools for teams; Tjosvold's *The Conflict-Positive Organization* connects to a whole research tradition on the dynamics of collaboration, competition, and conflict; Hirschhorn's *Managing in the New Team Environment* contains important links to psychoanalytic group theory; and Bushe and Shani's *Parallel Learning Structures* presents a seminal theory of large-scale organization change based on the institution of parallel systems as change agents.

As editors we have not dictated these connections, nor have we asked authors to work on higher-order concepts and theories. It is just happening, and it is a welcome turn of events. Perhaps it is an indication that OD may be reaching a period of consolidation and integration. We hope that we can contribute to this trend with future volumes.

Cambridge, Massachusetts   Richard H. Beckhard
New York, New York   Edgar H. Schein

Acknowledgments

There are many people to whom thanks go for this book. First are Dick Beckhard and Ed Schein for wanting to expand the venerable Addison-Wesley Organization Development Series beyond its behavioral science roots and to embrace the more multidisciplinary reality of the 1990s. Also, thanks to both for their patience during a nagging illness that delayed delivery of the manuscript. Mary Fischer, then the Addison-Wesley editor for the OD series, was both pleasant and insightful in helping to establish the original concept.

At Rath & Strong, Debbie Sarajian, Judy Galper, Cindy DiMatteo, Lisa Condon, and Dot Gheith were as always helpful and flexible under conditions of short time frames and the pressure of responding to the needs of the business (satisfying clients) in the midst of completing this manuscript. Meredith Allen was instrumental in the creation of the original project.

Dave Berlew, John Guaspari, and Tom Thomson provided their usual insightful critiques.

Jon Zonderman suffered through too many drafts, waited patiently, and did a great job of interviewing a number of busy people, as well as his usual good and humbling job of editing.

Finally, and most important, are clients who contributed everything—their time, their openness, their challenges, and their partnership. It is they who are changing organizations and making Total Quality a reality. Particular thanks go to these clients: Ed Fogarty at Colgate; Craig Weatherup, Mike Lorelli, Steve Bottcher, Gordon McPhaden, and Brenda Barnes at Pepsi Cola; Roland Pampel and David Dotlich at Bull HN; Jim Litts at

Johnson & Johnson; Paul Kikta of TRW; Richard Bovender, Jim Cavenaugh, and Dave Isbister at RJR; Pete Simone and Mike Werner at GCA/General Signal; Jim Kogen at Shure Brothers; Denny Schoener and Jim Lardner at John Deere; Pete Landry and Fay Tolman at Xerox; Dave Luther, Roger Ackerman, and Jamie Houghton at Corning; Tom Davis at Milliken; Ed Bessey and Frank Persico at Pfizer; Wayne Fortun at Hutchinson Technology.

Weston, Massachusetts   D.C.

Introduction

Much has been written on the need for better products and services. Joseph Juran and Edwards Deming have been sending this message since 1950. Armand Feigenbaum first used the term *Total Quality Control* in his book of that name in 1961. Especially in the 1980s, this subject has been carefully explored. If there has been an era of setting the stage for quality, it has been the 1980s. The American Society for Quality Control and the Association for Quality through Participation estimate that there were over 200 books in that decade that have the word *quality* in their title. In most of those books, the message is "Quality is important," or "If we don't improve our quality, the U.S. economy is going to suffer badly and our quality of life and position of economic dominance will decline." Strong messages—and they have been necessary. There is no question that the production of goods and services in this country had become sloppy and that many companies had taken the customer for granted.

Well, by all accounts, the message has sunk in. Total Quality is in demand today. Companies in every industrial sector are beginning to compete on the basis of quality, not simply on cost.

Today, cost is a given. In many industries, if a company is not cost competitive, it cannot even get on the playing field. The last five to seven years has seen enormous strides made by U.S. companies in driving down the cost of making and distributing their products as they strive to compete with their lower-cost counterparts in Asia, South America, and parts of Europe. In the 1980s, product quality moved from being just a challenge to being the next prerequisite for competitiveness. For companies that learned how to produce a high-quality product at a low cost, time became the next challenge. Beyond that is total dedication to the customer. The quality of transaction, of every transaction the customer has with the supplier, has come under scrutiny. (See Table 1.) The companies that will dominate markets in the 1990s and beyond will be those that can deliver high-quality, competitively priced products just when the customer wants them and do so in such a way that meets the needs of customers and exceeds their expectations. There is no question that the brass ring will belong to those companies. The vehicle by which they will reach that plateau has come to be called Total Quality.

Total Quality is typically a companywide effort seeking to install and make permanent a climate where employees continuously improve their ability to provide on demand products and services that customers will find of particular value.

Total Quality (TQ) has gone beyond being just a phenomenon. It is a movement spreading into every industry and sector in the United States and many in Europe as well. Starting in the early 1980s with some more forward-looking and innovative companies, its popularity has increased for three reasons.

The first reason is that some of the companies that started operating in a TQ way demanded that their suppliers do the same. Among the companies demanding changes from their suppliers are Ford, Motorola, Corning, Milliken, Xerox, and IBM. These sorts of businesses buy parts from thousands of companies; the message to those suppliers had been "operate under a TQ philosophy or you won't be a supplier to us any longer." In

Table 1
Competitive Realities of the 1990s

		Pre 1980s	*By Late 1980s*	*1990s*
Low	Givens	A useful product	Cost	Cost and product quality
Competitive Strength	Prerequisites	Cost	Product quality	Time
High	Challenges	Product quality	Time	Total customer dedication

addition to these large U.S. manufacturers, the Department of Defense has recently adopted Total Quality Management (TQM) as the mode under which companies that supply it materiel must operate.

The second reason is that the results some companies have been able to achieve through Total Quality are truly impressive. Dramatic reductions have become commonplace in the time it takes to get a product to the customer, in the cost of making and distributing the product, and the complexity needed to design and produce it. Improvement targets have not been limited to the production area; in the past few years, the same steps that have brought improvement in the factory have been started with some success in engineering, purchasing, marketing and sales, and human resources departments. Many companies in the United States embarked on TQ efforts out of competitive necessity. The market share that they once enjoyed, which in some cases was a symbol of their dominance, had slipped away. In most cases, this was due less to external factors such as the balance of trade and value of the dollar and more to factors those companies could have and should have better controlled (high cost, poor quality, long lead times, poor customer service, or just plain arrogance in how the customer was treated). Total Quality has provided a way for businesses to control these variables and, especially when TQ encompasses the tools and techniques of Just-In-Time, to achieve improvements never thought possible (80% to 90% reduction in lead time, 60% increase in productivity, 90% reduction in inventory).

The third reason TQ efforts have increased is that the values on which the concept is based are compelling to current industrial leaders, more so than to their predecessors. It is not by accident that the concept has spread at the time the leadership baton is being passed from the generation that grew up during the Depression of the 1930s and World War II to the generation that grew up in the 1950s and 1960s. Only a part of the success of Total Quality is due to its tools and techniques. The other, more important factor is that successful TQ efforts are based on values and basic assumptions about how to run a business enterprise that differ from the values and basic assumptions of most business leaders before the decade of the 1980s. These values and assumptions have to do with the role that employees play to make improvement techniques work, with the organization climate in which these people work, with the degree of teamwork and with the quality of transactions of those employees with each other, with suppliers, and, especially, with customers. It is apparent that one element that separates successful TQ efforts from those that have achieved average results is that the successful efforts display a particular set of values about the individual and the individual's role in the organization. TQ efforts in these companies encourage true employee involvement, demand teamwork, seek to push decision-making power to lower levels in the company, and reduce barriers between people. It is clear that when the leader has such objectives in mind in launching a TQ effort, the chance of dramatic breakthroughs is much better.

These values are at the core of Organization Development (OD), as well. In fact, TQ has provided the platform for the goals of Organization Development to finally be achieved. TQ has also added some new facets: It is multidisciplinary, it is more complete, more practical, more universally adaptable. Nonetheless, the core set of principles on which it is based are the same as those that form the basis for OD.

The purpose of this book is to explore what it takes to make TQ work, and to take the next step and build upon what has been written in the past to present the rationale for a TQ movement. The reason for presenting this book in the Addison-Wesley series on Organization Development is that the series has a track record for providing practical, no-nonsense handbooks for implementation and, also, that the essence of TQ is embodied in the precepts of Organization Development.

Contents

Part I
Opening the Door

1

Defining Total Quality

The man in the airplane seat in front of me displayed more and more anxiety as he recounted to the passenger beside him his experience in launching a Total Quality effort in his company.

It seemed like a great idea when I first heard about it in a speech at the industry meeting last spring. Your costs go down and things work better inside. Going for this Baldrige thing is something that will play real well in the market. So, I started to look for someone to help us get it done. The consultants we talked to never told us how much disruption we'd go through. I had no idea what was involved in this quality thing. Of course I didn't get that involved in it until the end of our search for a consultant—I had to delegate, get the troops committed, you know, and I didn't have the time anyway.

But it has been one problem after another over the past 18 months. I mean every part of your operation goes under the microscope. We got everyone to go through classes. Just learning a new language took an enormous amount of time. Then we had all these quality improvement teams go out to look for things to fix. Hundreds of people got involved in these. For a while, things were so disrupted that customers were waiting twice as long for service as they did before we started. Well, I hope all those problems are behind us, now. I don't know, maybe you have to go through this to get better.

Even though he ended on something of an upbeat note just as the plane landed, it seemed there was a big question in the mind of this leader as to whether his firm's prospects really would be as positive as he had hoped when he launched into "this quality thing." As I left the airport reflecting on the soliloquy I had overheard, feelings of sympathy for the employees and customers of this company mixed with frustration at hearing a story of disruption and confusion that never had to happen in the first place. The story spoke volumes about this particular leader and shed light on why the TQ effort had started on a chaotic note.

He decided to launch into this effort in too much haste and for the wrong reasons after hearing a speech on Total Quality. At best, one will hear only the outline of reality in a speech. While it may be intriguing to look further, it is hardly the basis on which to act. Whether it was the content of the speech itself, or simply what this fellow chose to hear, he walked away with a definition of Total Quality and, in particular what would result, that was distorted and, perhaps, simply wrong; reducing costs is not the reason to launch into TQ. While that should be one outcome, it should not be the primary focus.

The whole point of the Baldrige Award was missed by the executive. The Malcolm C. Baldrige National Quality Award has become something of a brass ring for American business. Many executives want to go after it for the right reasons—to use it as a way to become a better company—but many more, it seems, may be pursuing it for the wrong reasons — bragging rights or something that will "play real well in the marketplace." Not unlike marriage, parenthood, or any other commitment, if done for the wrong reasons it will hardly ever be satisfying.

This leader did not understand what was involved in pursuing Total Quality. The misunderstanding may have been the fault of the consultants whom he and his people met, or he may simply have not listened carefully enough. Regardless of the cause, however, it is reckless on the part of leaders to launch into any expensive change effort without understanding its parameters and likely impact; Total Quality means changing the way the business has operated and is always delicate and complicated. It is not something to decide on haphazardly.

He miscast his own role in launching a TQ effort. Portions of a TQ effort can and should be delegated, but the early stages are not among them. This is when the leader earns his salary, and also where he or she has the chance to show others that what he is asking them to go through is important enough to take the leader's time and attention as well.

The effort began with activities that should have occurred later in the process. Massive education is not the best way to launch an effort that seeks to have people behave differently on the job. First of all, it assumes that adults learn to practice new behavior best by hearing of a concept in a classroom setting and then going out to find ways to apply those new concepts. That form of education may be helpful to close gaps in knowledge, but not for changing behavior and the attitudes that underlie it.

It is also naive to assume that forming employee teams after a classroom experience will lead to real, positive, well-paced change. What makes much more sense is to gather data and analyze those data in such a way that employees gain more insight into problems. Then, form teams to attack the problems that both matter the most and are realistic to effect so that the new teams can achieve early successes.

Customers suffered. The disruption (perhaps even chaos) in the early stages of this particular TQ effort caused problems with what should be the major reason—and outcome—of any effort to achieve Total Quality: more satisfied customers. What happened in this company violates cardinal rule number 1 of Total Quality: Never hurt your customer while you are learning a new way to operate.[1] Rapid changes of normal practices will inevitably lead to lower service, missed delivery dates, slower response, and more mistakes and miscues.

Where should this leader have begun in considering a TQ effort in his company? How could he have better understood what he was getting into? The remainder of this chapter and Chapter 2 will answer these questions by exploring what Total Quality is; and, in Chapter 2, where it came from.

What Are We Getting Into?

It is not uncommon to meet with leaders of companies who have not yet launched a TQ effort who ask, "What are we getting into if we begin a Total Quality effort?" The CEO of one company put it in a particularly poignant way when he asked, "What am I going to find when I open the door?"

To be sure, especially in organizations that seem to be running smoothly, and in companies that are not in a financial or competitive crisis, the image of opening Pandora's box can easily spring to mind when one thinks of undertaking such a major effort as Total Quality.

Many people who have worked in organizations that have engaged in a TQ effort, as well as some consultants to such companies, are tempted to answer the question "What am I going to find when I open the door?" by replying, "One or two years of chaos and disruption that should lead to a better organization."

That is not an appropriate response. It is not necessary to go through a period of chaos to succeed in creating an environment where Total Quality can thrive. Does this mean that everything will be anticipated and will run smoothly and always as planned? Of course not. We are talking about change and the creation of a new state, a new character for the organization. That always involves some risk as the leader ventures into uncharted waters. Diligence is necessary along with flexibility and the ability to be nimble. There is such a thing as planned change, however, which can minimize disruption and certainly avoid chaos.

So, how can the question be answered? The point at which to start is with the definition of Total Quality that frames what this particular brand of change is and is not.

Toward a Definition of Total Quality

Total Quality can be defined in at least three ways. One way is by describing the unifying principle that is the basis for all strategy, planning, and activity in a company that embraces his philosophy. That principle, simply put, is *total dedication to the customer*. A company with a firmly established Total Quality mindset is totally dedicated to the customer's satisfaction in every way possible. In this organization, all employees are involved in improving its ability for that kind of dedication; all activities of all functions are designed and carried out so that all requirements of the ultimate customer are met and expectations exceeded.

A second way of defining Total Quality is to describe the outcomes that a TQ company strives for; the major results of the various activities its people seek to create or enhance. There are four categories in which these results fall.

- *Customers* are intensely loyal. They are more than satisfied because their needs are being met and their expectations are being exceeded.
- *The time to respond* to problems, needs, and opportunities is minimized. *Costs* are also minimized by eliminating or minimizing tasks that do not add value. Moreover, they are minimized in such a way that the quality of the goods and services given to the customer and the way the customer is treated is enhanced.
- A *climate* is put in place that supports and encourages teamwork and leads to more satisfying, motivating, and meaningful work for employees.
- There is a general ethic of *continuous improvement*. In addition, there is a methodology that employees understand for attaining a state of continuous improvement.

To take this second way of defining TQ a step farther, there are at least thirteen specific outcomes one can expect from a TQ effort. They are listed in Table 1.1, which also indicates to which broad category each applies.

A third way to define Total Quality is to discuss the various tools, techniques, and other elements that lead to the outcomes; in other words, to describe components of a TQ effort:

- Traditional tools drawn from Quality Control, Quality Assurance, and Reliability Engineering point to root causes of problems, clearly display those problems, and can be useful in making predictable the process for offering goods and services.
- The tools and techniques of Just-In-Time can dramatically reduce cost and time. These include ways to speed product flow, to pinpoint and eliminate activities that do not add value for the customer, to group tasks into work cells or product centers, and to alter the method of planning and scheduling work.

Table 1.1
Major Outcomes of Total Quality

	Customer More Satisfied	Less Time, Lower Costs	Climate Better	Continuous Improvement
Employees will better understand customers.	X			X
Goods/services will meet needs	X			
Fewer mistakes.	X	X	X	
Problems anticipated	X	X		X
Common problem-solving language	X	X		
Customers will feel better treated.	X			
Faster response time	X	X	X	X
Vendors more responsive	X	X		X
Better incoming materials	X	X		X
Closer manager/employee relationship		X	X	X
More innovation	X	X	X	X
People feel more ownership.	X		X	X
Commonly held vision of the future				X

- A number of elements from Organization Development are useful for TQ, including measuring the work climate, minimizing political and communication barriers to teamwork, developing management skills, innovating in design of the organization structure (formal and ad hoc), and increasing employee involvement in decision making.

- Finally, modern concepts of leadership are needed. The modern leader guides by creating a vision of what the organization can be and directing the establishment of a climate that encourages each employee to embrace that vision and make it his or her own, to personalize it so that it has meaning. Also, where the leader encourages teamwork and participation, and balances the use of one-alone decisions with those where participation is appropriate.

Table 1.2 summarizes the definitions. The definition that is best depends on the purpose being met in defining Total Quality. In addition to having the right definition, it is also essential to understand how it developed.

Total Quality in Historical Perspective

The Total Quality movement began to take shape in the United States in the late 1970s. It was driven by the frustration of some American industrial leaders whose companies were unable to keep adequate market share against foreign (mostly Far Eastern) competitors. These competitors produced consistently higher-quality products and were able to get them to market in less time than their U.S. counterparts, and at a lower cost. In response, a few of these leaders of U.S. companies set out to discover why. They, and at their insistence their managers, visited Japan to try to see what was different. What many saw was nothing new, but very different.

By and large, the individual elements of the way the Japanese had learned to manufacture were not new. They had been adapted from the West when Japanese businessmen conducted similar fact-finding missions in the decade and a half

Table 1.2
Three Ways to Define Total Quality

The Unifying Principle $\longrightarrow$	Total dedication to customers so that the customers' needs are met and their expectations are exceeded
The Outcomes $\longrightarrow$	Intensely loyal customers
$\longrightarrow$	Time is minimized so that costs go down
$\longrightarrow$	A climate that supports teamwork and more meaningful work
$\longrightarrow$	A general ethic of continuous improvement
The Tools and Techniques $\longrightarrow$	Quality Control, Quality Assurance, Reliability Engineering
$\longrightarrow$	Just-In-Time
$\longrightarrow$	Organization Development
$\longrightarrow$	Leadership

that preceded. Machine cells, group technology, sophisticated scheduling systems, Statistical Process Control (SPC) tools, and so forth, were all imported into Japan. In fact, the only technical element of Japan's manufacturing system that was not translated directly was "pull-through" scheduling, which supported a fundamental precept of their manufacturing philosophy—make things one at a time and only when they are needed.

Even here, however, the seeds had been sown as the touring Japanese businessmen witnessed activity in an American supermarket, where because of limited shelf space new canned goods were brought out only when a customer took a product off the shelf. The rate was determined by customers. It was not set by a schedule or a forecast of what someone in the back room thought customers would buy, but by customers actually taking something off the shelf.

Something else Americans saw in visits to Japan was even more profound: the way employees worked and related. They operated more in unison and were more involved. There seemed to be fewer limits and barriers between departments; engineers actually worked on the shop floor and manufacturing workers actually were a part of designing new products. Most of all, people we would call direct-labor employees, and others who typically enjoy little power in U.S. companies, had, relatively speaking, an enormous amount of influence over decisions that in the United States were the purview of higher ups.

Here again, the notion of cross-department teamwork and of involving employees in decisions was hardly new. It dated back to experiments in the 1950s in certain American and European companies and picked up momentum in the 1960s and early 1970s as Organization Development began to take shape, spawned by a few social psychologists, adult learning pioneers, and others interested in people's behavior inside organizations.[2]

It appeared that each individual element was not a new invention. Why then was there such a dramatic difference in quality, delivery, and cost? As people from the United States delved more deeply to answer this question, what emerged was the realization that the differences were in the way these familiar elements were being used, the philosophy that their use was based on, and in particular, the fact that they were being combined.

In the West, we thought about SPC as something entirely unrelated to team building. Responsibility was seated in different departments and language for each separated it and encouraged it to live a life of its own. Also, the mindset that dictated the use of these techniques was different. In the United States, for example, the quality of the product or service was often secondary to the cost of making or providing it, like options on a checklist in a zero-sum game where cost usually won out. In contrast, the best companies in Japan approached the issue differently. Instead of saying, "Keeping our costs down is more important than very high quality," they asked, "How can we provide very high quality, and do it in such a way that our costs don't get too high?" Indeed, many companies found that improving quality actually led to lower costs.

The other part of this mindset is equally important. Typically, the concept of the customer's importance as the driving force for all activities was foreign (pun intended) to American businesses. When improvement activities were launched in U.S. companies prior to 1980, the focus was internal—the expectation was that things would improve inside the company as a result of these activities and that was why they were being initiated. Costs would go down, thus adding to profit. If there was to be an effort to foster employee involvement, the reason was to increase productivity so that (you guessed it) costs would go down and more money would go to the bottom line. The idea that from improvement efforts savings would be "invested" in reducing prices and capturing more market share was seen by some as heresy. The problem was that the current way of thinking was not working particularly well. Wickham Skinner called it "the productivity paradox" when he found that while larger and larger amounts of effort and money went into productivity improvement programs in the 1970s, productivity continued a relentless decline.[3]

What slowly began to sink in for Americans who observed how the Japanese operated was that there was much less inner-directed concern. Instead, in Japan there was an outer-directed, customer-oriented concern that drove internal improvements. This was supported by the belief that if the customer was satisfied, you were doing a good job, and that trade-offs should be decided on this basis above all others. Doing so meant that customers were listened to more and it was their wants that determined to a much greater degree what was designed and produced.

Another interesting discovery was the way the Japanese had learned to manage time. They were relentless in reducing the time of the processes that made up their businesses. Stalk and Abegglen have pointed out that it is in how the Japanese manage time more than anything else that has enabled them to gain competitive advantage.[4]

Yet another observation from studying the Japanese was that there seemed to be an intense and ongoing dedication to improving everything that could result in a better product produced in less time. Schoenberger pointed this out in 1982. "In the Western system goals tend to be static. [They] serve as standards, and [the] focus is on control, or minimizing variance from the standards. On the other hand, as [Dr. Joseph] Juran notes, 'Over the years the accumulated experience of the

Japanese has developed its own imperative—the precious habit of improvement. Control keeps things stable, but while the Western company is maintaining stability, the Japanese company keeps improving.' "[5]

So what did all this observation and experimentation say? It said that there had emerged a new paradigm in manufacturing, one where

- The tools and techniques were familiar.
- Employees were using them more uniformly and more in unison.
- There was more cooperation among departments and different specialties.
- Employees who had direct contact with the product had more influence.
- There was a different mindset that guided behavior; one that caused people to:
  — strive to continuously improve,
  — hold quality and time improvement as sacred, and
  — focus first and foremost on the customer.

These learnings represented a significant departure from how manufacturing companies had been run. It was another chapter in the ongoing search for a formula for organizational excellence. What Americans learned from studying the Japanese in the late 1970s and early 1980s was born of a competitive concern. It was a watershed after which what had been separate disciplines began to merge into a multidisciplinary approach to organizational excellence that encompassed technical, physical, behavioral, and leadership elements. It is this multidisciplinary approach that has come to be called Total Quality.

This is how Total Quality developed over fifteen years, but to understand it fully we must also understand where it came from. In one sense, Total Quality is the latest, most comprehensive, and most complete approach to organizational excellence. It is another way to achieve better and longer lasting results than the other approaches that have preceded it. Chapter 2 explores the lineage and interplay of various approaches as groundwork for Total Quality.

References

1. This rule was first stated by E. Hay in *The Just-In-Time Breakthrough* (New York: John Wiley & Sons, 1988).

2. See bibliography for a list of references.

3. Wickham Skinner, "The Productivity Paradox," *Harvard Business Review,* July-August 1986.

4. James C. Abegglen and George Stalk, Jr., *KAISHA: The Japanese Corporation* (New York: Basic Books, 1985).

5. R. Schoenberger, *Japanese Manufacturing Techniques* (New York: Free Press, 1982).

2

Some Background—from Taylor to the Customer

To introduce some ideas of where Total Quality came from, let me use an analogy to the sport of baseball. I apologize to readers who are not baseball fans or who live in countries where that sport is not popular. The analogy is not a bad one, so bear with me.

A team that wins a baseball game does so by scoring at least one more run than the opposing team. A run is scored by a player touching four goals, called bases. Going to first base is good, going beyond first to the second base is better, and being able to get to third base is impressive. But even getting to third base doesn't matter in the final analysis, because the only thing that counts is when a player goes beyond third base and touches the fourth base, called home plate. Each of these bases must be touched in sequence before a run is scored and credited to the team of the player who accomplishes this feat. Figure 2.1 depicts this relationship.

Think of home plate (the base that must be touched for a run) as the customer. Touching the customer is success. Just like a run in baseball, this is the reason for playing—it is the point of the whole game. Third base is the company's strategic imperatives, those things that must be achieved in order for the business to thrive. Second base is the collection of techniques and approaches that foster teamwork and create a satisfying, motivating work environment. First base represents the statistical tools and techniques that can be used to measure the process through which the product or service is offered, to predict failure, and to point to root causes of problems.

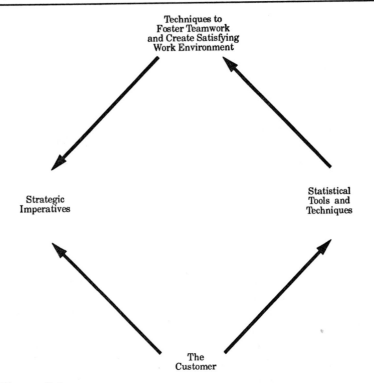

Figure 2.1
The Four Bases of Total Quality

Getting to first base, using statistical tools and techniques, is good, and success cannot be achieved without them. But in and of themselves, statistical tools are not enough.

Proceeding to second base adds important elements on the people/organization culture side. These are essential to success and combining them with the statistical tools creates an enormously powerful force. But even this force will not bring success. The issues on which that problem-solving force are used must be important to the business and to realizing its strategy.

When these three components are combined, and when the customer component is added, you've got a powerful operational force aimed at what is crucial for the business, all focused on getting to the customer. Let's look at each component a bit more closely.

The Technical Side—Component One

Choosing a starting point to trace the technical roots of TQ is harder than it may seem. The construction of the great pyramid at Giza, the efficiency of the Roman legions, Napoleon's command structure as his armies conquered Europe, Max Weber's organization design that became the modern day bureaucracy—all can be cited as procedural and/or technical examples intended to make organizations perform more effectively. For our purposes, however, it may be best to go back to the turn of this century and the ideas of Frederick Taylor.

Taylor's ideas, which he called Scientific Management, were an early industrial attempt at organizational improvement, although they were based on values that are not generally highly regarded today. Taylor held that the way to get more production from workers was to control them tightly and to break down the actions and activities expected into small, discrete steps and substeps, install ways to measure those elements, and micromanage time and activity relentlessly. One basis for his system was a belief that workers could not be trusted to make decisions, hence needed strict rules. As antithetical as this may be to our current ways of viewing organization life and the role of the worker, Scientific Management propelled the development of an enormously powerful industrial machine that was the standard and the envy of the world for decades. It was not Taylor's concern or objective to enhance employees' quality of life. Rather, the intent of his system was to organize and systematize the process by which a product was made so that roles and responsibilities were clear and measurable, and so that production was maximized. It did that.

Industrial Engineering resulted, with its techniques to measure output and set standards of production against which workers would be measured. It created individual, and later, group incentives to encourage workers to surpass those standards. As they did, standards had to be reset, which in turn called for more Industrial Engineering.

The next wave of development came as a result of World War II. The effort to produce materiel reliable enough not to fail in combat conditions, and at a faster-than-ever pace, caused great strides in quality and compressed the development time of new ways to make a product. The first step was inspection, inspection, and more inspection. In the late 1940s and early

1950s this evolved into the use of statistics to predict failure rates, plot conformance to specifications, and control the production process so that it predictably operated within preset limits of variation. It was in this transition from inspecting something already made to predicting nonconformance and plotting variables that Quality Control evolved into Quality Assurance and Reliability Engineering disciplines, often grouped under the title of quality engineering. These disciplines paved the way for the diagnostic techniques that make up Statistical Process Control (SPC). SPC techniques allow sampling rather than 100% inspection and point to the most likely root causes of quality and variation problems. Appendix B goes into greater detail on the techniques taken from quality engineering that are in most common use in TQ efforts.

By the late 1950s, business volume had grown and production had increased as consumer appetites grew. The results were larger-than-ever inventories, warehouses to put them in, and complex production-scheduling requirements. The response was modern materials management, which created algorithms to pose scheduling scenarios and then created categories into which data could be sorted. Critical Ratio Scheduling was developed, and as a result Material Requirements Planning (MRP) emerged in the early 1960s as the umbrella for these scheduling techniques and became more refined as the computer developed through the 1960s and into the 1970s. MRP became the primary tool of the production scheduling department (variously called materials management or production control). This gave rise to yet another specialty function in American manufacturing (in addition to industrial engineers and Quality Control specialists) thereby adding to the ratio of so-called indirect labor to total employees.

Computer Integrated Manufacturing (CIM) gained attention as a manufacturing concept in the mid 1970s. Automation of equipment and of information was nothing new; companies in the United States, Europe, and Japan had been automating elements of their operations for decades. What was different with CIM was the idea that all these automated elements (called islands of automation at the time) must be linked together. Even though Joseph Harrington of Arthur D. Little had suggested this years before, it took the equipment and software capability of the 1970s to bring it closer to reality. CIM received a lot of attention as an organizational excellence strategy in the late 1970s and early 1980s as companies worldwide were desperately working to improve.

Unfortunately, it was oversold as a concept and expectations were unrealistic. By and large, software programs had been developed as stand-alone elements not ever intended to communicate with one another, and most were based on proprietary rather than common operating systems. Also, equipment manufacturers found it difficult to get costs down. The catch-22 for many was they needed to sell in large quantities to reduce costs but couldn't sell in large quantities because costs were too high. Ironically, it was to be Just-In-Time, which eschews automation, that would reduce costs for many of these automation equipment manufacturers during the 1980s.

In the mid to late 1970s, manufacturing resource planning (MRPII) appeared as a more sophisticated and more complicated way of scheduling. It also provided the potential for a uniform measurement of internal efficiency. MRPII, like MRP, could make things run more smoothly inside a manufacturing company. However, MRPII had these problems: (1) it tended to require increasing overhead and giving more responsibility to staff specialists; (2) converting to it was expensive (often several million dollars of software and consulting time); and (3) like MRP, it was based on the assumption that inventory was inevitable, something that was a fact of life and there to be managed so it would not get out of control. These notions were changed by Just-In-Time in the early 1980s.

Just-In-Time (JIT) emerged in the United States about the same time as Total Quality. It was initially, mistakenly, seen as only a way to reduce inventories. While inventory reduction is one of JIT's benefits, it is much broader than merely a technique to achieve this one gain.[1] It became popular starting in the early 1980s and eclipsed TQ in popularity for several years. JIT caught on more quickly than TQ for two reasons: (1) it could gain dramatic results in cost reduction quickly, and (2) it appeared at a time when American manufacturers were desperately trying to make up lost ground in the fight for market share, and many were scared. Just-In-Time comprises seven elements:

- Lead time reduction
- Productivity increase

- Cost-of-poor-quality reduction
- Purchasing material price reduction
- Inventory reduction
- Setup reduction
- Space reduction

The benefits Just-In-Time promised are impressive, even unheard of: 80% to 90% reduction in lead time; over 90% reduction in work-in-process inventory, and 90% reduction in finished goods; up to 60% increase in productivity of indirect and salaried employees; 60% reduction in cost of poor quality; up to 50% reduction in the price of purchased material; up to 94% reduction in setup times; up to 92% reduction in cycle time. These improvements were all internally focused and all important to be able to compete effectively in the competitive era of the 1980s and 1990s. JIT said that the best way to improve was to eliminate waste, and one of the biggest examples of waste was inventory. The key was to eliminate inventory, not manage it. This became the demarcation line where true JIT separated from contemporary ways to manage and control inventory.

The automobile companies made an early commitment to try JIT and required their suppliers to do the same; since these combine to make up about 8% of the total of the U.S. industrial output, Just-In-Time began to spread. The more it spread, the more it became apparent that the real benefits from JIT came from a combination of its seven elements; that is, while gains in each case are worthwhile and will bring some improvement, truly impressive and significant results that have an impact on the overall competitiveness of the business came from working on all elements at the same time. In order for such coordinated activity to take place three conditions had to be met.

First, the process through which the product was made had to be predictable, and that meant that the basic ingredients of quality engineering had to be in place. Second, there had to be a particular organization climate that encouraged teamwork across department lines, the pushing of decision-making authority to lower levels, and a relentless drive to be constantly better. Third, it required a leader with the courage and vision to allow challenges to time-honored ways of doing things.

The most successful leaders took on the task of meeting these conditions and gained impressive results. As they remade their companies into lean, flexible competitors, the best went beyond cost improvement and worked on ways to reduce time, applying JIT techniques to shorten the new-product development cycle and lessen internal bureaucratic processes. They also demanded their suppliers operate in a JIT fashion so that they could eliminate preproduction inventory, and also eliminate incoming inspection as the suppliers learned to deliver product on time that met all necessary specifications. Just-In-Time has proven to be one of the more significant ways to achieve organization excellence in the modern industrial era.

As Just-In-Time was being used and refined, there emerged a vigorous emphasis on product quality. The realization had sunk in that customers cared about quality and reliability of a product as much or more than they cared about cost. Many leaders finally realized they had been losing market share because customers found they could get better products and services at the same cost elsewhere.

Statistical Process Control became popular once again as people learned (or relearned) the principles of creating a stable, predictable process through which to make a product.* This is when they began to listen to such people as Edwards Deming and Joseph Juran, who had preached the quality assurance gospel since the 1940s. Deming and Juran had been, by and large, teaching and consulting in Japan and became national heroes there.

This emphasis on product quality combined with the interest in Just-In-Time by the end of the 1980s. Quality tools and techniques concentrated on predictability and stability. JIT concentrated on cost and time, and also provided a philosophy that stressed adding value and reducing waste while continuously improving.

---

*It is interesting to note that Rath & Strong's Quality Assurance and Reliability consulting practice, which had begun in the years immediately after World War II and had grown substantially during the 1950s and 1960s, was representative of how an emphasis on quality sunk to a comalike existence before 1980. It went from a robust consulting practice in 1970 to be practically nonexistent by 1979. Not only was there little interest in product-quality improvement, but we did not do a good job of explaining to the marketplace the connection between product quality and market share. By 1979, for all practical purposes, there was no Quality Assurance consulting market left in the United States.

The People Side—Component Two

These technical attempts to improve the way organizations operated were happening in parallel with other attempts on the behavioral and organization side of the equation that emerged under the title of Organization Development. Here, roots can be traced to the late 1940s.

The years after World War II saw a number of government-sponsored programs to help the reentry of American servicemen into civilian life and to develop a new postwar American society. One such program was to develop community leaders to facilitate understanding of and compliance with the Fair Employment Practices Act. The federal government hired educators from various institutions to conduct seminars. One was at State Teachers College in New Britain, Connecticut, in the summer of 1946. It proved to be one of the most important steps leading to Organization Development, which would be formulated during the next two decades.

Educators from Columbia University, the Massachusetts Institute of Technology, and the National Education Association were hired to conduct this seminar. The training leaders were Ken Benne from Columbia, Lee Bradford from the National Education Association, and Ron Lippitt from MIT. Researchers at the workshop included Kurt Lewin and Murray Horwitz.

Accidentally, they stumbled on the discovery that by involving students in evening discussions of the day's events, participants derived important understanding of their own behavior and of the behavior of the group as a whole. It became increasingly apparent that groups, like individuals, went through stages of development. These stages could be understood through analysis of events and, in particular, feedback to people of how they had just behaved and the impact that behavior had on others in the group. While the focus of the day was on imparting knowledge and looking at past events, these discussions centered on what had just happened; the fact that they were being held by the people who were involved rather than just observers, heightened interest and learning.

As Ken Benne observed:

> . . . group discussion of their own behavior and . . . its consequences had an electric effect both on the participants and on the training leaders. What had been a conversation between research observers and group

leaders [of what had taken place during the day] was . . . widened to include participants who had been part of the events being discussed . . . before many evenings had passed, all participants . . . were attending these [discussions]. Many continued for as long as three hours. Participants reported that they were deriving important understandings of their own behavior and of the behavior of their groups. . . . it seemed that a potentially powerful medium and process of re-education had been somewhat inadvertently hit upon. Group members, if they were confronted . . . objectively with data concerning their own behavior and its effects, and if they came to participate nondefensively in thinking about these data, might achieve highly meaningful learnings about themselves, about the responses of others to them, and about group behavior and group development in general . . . the notion was to supplement there-and-then content with the collection and analysis of here-and-now data concerning the members' own behavior.[2]

These educators continued to explore ways to involve adults in their own learning during the subsequent academic year and received a grant to conduct a three-week session at Gould Academy in Bethel, Maine, the following summer. The medium for that session was the Basic Skills Training (BST) Group, where an observer fed back what had been observed for discussion as the group was meeting. The role of the leader was to facilitate the group in learning from these observations; that facilitation role was in addition to the leader's more traditional role.

Development of this form of learning platform continued over the next few years, fueled by grants from the Carnegie Foundation and the founding of the National Training Laboratories (later to become NTL Institute for the Applied Behavioral Sciences) as a part of the National Education Association. What evolved was something called the T Group, or Training Group. Lee Bradford described the T Group in this way:

[It is] a relatively unstructured group in which individuals participate as learners. The data for learning are not outside . . . or remote from their immediate experience within the T Group. The data are the transactions among members, their own behavior in the group, as they struggle to create a productive and viable organization, a miniature society, and as they work to stimulate and support one another's learning within that society.[3]

A relatively new aspect of learning emerged as the T Group evolved. As a "minisociety" formed and as people's behavior was observed and fed back for the whole group to analyze, norms of group behavior were changing. It was no longer forbidden to discuss someone's behavior and the emotions that it caused in others. It was seen as valuable to let those emotions surface, and to deal with them and use them as sources of important learning.

The T Group also focused participants more on learning from each other than its predecessor, the BST Group. Rather than having the objective of the training to do something back home, the focus was on the events happening between group members and those happening as the group itself evolved as, as Bradford put it, a miniature society. The popularity of the T Group fueled interest in action research. The two fit nicely together, since both require the learner (whether T-Group participant or researcher) to take initiative to determine what needs to be learned and the responsibility to come up with ways to learn it.

From the late 1950s through the 1960s, four T-Group notions grew in popularity: (1) learning from the dynamics of people interacting, (2) group members' taking responsibility for their own learning and the legitimate exploration of feelings as important ingredients in group development, (3) feedback of just-happened behavior, and (4) changing the role of group leader to include the task of facilitating discussion and inter-personal/group growth.

The reasons it is important to understand the development of the T Group are that, by and large, the people who shaped Organization Development came from this tradition during the formative years of the applied behavioral science movement, and also because the principles of T Groups were the basis for Organization Development.

In 1969 Warren Bennis provided one of the early, lucid definitions of this emerging field of Organization Development (OD). He said,

Organization Development . . . concentrates on the values, attitudes, relations, and organizational climate—the "people variable"—as a point of entry rather than on the goals, structure, and technologies. . . .

[It involves dealing with] problems of communication—particularly upward, inter-group conflict, leadership—particularly problems of succession . . . [and] questions of satisfaction and the ability of the organization to provide . . . appropriate . . . inducements [to motivate its people].

[It] relies on an educational strategy which emphasizes experienced behavior.

The T-Group format, including feedback of just-happened behavior and dealing with people's emotions, was the basis for group work used extensively in Organization Development projects.

[It sets out to achieve] a set of normative goals . . . most commonly sought are:

- Improvement in interpersonal competence
- . . . human factors and feelings come to be considered legitimate
- . . . increased understanding between and within working groups . . .
- . . . more effective team management . . .
- . . . better methods of conflict resolution [instead of] the usual . . . methods which rely . . . on suppression, compromise, and unprincipled power . . .
- . . . organic rather than mechanical systems [where relationships, trust, interdependence, and multi-group membership replaces an exclusive emphasis on the individual, on rigid authority–subordinate relationships, and on conflict being resolved through suppression or arbitration][4]

Organization Development relied on the ability to diagnose the climate in which people worked and to gain insight into the organization's culture. It was the diagnosis of the human part of the organization and the humanistic values that it was based on that gave OD its unique flavor.

As this method of understanding the human side of organization life was taking shape, a related development effort was in process—management training focusing on interpersonal skills of the individual with management responsibility rather than just education that transferred concepts. The main proponents, many of whom came from the same tradition as those in Organization Development, concentrated on how to design programs for people to learn new interpersonal and influence skills and to change behavior, rather than large-scale, organizationwide planned change.

One example was Achievement Motivation Training, designed for setting goals and preparing people to establish small businesses or perform other entrepreneurial tasks. Another example was the Managerial Grid, which offered personal diagnostic tools to determine concern for people and for task accomplishment as the manager sought ways to become more humanistic. Synectics was a brainstorming and creativity-enhancement training program originally designed to help with new product development. Kepner-Tregoe offered a systematic problem-solving/decision-making model to handle decision making as the computer and other technical developments made the task of managing more and more complex. These were just four of the more popular training designs that were developed in the 1960s to help individuals handle complexity more effectively and better relate with each other as they did.

Many of the management training developments came from a view of how adults learn that was quite different from the traditional view. Malcolm Knowles, then at Boston University, was a true pioneer in this regard. He pointed out that while adults learn quite differently from children, the process we use to train adults is based on pedagogy, the art and science of teaching children (*pedagogy* is derived from the Greek PAID, meaning 'child,' and AGOGOS, meaning 'leading'). Knowles coined the term *andragogy* (from the Greek ANDR, 'man,' and AGOGOS, 'leading') to distinguish the new discipline of adult education from the traditional discipline of teaching children. He stressed the role and responsibility of the learner; and, more important, that of the teacher to allow and structure ways for the learner to influence his or her learning process and to assess learning needs. Prior traditional educating put all the responsibility on the teacher to transmit information and on the learner to listen to the teacher. Knowles pointed out that lecturing may work with children (which is debatable) but not with adults. Adult education had to take into account the learning needs of the student and to encourage give-and-take dialogue or in other ways to engage and ensure the learner's involvement.

There were attempts in the 1960s to bring more closely together Organization Development (with its emphasis on systemwide cultural change) with management skills training. One such attempt was the Managerial Grid, which was posed in 1961 as a six-phase program that went from individual awareness and interpersonal skill development (phase I), to intragroup teamwork development (phase II), and teamwork between groups (phase III), to create a theoretical model of how the organization should operate and of how the top team should make decisions (phase IV). The fifth phase involved designing the ideal organization change process and assigning employees to conversion study teams in each of the main functions (marketing, R&D, sales, and so on), and also implementing changes the teams recommended. The final phase was an organizationwide critique.[5]

Another, less programmatic attempt to merge OD and management training was at a consulting firm called the Behavioral Sciences Center that was part of Sterling Institute (it later separated from Sterling and became McBer & Co.). In the late 1960s, it brought together a group of trainers and Organization Development consultants and put them together on large OD efforts, mainly on economic development projects for poverty programs for the U.S. government in America and in developing countries. The training components here were Achievement Motivation Training, based on David McClelland's research, and team building based largely on T Groups.[6]

In addition to OD and management training, a third track was also being laid by organizational theorists. These people established theories of the organization as an open system, one that should provide employees with the opportunity for self-actualization at the same time as they were providing the organization with productive, profitable work. Early development in this regard was at Tavistock Institute in London.

Based on the work of Ludwig Von Bertalanffy on general systems theory dating from 1940, the researchers at Tavistock (Eric Trist, A. K. Rice, and others) suggested that social scientists shift away from thinking of organizations as purely social systems to thinking that also included the technology of work, so that the social and the technological parts of the business relate to each other. They also suggested that the enterprise cannot be thought of as independent of external forces which act on it but must be seen as an "open system." Trist pointed this out in 1959.

> In the realm of social theory... there has been a strong tendency to continue thinking in terms of a "closed" system, that is, to regard the enterprise as sufficiently independent to allow most of its problems to be analyzed with reference to its internal structure and without reference to its external environment.[7]

Early Tavistock studies of coal mining in Britain showed that the social and psychological development of groups could be understood only by understanding the detail of how the production system operated and the technology of extracting coal from underground. This broke ranks with traditional social science research.

The work at Tavistock was a precursor to a brand of consulting that would begin to take shape in the United States in the mid-1960s. Dave Gleicher at Arthur D. Little, the consulting and research firm in Cambridge Massachusetts, started a group of Organization Development and management training consultants. The pioneering aspect of this group was that it was the first attempt (as far as I know) to merge OD and training with consulting on technology and operations management.

A couple of years later, the same sort of experiment was attempted at Rath & Strong in Lexington, Massachusetts, several miles outside of Cambridge. Rath & Strong, established in 1935, had been a traditional management consulting firm with services in industrial and manufacturing engineering, quality control and assurance, and materials management and distribution. While its consulting projects were generally highly regarded, results were not as long-lasting during the late 1960s as they had been before then. Six or twelve months after working on a yield problem, a productivity problem, or installing an information system, with both client and consultant satisfied, the same problems would reappear.

This recidivism caught the attention of the people at Rath & Strong. The response was to try what Arthur D. Little had done several years before. An Organization Development and management training group was formed in 1972. This time it worked, although it took some time. Ultimately, behavioral scientists and technical consultants worked hand-in-hand diagnosing, analyzing, feeding back, and implementing improvement projects in multidisciplinary fashion.

These are just some examples of experiments to further develop the people side of the equation through combining OD with management training or merging both with other forms of consulting. There weren't many real, serious attempts, and those who tried for a higher order, more comprehensive change approach were pioneers. But just as long-lasting, truly comprehensive change was hard to come by with clients in those years, it proved at least as difficult with the consulting firms that were trying to get clients to make fundamental changes.

For the most part, the Managerial Grid remained a training program (with the exception of such companies as Humble Oil), with most Grid clients using the first two phases (interpersonal awareness of managerial style and team building) and occasionally the third phase (intergroup teamwork). McBer was torn apart by internal political rifts and too-slow reaction to government cutbacks for consulting in 1970. The experiment in multidisciplinary consulting at Arthur D. Little had failed, as bonds were never solidified between the OD group and other, more traditional consulting divisions in the firm. While multidisciplinary consulting did eventually take hold and succeed at Rath & Strong, it took much longer than it should have (it took eight years before it became ingrained) because of interdisciplinary jealousy, lack of adequate strategy and vision, and little teamwork.

In spite of these shortcomings the OD field continued to develop, and many companies took its principles seriously and were successful at implementing them. One of the early examples was the Red Jacket Manufacturing Company in Davenport, Iowa, where an OD effort started in 1953. Its young president, Jim Richard, was one of the early clients of the people who shaped OD (Argyris, Bennis, and others) and participated in the early small-group experiments such as T Groups. He was driven to create an environment where people could express themselves as individuals and be satisfied in an increasingly organized and impersonal society that was putting more and more constrictions and formal structure on employees.

As a midsized manufacturer of pumps in a highly competitive industry, Red Jacket also had to ensure that product quality, cost, and delivery were meeting customers' needs. Richard constructed a participative environment where workers had more power than most of their counterparts elsewhere, where various forums opened lines of communication, and where teamwork was emphasized through various training methods.

He reported,

> The positive effects of this were remarkable and richly rewarding. The foremen and staff men changed from passive, dependent, and acquiescent men, to men who were effective, self-starting, responsible, and deeply involved . . . we have made some real efforts to shift the emphasis of power. Operating control has been significantly diffused from a few to many. The positive results have been clearly to relieve men of a cog-like feeling and a sense of dependency.[8]

Richard took learnings from his experience at Red Jacket to Polaroid in 1959 and started its OD effort as the first vice president of human resources.

Humble Oil (later Exxon) began its OD program in 1956. It combined various kinds of laboratory training, the Managerial Grid, participative goal setting, group problem solving, early identification of managerial potential, career development, team building, a variation on the Scanlon Plan, and employee attitude surveys. It also funded centers for developmental research on many of the OD techniques of the time. The OD effort at Humble started with T-Group training.

One of the first examples of the transition from training to more systemic efforts was at Humble's Baton Rouge, Louisiana, refinery. Because of significant cost pressure, there were substantial changes underway in manning practices; due to methods changes and automation there had been layoffs of up to one-third of the work force in some units. Results had been poor communication, generally low morale, fear of job loss, and quality and safety problems. The laboratory training helped alleviate these pressures and turned the climate into a more collaborative, problem-solving one. Baton Rouge accomplished its work-force reduction targets with fewer upsets than anticipated and went on to job enrichment and enlargement efforts as costs were reduced.

This success caused other Humble refineries to try the same approach. The Managerial Grid system of instrumented Organization Development was begun in 1961 at Humble. It appealed to management because it had the potential of something that could be led by line managers rather than outside trainers or consultants, on whom the T-Group training depended. OD spread to other Humble units and was ingrained in the company's fabric sufficiently by 1970 that formal Organization Development programs were phased out in the early 1970s.

While these experiments were taking place in the United States, companies in Europe were adopting similar approaches. One pioneer was the Petrochemicals Division of Imperial Chemical Industries Ltd. (ICI) It was one of the early efforts at comprehensive organization change using OD techniques. It affected the unit's strategy, its organization structure, the climate, management style, and various systems. Table 2.1 correlates categories of emphasis with OD (and other) approaches that the Petrochemicals Division employed.

This effort was an early attempt to merge training and OD elements into a truly planned strategy, taking into account the unit's business strategies and goals. Rather than training in T Groups, it began with diagnosis classified in seven headings: plans and objectives, organization structure, climate, management style, management (effectiveness), work methods and equipment, and career development.

A manager involved said, "In the past, faced with a plethora of . . . techniques and feeling that it ought to be doing something, management has tended to try this technique or the other with far too little thought as to whether it is really appropriate or not." ICI managers and consultants took a different, more planned and systematic approach.

It may also have been the first time that the notion of the internal customer appeared.

> This applies particularly to service sections who . . . set themselves up as an end in themselves and forget that their main purpose in life is to provide such a service as allows their "customer" sections within the organization to operate effectively and with overall maximum economy. It is often . . . useful . . . for the service section to define its roles as it sees them and then to check [out these conclusions] with its customer sections. This often leads to considerable

Table 2.1
*Classification of Problem Areas and Relevant
Techniques and Approaches*

Problem Area	Relevant Techniques and Approaches
1. Overall planning objective setting	Market research Operations research Long-range planning Mathematical modeling, etc.
2. Organization —planning (long term) —structure (short term)	Organization planning Systems engineering Organization study approaches, etc.
3. Climate management style	T Groups Blake's Managerial Grid seminars Coverdale Training Reddin's 3-D Grid In-company management training and teamwork development Job enrichment, etc.
4. Management	Management by objectives Target setting Planning techniques; CPS, etc. Management job descriptions
5. Work/equipment/ methods	Method study Critical examination Planning techniques Methods change Value analysis Variable factor programming Group capacity analysis Short interval scheduling, etc.
6. Career development	Manpower planning Management succession programs Staff assessment/career planning etc.

Source: I.L. Manaran, D. Shaw, and B. Wilson, *Managing Change,*
Management Guide No. 3 (London: British Institute of Management,
1971).

changes . . . once the roles are clear, the customer can be asked 'Are we fulfilling the agreed role properly?' [9]

Back to Total Quality

The people side of Total Quality is a direct descendant of Organization Development. To truly understand TQ and to be able to make it a reality, one must be expert in creating change on the people side of the organizational excellence equation. The values on which OD is based, its dedication to human learning, its elements of adult education and management training are all necessary parts of a true, successful TQ effort.

The technical developments since Frederick Taylor suggest the lineage of the procedural, statistical, and mechanical elements that make up another facet of Total Quality. They draw statistical tools from quality engineering and utilize the philosophy and techniques of Just-In-Time (a combination of techniques that is much more contemporary and refined than the industrial engineering and materials management fields from which JIT grew). The combination creates an operations hybrid that is potentially more powerful than any operations methodology that has come before. What provides the promise of making that potential a reality is the people side and the cultural change that comes along with it that can truly alter the very character of the organization.

These are two vital components of Total Quality, one technical, the other people-related. They have been combined to create this powerful organizational excellence paradigm of the 1990s.

But conceptually, what makes this 1990 model any different from the multidisciplinary approach of 1972 or, for that matter, from the sociotechnical theories from Tavistock Institute? Sure, the OD part is updated and more attuned to a modern, more rapidly changing, volatile world and JIT combines (and changes for the better) previous techniques that only were concerned with cost reduction. But are there other factors added that give TQ a unique flavor rather than simply being a new name for what has been tried before? The answer is yes. There are two other major components that must be added to Total Quality to make it full and robust.

Strategic Imperatives—Component Three

The third major component to be added to make true Total Quality is that the focus of TQ attention inside the organization must be on the strategic imperatives of the business. The logic train should go something like this—the business strategy and the approach to current market conditions (both reflecting the overarching concern for the customer) should point to the vital few imperatives that must be addressed for the enterprise to thrive, which, in turn, should point to the discrete processes on which those imperatives depend. It is these processes that should be the focus of improvement activity.

In the embryonic days of Total Quality, "Quality Control circles" were fairly common. These were typically small groups of employees brought together to find problems to work on; they were then given the license to work on them. They were mainly employee-involvement mechanisms and were generally not guided by strategy or concerns for the customer. The biggest criticism of these groups was they tended to quickly lose focus and start addressing problems that were not very important. Many a plant manager has bemoaned the fact that the QC circles that were supported by his budget were working on the placement of water fountains and redividing the parking lot.

This emphasis on processes is extremely important. A process is a linear string of activities related by (1) the dependence that one activity in the process has on ones that have preceded it, and (2) the fact that they are all combining and building toward the same end. Such processes cross department lines. Examples include the new-product-development process and the process by which customer complaints are handled. Such sets of activities involve many people from many departments where the quality of one person's input is largely a function of the work of those who have gone before.

Improving a process is a matter of the leader managing a sequence such as the following:

1. Identify the process, its mission, and the part it plays in the overall business.
2. Ensure that the process to be worked on is connected to a business imperative.

3. Enlist the help of people who are involved in the process and make sure a top manager assumes stewardship to improve it.

4. Map the existing process in a way that identifies precisely the degree to which each step adds value.

5. Envision what the best possible process would look like and what it would feel like to be a part of it. (This can be done through benchmarking or by vision clarification workshops.)

6. Define the problems to be solved in moving from the current state to the ideal and establishing specific, measurable, realistic, and challenging goals.

7. Establish task teams, made up of the right people, to work on pilot programs to achieve those goals.

8. Train those task teams as they address their assigned tasks in both technical and teamwork skills.

9. Measure results and in particular keep the focus on improving the whole process, not just a part of it.

10. Reward and celebrate results.

Concentrating on the imperatives of the business and looking at the cross-departmental processes that they rely on will help groups of employees avoid the Quality Control Circle syndrome. Highlighting the imperatives of the business requires gathering and analyzing data. Working on the processes means mapping them out in detail and homing in on the parts that must be improved. Not only does this approach lead to a better overall operation that is more responsive to customers, but it also means that the work force will be more aware of what is important to the business and more skillful at improving those things.

The External Customer—Component Four

The final component to TQ that gives it potency and makes it unique is the external customer. Past approaches to organizational excellence were independent of the customer. Organization Development has been inward looking and insulated in this regard, totally focused on the internal climate and the interactions of employees. Some of the technical elements go even a step farther toward total concern with the internal climate alone by being so conscious of cost that the customer may even be hurt (by inventories that raise costs and prices, by acceptable quality levels that actually encourage some bad product to reach the marketplace, or by industrial engineering practices that ingrain bad habits that negatively affect service). While none of these traditional practices were purposely intended to hurt a customer, they were created and used with only internal, cost-related considerations in mind, not with the customer in mind.

In fact, in the early days of Total Quality the customer was not very apparent either. So much change was needed and there was so much work to do inside the factory, the distribution center, the R&D center, and, eventually, in the office that all attention was devoted inside the business itself. This is one reason that sales forces and marketing departments have often not been touched by TQ, even in companies well known for their TQ efforts. One reflection of this is that in the late 1970s and early 1980s many TQ efforts were anchored by cost-of-quality programs and there was enormous effort expended on measuring how much quality actually cost. It was thought that top management would only be intrigued enough to pay attention to TQ if the cost ramifications were made apparent. This reinforced the notion that TQ was internally oriented and cost-driven.

By the 1980s, some consultants and their clients took a step in the right direction by focusing attention on the cost of *poor* quality rather than all the costs to produce a good-quality product. Cost of quality is traditionally made up of appraisal costs, detection costs, costs of rejects and of returns, cost of responding to customer complaints, warranty costs, and so forth; in other words, all costs connected in whatever way with product quality. Trying to calculate, communicate, and maintain total cost of quality is both confusing and cumbersome since doing so well and consistently requires significant changes to the accounting system. Cost of poor quality on the other hand, means the costs that would disappear if there were no quality problems. It is generally accepted that cost of poor quality can be from 20% to 40% of total sales, while the other quality costs— department costs, education costs, appraisal, etc.—are usually less than 5%.

It has only been in the last few years (since 1988 or so) that the customer component has taken shape on a large scale. Customer surveys, focus groups, one-on-one meetings between top managers of supplier companies with customers, and other ways to clarify the voice of the customer are becoming more common. This is not to say that these are new developments. Surveys, focus groups, etc. are information-gathering tools that have been used for many years. The differences today in the best examples of TQ are that they are being used by top-level managers, that they are part of overall company improvement efforts, that data are being translated to all employees, and most important, that the reason they are being used is to involve customers in the process of improvement so that their voice is both dominant and clear. In times past, customer data were used as input for the marketing department in product positioning and not for important product development and strategy, nor for feedback to the people who made and distributed the product.

Emphasis on the customer seems accepted as an important element of TQ in the 1990s. But it has not yet gone far enough in most cases. The customer and concern for meeting customers' needs and exceeding their expectations while producing what has been promised, must be the driving force behind Total Quality. Doing so provides for customer loyalty, which translates into market share. Also, there is an enormously powerful impact on the internal climate. As employees better appreciate that the customer is a real, live person who depends upon what they, the employees, do and how they do it, increased meaning is given to their efforts. That meaning leads to the resolve and determination to make the often difficult changes that are required.

Figure 2.2 depicts this view of the development of Total Quality.

In Summary

- Total Quality is part technical—largely Just-In-Time combined with the right diagnostic tools from quality engineering.

- TQ is part cultural—largely drawn from the field of Organization Development, including adult education

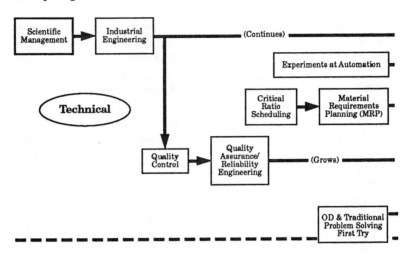

Figure 2.2
One View of the Evolution of Total Quality

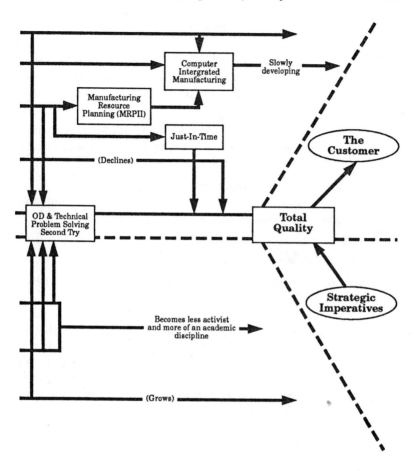

1970s   1980s   1990s

and management training and sociotechnical system theory.

- TQ concentrates on, and helps employees to focus attention on, strategic business imperatives and within that context on improving cross-department processes.
- TQ is a function of the customer and springs from a deeply held concern to meet the needs of and exceed the expectations of the customer.

How any organization mixes these ingredients is an individual decision. The recipe depends on where a company begins and the conditions under which it operates.

So, What's Behind the Door?

Let's turn back to the CEO's question "What will I find when I open the door?"

First you will find new ways of looking at your organization. You will find teams of people working together to solve problems that will have an impact on how well the business operates and to streamline and enhance the business's processes. You will find activities taking place that cross departmental and functional boundaries, rather than all activities taking place within functions. You will find data being gathered and turned into information in different ways than previously done, then analyzed in different ways so that they are more useful.

You will find people learning, to be sure; learning and mastering the tools and techniques of quality engineering, JIT, teamwork, and group problem solving. You will find people struggling to incorporate the philosophy of Total Quality into their daily work. You will notice, though, that this struggle is not damaging the climate, but is causing a certain enthusiasm among employees.

You will find people trying to do the right thing in the right way for the right reasons the first time around.

But most of all, you, the CEO, will find a lot of hard work that you must engage in. You will find your role as a leader more challenging and broadened. You will find that the imperatives of the business must be defined for your company in a way that can be understood not only by stock analysts and company directors but by secretaries, stock room workers, and skilled production workers. You will find it necessary to create a vision of what the company will look like in the future that is compelling for every worker, where every worker knows where he or she fits in, and what the customer will get out of it.

In short, you will find people striving to make Total Quality not an end in itself, but a means to a better and more satisfying company. If you find all of this, Total Quality will have been defined for you and your company. But I would hope the definition is something close to this:

Total Quality describes the state of an organization in which all the activities of all functions are designed and carried out in such a way that all external customer requirements are met while reducing internal time and cost, and enhancing the workplace climate.

These first two chapters have attempted to frame the definition of Total Quality and discussed it from the perspective of the organization trying to implement it. In Chapter 3, John Guaspari looks at it from the outside, from the perspective of the customers.

References

1. See bibliography for more on JIT.

2. Lee Bradford, Jack Gibb, and Ken Benne, *T Group Theory and the Laboratory Method* (New York: Wiley, 1964), pp. 82-83.

3. Ibid., p. 91.

4. W. Bennis, *Organization Development: Its Nature, Origins, and Prospects* (Reading, MA: Addison-Wesley, 1969).

5. See J. Blake and J. Mouton, *The Managerial Grid* (Houston: Mouton Gulf Publishing, 1964).

6. See D. Berlew and W. LeClere, "Social Intervention in Curacao," JABS, 10, 1 (1974).

7. Eric Trist, "On Socio Technical Systems," in Warren Bennis, Ken Benne, and Robert Chin, *The Planning of Change* (New York: Holt, Rinehart, Winston, 1968).

8. "A President's Experience with Democratic Management," *Occasional Papers,* No. 18, A. G. Bush Library, Industrial Relations Center, University of Chicago, June 1959.

9. Manaran, Shaw, and Wilson, *Managing Change,* Management Guide No. 3 (London: British Institute of Management, 1971), p. 21.

3

The Customer's Perspective of Business Quality: Starting Off on the Right Foot

John Guaspari*

"In a closed system..."

Anyone who ever took a freshman physics course in college will remember that four-word phrase. (And anyone who actually got through the course at some point figured out what it meant.) The first step in solving a problem was to define the system. You drew a dotted line around a combination of theoretically elegant but practically impossible weightless ropes and frictionless pulleys, thereby bounding the system—stepping back, assuming the proper perspective, and defining the area under investigation. Then you put your analytical hat on and went to work applying the various theories, laws, corollaries, and lemmas of mathematics and physics to solve the problem at hand.

A lot of progress has been made in the understanding of the "physics" of quality, and much of it has come from a better understanding of the area under investigation; we've gotten better at bounding the system. It wasn't all that long ago that when we talked about quality problems (and to the extent that we were even particularly worried about quality problems) we would see them as people problems, as in "George messed up" or "Jane didn't try hard enough." We drew the dotted line around people, the individual components of the system.

*Vice President, Rath & Strong, Inc.

Happily, it can be reported that that has changed. The accepted wisdom now holds that in the great majority of cases, the Georges and Janes of the world generally do things right, try hard enough, and genuinely care about quality. The loftier explanation for this has to do with matters of pride and self-esteem. The more prosaic rationale holds that doing rework and correcting mistakes is boring and a pain in the neck. Regardless of the impetus, however, the dynamics of the situation point toward individuals doing quality work.

We now say—correctly—that quality, properly understood, is a "process" issue and that the vast majority of quality problems are endemic to the system by which work is carried out in an organization. That notion, as far as it goes, is an important breakthrough in the area of quality progress. It gets the population of the organization in question, particularly the management population, focusing on "how things work" rather than "who messed up," and that is categorically a good thing.

What is not such a good thing is the failure to take the next step. Quality is a process issue, and the questions we choose to ask, the way we bound the problem at hand, where we draw the dotted line, are themselves parts of the process. Asking of ourselves, "How do things work around there?" is an important starting point. Probing further into "To what purpose?" represents a critical follow-up question.

Consider an example. If one were to cite Acme Manufacturing, Inc., which had achieved failure rates of zero, scrap rates of zero, first-pass testing rates of 100%, and infinite productivity, you might assume that this was an operation that had its act together. But might the fact that Acme had mastered the art of turning out perfect 8-track tape players mitigate your enthusiasm for their operating excellence?

If one were to describe the performance of the Ajax Delivery Company, which offered a guarantee of third-day delivery—right to your doorstep, never late, never a billing error, never the slightest deviation from their promise of performance—you might think pretty highly of them. But suppose the product they're delivering is the daily newspaper?

Are these examples unrealistic? Only in degree. Quality *is* a process issue, and the serious study of quality calls for an intensive focus on the thousand-and-one process details by which work is carried out in an organization. It is precisely the intensiveness of that focus that can cause us to lose the bigger picture and focus so closely on the "what" and "how" of quality that we lose track of the "why."

Peter Drucker has written that "the purpose of a business is to create and keep customers." Total Quality is the most powerful vehicle we have at our disposal to see to it that Drucker's dictum is observed. But unless we take a broader view and ensure that our quality actions are informed by the realities of the marketplace, unless we include the customer inside the dotted line that bounds the process under investigation, the results of our TQ efforts can be that we will simply go out of business more accurately and efficiently.

Taking the Customer's Perspective: A Critical Element of the TQ Process

Seeing to it that our TQ efforts are informed by our customer's point of view can have a dramatic, positive effect in two ways.

First, it will ensure that when we spend time on quality matters we are dealing with the imperatives of the business. One of the major hurdles to be cleared with any organizational quality effort is the extent to which people see quality as an ancillary issue: "I've got a job to do. I haven't got time for all this quality stuff." And if quality is perceived as a technical abstraction rather than a bedrock business issue, this tendency will be exacerbated. Inseparably attaching quality to customer issues lends an important air of validity and undeniability to quality efforts: "If our customers are saying we need to improve. . . ."

Second, there is a strong sense in which people will take the need for quality efforts as a personal indictment: "Are you telling me that I'm not doing a good enough job? That I'm not trying hard enough? That I'm not committed to the cause?" Whether those charges are valid or not (and in most cases these days they aren't) is less relevant than the fact that people perceive them that way, and they must be dealt with.

Attaching Quality to the Business Imperatives

What, *really*, is quality?

Historically, definitions of *quality* ran to things such as "hitting specs," "fitness for use," "conformance to requirements." Those definitions are fine, as far as they go.

Let's use "conformance to requirements" as our working definition of quality. It is the one espoused by Philip Crosby and the best of what might be thought of as the "standard definitions of quality."

Conformance to requirements. Correct, but it begs a critical question: namely, "Says who?" Consider. One set of requirements to which we must conform is what will be called here the "specifications" component to quality. These are the numerical targets that we establish and against which we make measurements to run the business, and which we *must* establish and against which we *must* make measurements to run the business. The part shall be x cm by y cm, the order shall be processed within z days (or hours or minutes). Having such specifications, clearly defined and effectively communicated, is essential to any effort to achieve quality. Absolutely necessary.

Necessary, but they are not sufficient. Suppose you were to go to a store to buy, say, a set of tires for your car. The clerk tells you that the tires will last for 50,000 miles. You buy the tires, but lo and behold, they wear out after just 35,000 miles. How do you feel about the quality of those tires? An emotion somewhat south of "delight" would probably apply in such a case.

Now let's go back in time. Assume the first purchase never happened. You enter the tire shop, are steered to the same set of tires, and are told: "These tires will last for 25,000 miles." So you buy them, and, 25,000 miles later, they're still in good shape. In fact, they last for a full 35,000 miles!

Now how do you feel about the quality of those tires? Probably a whole lot better. But why? They're the same tires, the same performance, the same mileage before they wore out. For all you know, they were built to the same specs. But as the customer you're probably not terribly interested in those specs. If you wanted to worry about the thousands of details that go into the manufacturing of tires all day every day you'd be in the tire business. But you're not. As a customer, you are implicitly saying to Goodyear, or Goodrich, or Firestone, or Michelin, or Pirelli, or you-name-it: "Here's my money. You worry about the details."

Your reading of—your *feel for*—the quality of the tires has changed dramatically in the two cases. Owing to what? Owing to the tires' performance relative to your expectations. Which leads us to a refinement of the standard definition of quality:

Quality is that which meets the customer's expectations.

The definition is fully consistent with "conformance to requirements" and "fitness for use," but more useful—and usefulness and efficacy in implementation are the issues here, not theoretical elegance—if you accept the premise that institutional focus is a critical part of the TQ process to be managed.

- In the final analysis, quality is what the customer says it is.

- Customers make quality judgments based not on a detailed reading of the supplier's operation specs, but on a much more impressionistic scale: "Did you or didn't you give me what I thought I was paying you for? Did you or didn't you meet my expectations?"

If you doubt these assertions, consider how you make decisions as a customer. Consider the role that expectations play in determining your level of satisfaction.

The Quality of What Is at Issue

We tend to think in terms of the quality of the products we build or the services we offer. But customers don't buy products or services. They buy answers to needs—the ability to do something they couldn't have done without us and for which they're willing to give us money.

Quality is a function of expectations. As was demonstrated in the preceding tire example, we have expectations for the products we purchase. But we also have expectations for the delivery date of the product. And that the explanatory product literature will be clear (and, for that matter, present). And that the invoice will be timely and accurate. And that the advertisement that drew us to the product in the first place will be a fair and reliable representation of the product. And that when we have to call the supplier with a question, the phone will be answered within a reasonable number of rings. And that the person answering the phone will be gracious and capable, connecting us directly to the party who can help us without our having to run a telephonic gauntlet. And on and on it goes, with the customer gaining impressions about the supplier organization based upon its performance relative to his or her expectations for not just the product, but every aspect of the experience of doing business with that organization, what can be thought of as the quality of the total transaction.

This is where many TQ efforts fall down. It is often assumed that the "Total" in "Total Quality" means extending quality efforts beyond the factory floor and into all functional areas of the organization. So, yes, manufacturing has a quality effort in place. But since Total Quality is the goal, so does engineering. And marketing. And sales. And accounting. And administration. And human resources. And finance.

Suppose each function pays explicit attention to the quality of the work in its area, vigilantly applying the proven and powerful techniques of quality. Will that lead to improvements? Almost certainly. But—and this is a critical question—will this *necessarily* mean that when all the pieces come together, it will yield the best possible result from the customer's perspective?

The answer, unfortunately, is no. As customers, we aren't interested in whether or not *each* function performs well. (As a matter of fact, as customers, we aren't particularly interested in anything about those functions.) Our interest as customers is that *all* of the functions perform well.

Our business objective ought to be more a matter of integrating functional efforts than summing them. It is the seamlessness of the total transaction that matters to our customers and not the results of our "Quality Department of the Month" competitions. How do you feel when you call ABC, Inc. with a question and are told: "Oh, that's not my area. You'll have to talk to someone in accounts receivable about that." Would your feelings change appreciably if it could be demonstrated to you that the person to whom you had spoken was "right?" That the internal rules and regulations had been followed to a tee?

Building seamless Total Quality transactions is a difficult goal to reach. It becomes impossible if it's not made clear to everyone in the organization. Getting people to take the customer's perspective can enhance that clarity enormously.

___

Uncovering the Real Opportunities of Quality

A bit of a devil's advocacy.

"You've written that 'Quality is that which meets the customer's expectations.'"

"That's right."

"But I don't want to just meet my customers' expectations. My objective ought to be to exceed them."

"Mine too."

"Then the logic of your position breaks down."

"How so?"

"Well, if quality means 'meeting' expectations, yet your goal is to exceed them. . .?"

"The only way the logic breaks down is if my goal is quality. And I don't think it should be."

"Excuse me?"

"Look, Quality does mean meeting expectations. We ought to be trying to exceed customers' expectations to truly make the customer delighted, ecstatic even. Therefore quality—merely meeting expectations—can't be our objective. It's a critical way station, to be sure. But it's not the destination."

"Then why can't quality mean 'meeting or exceeding expectations' so that when you exceed expectations, you're delivering even more quality?"

"Because then you let the genie back out of the bottle. In the beginning of the Total Quality involvement, it was written that 'quality means conformance: either you've done it or you haven't.' This was an invaluable contribution. Quality became a digital issue—one or zero, yes or no, plus or minus. No longer was quality a matter of subjective judgment. Quality as 'conformance to requirements,' which can be refined in customer terms to 'meeting expectations,' enables us to get our arms around it, measure it, and manage it. If you tell people that quality means meeting expectations, you've told them something specific. Tell them 'meet or exceed' and all of a sudden things get vague again."

"But shouldn't we want people to deliver more quality?"

"Can't be done. Now it's my turn to say that the logic of your position breaks down."

"How so?"

"Look. Suppose I had two lamps here in front of me. The lamps are exactly the same in every aspect except for one. Into one lamp I've screwed a 60-watt bulb, and into the other lamp I've screwed a 100-watt bulb. The question is, which lamp is more *on?"*

"They're both on!"

"Exactly."

"But the question doesn't make sense. If you were to ask me, 'Which lamp is throwing off more light?' or 'Which lamp is consuming more power?' I could answer that. But to ask which lamp is more 'on' is illogical.

"Again, exactly. Quality, properly understood, is, like a lamp, an 'on/off' proposition. Just as talking about which lamp is more 'on' makes no sense, neither does talking about delivering more quality. Once expectations have been met, quality 'switches on.' To be sure, you can go beyond expectations, and in the process you've delivered more of something. But it's not more quality, it's more of something else."

"Well then what is that something else?"

"Value."

"Value?"

"Value. Remember, we started all of this by talking about the importance of seeing things from the customer's perspective. Well, to customers all that matters is value, the ratio of "what I got" to "what it cost me." You can put that in a simple equation as: Value = Got/Cost."

"But isn't quality built into that value equation?"

"Absolutely. The point at which quality is reached—or, if you prefer, 'switches on'—can be thought of as minimum acceptable value. It's what gets you into the game. But to truly stand out you have to deliver more, you have to provide added value."

"Are you saying that we should forget about quality and focus on added value?"

"No. I'm saying that we need to understand the relationship between the two. The concept of added value only makes sense once we've gotten our quality house in order. Viewed this way, quality becomes the foundation on which we build our efforts to deliver added value and in the process achieve competitive advantage. And that ought to be our business objective."

"But doesn't this approach beg the question of quality versus cost trade-offs?"

"Quite the contrary. Bear in mind that cost is in the denominator of the value equation. This approach will force you not so much to make trade-offs as to explicitly address the most fundamental business question of all: What are we giving our customers and what is it costing them? Answer that right, and we're successful. Get it wrong, and we've got problems. But realize what's happened here. Our quality efforts, which provide the basis for our value-added efforts, have now got us addressing bedrock business issues instead of assessing blame and looking for scapegoats."

"I don't know . . . all this business about customer focus and added value. Won't it incline us to give away too much?"

"If you give away a lot and don't charge enough for it, you will go out of business. That's not good for you, and it's hardly added value for your customers. So there would seem to be a built-in safeguard. If you give away a lot and charge too much, then the value your customers receive— got/cost—is low, not high.

Two summary points to consider about value: 1) We've defined value as "what the customer gets per what it costs the customer." But bear in mind that that customer "gets" more than a physical product. He or she gets a sense of confidence in a supplier. A sense of assurance that the supplier will be there when needed and that when the next generation of products comes along, they'll be taken care of. When service is required, it'll be there. Those assurances are part of the package customers get and for which they may be willing to pay. And turning that "may" into a "will" has to do with the degree of understanding of one's customers. That's a pretty basic issue, one that a value-based approach to quality forces us to consider. And what this all "costs" the customer is more than money. It can be time, aggravation, frustration, inconvenience. All are part of the value of a total transaction. All must be factored in. 2) This is not a panacea. It will not magically provide all the right answers. But it will make us far more likely to ask the right questions, which is a major piece of progress.

Tending to the Effect of TQ Efforts

Sample testimony of an individual who finds himself or herself a part of a TQ effort:

> I understand that quality makes good sense. I understand that there are significant business benefits to be realized and that we ought to go after them. I understand that there are techniques to be applied and that we ought to apply them. I understand that there are measurements to be made and that we ought to make them. Intellectually, I've got it, I grasp it, I understand. But somebody please tell me why it is that if quality is so good, if quality is so right—why is it that whenever anybody talks to me about quality, it doesn't make me *feel* good. Why is it I feel threatened, defensive? Why is it I feel my back go up? Why is it I feel like, when we make all those measurements, what's really being measured is whether or not *I* measure up?

In fact, that set of emotions is almost universally felt: not always expressed, but almost always felt. It knows no bounds, industry, function, nor hierarchy. If you believe a key element of the quality orthodoxy, which holds that "quality is everybody's job," then the fact that a significant percentage of that same population of everybody doesn't exactly turn its attention to TQ efforts with bells on represents a significant problem.

We say we want buy in to quality, that we want everyone to take ownership of quality. Well, if large numbers of people are buying in to quality in the same way that they buy in to filing their income tax returns on April 15 or buy in to their biannual visits to the dentist and all the potential for excitement that a root canal holds, then we will not realize the potential that TQ truly does have to offer.

Why the disfunction? Again, it has to do with the way we bound the issue of TQ, with where we draw the dotted line. Yes, it's essential that we understand and apply the technologies of quality. But if we believe that the agent which truly makes TQ progress happen is the people who produce the product or service, then we must also account for the psychological impact our quality efforts will have on those people. We must square the intellectual with the visceral, tending to both the content and the affect of those TQ efforts.

Is there an approach to quality that will cover all of the bases, a perspective that will help us see our way around these obstacles in our path to TQ? Yes. And it's the same perspective that was discussed in ensuring that TQ was directed at the imperatives of the business.

It's the customer's perspective, and the reason for its power comes from the fact that it is a universally shared perspective. Everyone in any organization—all job functions, all hierarchical levels, all ages—has a lifetime's experience at being a customer. We all know what it is, what it means, what it feels like (and "feels like" is a key phrase) to be a customer, whether at a bank or in a restaurant or with an insurance company or a computer supplier. We know—deep down, emotionally, viscerally—what pleases us and causes us to go back for more. We know what displeases us and causes us to consider alternatives. Yet we can get on the job and lose sight of that invaluable body of knowledge. It's not because we don't care or aren't committed or aren't devoted to the cause. Quite the contrary. It's usually because we do care so much and get so wrapped up in the details of what we're doing and how we're doing it that we lose sight of why we're doing it in the first place.

Quality is important because it is the thing that assures that we will deliver the value for which our customers are paying us. People understand that intellectually and feel it viscerally. Along with aligning our efforts with the imperatives of the business, looking at quality from the customer's perspective enables us to achieve true buy-in. No longer is quality perceived as "management standing in judgment of me." Now it becomes "our customers standing in judgment of us."

That is by no means an easy challenge. In fact, if anything, it's tougher. It is not that people are unwilling to take on tough challenges; rather, they are less inclined to take on challenges that don't feel right. The fact that we've all had a lifetime's experience as customers is pivotal in passing that "feels right" test. The fact that taking the customer's perspective does tend to both the content and the effect of TQ efforts is pivotal in passing the more rigorous business test.

Why Worry About "Why"?

Quality is a process issue. The perspective we take toward quality is in itself a part of the process. By taking the customer's perspective, we will be more likely to hit our business targets, since it will point us toward the following notions.

1. To the customer, quality is a function of expectations.

2. Customers have expectations for the total experience of doing business with us—for the total transaction.

3. What customers are after when they enter into transactions with us is maximizing the value received.

4. Total Quality is the base on which customer value is built.

5. We are better able to achieve true commitment to quality since it enables us to channel the energies of a lifetime's experience as customers onto quality issues.

Of course we must understand and apply quality technologies; we must be able to address the "what" and "how" of quality. But quality will ultimately be achieved through people, and people need to know "why." So let's close with the simplest, most direct formulation of "why": The customers have the money. We want it. Our job is to figure out how to get them to give it to us in a world of choice and in a world of change.

And one of the changes that is inexorably occurring is the fact that unless TQ efforts are informed by a laser sharp customer focus, they will fall short. The operating results won't be there. The competitive edge won't be there. And worst of all, you won't, in fact, know why.

Part II

How to Successfully Implement Total Quality

4

Total Quality and the Character of the Organization

So far, a description of Total Quality has been offered from both the view of the customer and the view of the organization. This chapter will delve more deeply into the sort of place a company dedicated to Total Quality can be by describing facets of the organizational character of such a place.[1] It will then offer some ideas on finding out how your organization measures up to these characteristics.

Not Organization Culture

The Random House College Dictionary defines culture as "the sum total of ways of living built up by a group of human beings and transmitted from one generation to another." Culture as it applies to organizations, and to Total Quality in particular, has become a popular topic. Hardly a speech or article on TQ occurs today without the terms "corporate culture" or "organizational culture."

On one hand, this is a positive development because it raises this amorphous but important concept to a higher level of recognition. It has only been within the last decade that this has been the case outside of some academic circles and the Organization Development movement. Talking about this notion will inevitably lead to more research, more practical experimentation, and greater benefit to those companies anxious to improve.

On the other hand, there is a clear danger in the belief that the culture can be altered permanently by any single individual or, for that matter, by an organization improvement effort. Too often today, the term "culture" is used in a way that implies the culture of the organization can be changed easily, or at least can be changed whenever one's mind is made up to do so. Anyone who has actually tried to lead such an effort knows that in reality this sort of change does not take place in the short term, and certainly not because people will it to happen. The culture of an organization (like the culture of a society) is not something that a single leader creates, nor is it something that managers control and make predictable, like a budget or a project with a starting point and a completion date. The culture is something that every person in the organization contributes to and has a role in either perpetuating or changing over a very long period of time.

The organization culture is a function of

1. the collective action of all employees—not just the ones at the top, not just the "stars," not just the union, but everyone,

2. years of actions taken, decisions made, policies cast, recast, and discarded, with each successive generation changing somewhat but not entirely that which has been laid before; the new generation adds something new, its own unique layer for future generations to add to or chip away at when it has its turn, and

3. both the formal policies and procedures and also the informal lore, as in, "the way things are around here." Because informal lore occupies a more important role, to attempt a TQ effort (which seeks to alter the character of the organization in fundamental ways) by only concentrating on the policies and procedures, as some advocate, is naive and potentially destructive.

But, Rather, Organizational Character

For the purposes of striving for Total Quality, it is more precise and appropriate to focus not on the culture of the organization, but rather on its character. The Random House Dictionary says that character is the "aggregate of features and traits that form the individual nature of some person or thing." It is certain types of traits and features that Total Quality seeks to bring about, distinguishable from those that preceded it.

The TQ-induced organization character is one that has the 12 attributes described in the following paragraphs.

1. Decision-making authority and responsibility are at the lowest reasonable level. *Authority* here means just that: the power to make the decision and the belief by people assigned the authority that that power is vested in them, and that they are responsible for the results of the decision. *Lowest level* here obviously means of the organization chart, and *reasonable* means that the leader must exercise some judgment and not expect people at a level that is too low to make decisions they are either unprepared for or don't have the information needed to make.

2. Problems do not wait to be solved and, more important, potential problems are anticipated and addressed before becoming problems. This is the case partly because decisions can be made at levels where problems and the signs that precede them can be dealt with quickly.

3. There is relentless activity at reducing time and improving the quality of what is provided to the customer while, at the same time, enhancing the organization climate. All such improvement activity is measured by its ability to tangibly improve how the business operates to satisfy the customer.

4. The entire TQ effort is seen as a means to a better company. It focuses its attention on a vision of the ideal, realistic company of the future that is commonly held. It is in large part the belief in this future vision that provides the glue that bonds people together and enables them to move in unison toward a company they have been able to picture in their minds.

5. In terms of employees in a TQ company, one should expect to see

   a. a widespread attitude of wanting to excel and being willing to do what is needed to constantly improve.

   b. employees going out of their way to make sure the right tasks are completed in the right way.

   c. a widespread spirit of discovery and inquisitiveness.

   d. people excited about their work and viewing it as important, relevant, and meaningful.

   e. a certain degree of purposeful impatience, which triggers a drive to get the job done now—this is the enemy of complacency and procrastination.

6. Even though employee involvement is the norm, improvement efforts are directed by leaders and managers, starting at the top.

7. A lot of work goes on in small groups. Operating in cross-functional task teams should be the norm and should be an immediate reaction to issues that involve more than one department.

8. Teamwork is the operating mode by which things get done. Teamwork is defined so that it has the same meaning to all, and there are special training programs to sharpen teamwork skills.

9. There is constant communication of company progress, successes, and failures. The strategy is widely known and understood. Data on customer satisfaction are shared often and with everyone.

10. While there is a dedication to helping co-workers, this does not overshadow concern for the external customer. There are many companies that emphasize the notion of an "internal customer" often to the detriment of doing what is best for the external, ultimate customer. (It is preferable for leaders to emphasize the preeminence of the external customer and to refer to "internal clients" rather than internal customers.)

11. Heroes and the lore of the company emphasize customer satisfaction, extraordinary service, taking substantial personal risk to make sure what is shipped is right, and so forth.

12. Of course, the leader has the most significant role to play. He or she must purposefully put in place ways to promote

    a. a belief that the employee has the right and the responsibility to improve his or her immediate surroundings, to change whatever affects the ability to do the right job and is within his or her control,

    b. a sense of ownership in the product or service delivered to the customer,

    c. the ability of the people, and through them of the systems, to innovate and to create something new that adds value,

    d. a feeling of co-dependence—that "We are all in this together" and the good of the whole supersedes that of the individual,

    e. the desire to change and to improve what currently exists, and

    f. commitment to a commonly held vision of the sort of company that could be.

Listing these attributes in this manner makes a TQ character sound utopian: one big happy family with every employee eager to please, all going in the same direction, anticipating problems, and pouncing on opportunities as soon as they pop up. It is not as farfetched as it may seem, as anyone can attest who has been through Disneyland; talked to employees at Stu Leonard's grocery store in Norwalk, Connecticut; met with pilot and quality-improvement teams at Hutchinson Technology, Xerox, Motorola, Florida Power and Light, or Milliken. It is certainly not common for a business to have these characteristics; many more have tried than have succeeded. But what the past decade of experimentation has proven is that it is possible to create an environment that can lead to such a culture, not all at once and, perhaps, not easily, but it is a task that can be achieved.

While the term *organizational character* as it is defined here should be the focus of activity of a TQ effort, what is the relationship between TQ implementation and the organization's culture? If Total Quality can have a positive effect on the character of the organization, that is, on how the organization "acts," what impact might it have on its culture? To find out, let's look at an example of a culture in the process of changing.

Changing an Organization Culture

An executive I will call Jack was hired as the president of a large consumer products company three years ago. He had actually begun his career at the firm just after business school years before. He left to succeed in three other corporations, each time taking on larger and larger responsibilities. When he was hired back after 25 years, the company where Jack had first been hired had changed quite a bit. Rather than the energetic, team-oriented place he had remembered, where going to work each day was fun, what Jack found was an organization where departments rarely cooperated, the dominant operating mode was low risk taking, fingers were pointed at one another when something went wrong, and behavior was generally self-serving and self-centered. One of the first things Jack noticed when he began holding review meetings was that those making reports about accomplishments used the term "I" almost exclusively, hardly ever did he hear what "we" had accomplished; a sure sign of a climate not geared to teamwork. Jack realized that in addition to getting the volume and profit growing again, there was a significant job to do in changing attitudes and behavior.

Let's now "fast forward" to the present and walk through headquarters. In the place of the drab, lifeless environment of three years ago, today office furniture is bright. Offices and modular work areas that formed an incomprehensible maze and served only to separate departments have been rearranged in a more open configuration. People walk faster than they did before, seemingly with more purpose and direction. There is more energy in conference rooms as people debate issues more forcefully. Laughter is evident, a dramatic contrast to the moroseness apparent three years before. One also notices that the people in significant decision-making positions today are of a different sort, people who bring enthusiasm and optimism to their jobs. There are more meetings, more opportunity and requirements to plan and solve problems in groups. Employees know how the business is performing. They receive a memo from Jack each month describing the current conditions and challenges and comparing the results of the previous month and year-to-date results to target.

The most significant, and important, change has been in the performance of the business. Market share is up. Even though volume has stayed more or less even because of a flat market, profits are dramatically higher. One reason is that costs are down, but the other, more important reason is that decisions are being made faster, execution is more smooth and complete, and there are fewer mistakes. Emphasis has been put on doing what adds value. The customer is emphasized in a positive way, replacing the former belief that customers were necessary pains-in-the-neck to be tolerated.

While dramatic change in the behavior of people in this organization has occurred, some vestiges of what existed previously remain. People from the old regime have been retained because they possess skills or knowledge important to the business's success. These long-time employees have not entirely embraced the new norms and occasionally are roadblocks to progress. They tend to be less open, to refuse to confront issues or people openly, and still act in what can only be called a political manner. It is not uncommon to see even new employees act in a way that is more like the company's former character. There is occasionally miscommunication, or no communication at all, which leads to some lack of trust and teamwork.

While Jack's era has spanned three years, the sort of behavior that one sees today at his company has certainly not been taking place for three years. It took six months to become reacquainted with the business and to tour sales offices and factories. It took a year to replace people who it was decided would not succeed in the new environment that Jack was constructing. The new people who have been hired needed some time to get on board and to establish themselves.

Training programs are just now being delivered to ensure consistent problem-solving approaches and language, and to help quicken the pace of teamwork. The formal reward system has yet to change a great deal; while formal rewards such as promotions have been affected, the pay system remains more or less as it was. Measurement of performance has begun to change but not been solidified nor made a part of normal, to-be-expected activity.

Has the culture of this organization changed? No, not, at least, by my definition. The reason is that the new behavior has not been taking place long enough to become truly ingrained. A culture changes when the basic assumptions and values are altered, and that happens only when certain behavior that reflects those attitudes has taken place long enough that it becomes the accepted way of operating, so natural that it is taken for granted and is passed down from one generation to another.[2] Also, cultures change when solidifying mechanisms such as training programs and new measurement and reward systems are used to reinforce new attitudes and behavior.

What Jack has accomplished so far is a change in the character of his company. That new character will bring about a new culture if it is reinforced and if the new behaviors are institutionalized over a long period of time. How long a time depends on a number of factors, but one or two years is hardly long enough for behavior to be considered permanent. It will not be permanent until the new behavior is legitimized by significant reinforcement, lack of any steps from leaders to force reversion to old behavior, and a reward and measurement system that reflects the values on which the new behavior is based. The values on which Jack is basing his new organization (as well as his success) have been laid out and described by him in some detail. He has written them, spoken about them, and reinforced them in many ways. But changing behavior takes time and most people must try new behavior, experience how it feels, wait to see what happens to make sure the boss means what he says, and then try it some more.

There's also another factor: financial results. The reality of permanent behavior change in a business organization is that it will simply not last unless the new way of operating, the new character, brings better business results. Such results include developing products faster; reducing costs without firing people but by operating differently; increasing market share because the customer feels specially treated and is more loyal; achieving more profit and the pride that goes along with it; rewarding people more substantially than in the past. These are results that lead to lasting behavioral change, and, if these results continue over time, to eventual change in the culture itself. From the point of view of the business enterprise, the most important measure of a Total Quality character is whether the organization which acts that way achieves truly remarkable, tangible results and is able to sustain those results.

Sustaining Results

An example that makes the point is Motorola. Chairman Robert Galvin has put it this way.

> A decade ago [we] were growing and enjoyed [a larger market share than competitors]. But some officers reported that customers were dissatisfied . . . and some competitors were outperforming us. . . . We listened. All company officers met on this issue. That meeting stirred a corporate management conviction to set much higher quality expectations.
>
> We were already a participative management company [and there was not much trouble getting people to sign up]. Plans were drawn to involve customers and suppliers . . . to . . . achieve total customer satisfaction.
>
> We set an initial goal to reduce defects, paperwork, delivery, etc. to one-tenth [what they were at the outset]. For example, our . . . yield on a transistor was 5,000 defects per 1,000,000 devices, not bad when translated into 99.5% good, but too bad for the user. [Our first goal was] to reduce defects 10 times or down to 500 per million. . . . [Many people contributed] new concepts on creating and controlling quality. We listened. We [also] went to other organizations benchmarking the best-of-class of each function. We listened. In time, we began a series of fundamental changes.
>
> - Quality [had] the first order of attention on meeting agendas, reviews, plans, compensation, and rewards.
> - We clarified responsibilities and identified champions.
> - We organized to a more manageable size . . . and integrated functions.
> - We established regular quality systems reviews.
> - In a few businesses we . . . [changed] every standard, expectation, process, and system. . . .

To accomplish these [changes], and to move to the most challenging standards, we continuously informed and hoped to inspire our people . . . they listened . . . [and] responded.

[We conducted] massive training.

- We trained ourselves in processes.
- We shared experiences.
- We brought in the best teachers of the new ideas.
- We [learned] how to better design for quality, for manufacturability, [and] to analyze for quality results [through] statistical process control.
- We studied the latest techniques in cycle time management.
- We teamed [together] the best people to employ these . . . skills.[3]

Motorola President George Fisher adds a comment on the firm's results. "We once measured defects in parts per thousand. Now we measure them in parts per million . . . and in some areas, parts per billion. We have surpassed our goal . . . of improving quality tenfold. Our new goal is to improve one hundred fold on the way to achieving [a quality level of] six sigma by 1992. This translates into 99.9997% product or service." He goes on to say that there are two keys to achieve such tough targets. One is an integrated approach to the business where the organization structure has been flattened and elongated levels have been taken out and suppliers have been added. "It takes a horizontal organization to serve the customer," he contends, and then points out that when such a structure is adopted, "the manufacturing function becomes more pivotal. Marketing, design, and manufacturing people form teams to develop products that meet customer needs and can be produced quickly, reliably, and efficiently . . . an integrated approach enables us to design in quality from the beginning." He attributes such progress to the second key to achieving tough targets, a participative and cooperative culture and goes on to say that the job still is not quite done. "The ability of a large corporation to work as a team across functional lines is still one of the most difficult transitions."[4]

Milliken offers yet another example. CEO Roger Milliken changed his management style in the early 1980s and made customer responsiveness the core of a Total Quality effort. "We had a communication problem and I realized that management was the real problem." He streamlined company management, gave more authority to employees, and implemented a team approach to production. The results showed up in increased profits, less absenteeism, and expansion of markets. "Continuous education and training of (our employees) is the master key that unlocks the door to quality improvement every day. Our long-term plan calls for management change . . . and that requires enabling and empowering each and every [employee] to make customer satisfaction [the number one] goal."[5]

Training has played a significant role in any company that has succeeded in establishing a new organizational character. IBM was one of the first major companies to make manager training mandatory. It began before the depression of the 1930s with the IBM School House in Endicott, New York, where all salesmen, and eventually others, were trained in intensive programs, some lasting 12 weeks. Today, 40 hours a year for every manager is mandatory. Milliken estimates it spends $1700 per employee per year on training; at 13,000 employees, that's $22 million. At Corning, almost $5 million dollars was spent setting up the Corning Quality Institute at the start of its TQ effort, and that was a period when Corning was just breaking even.

Learning Programs for TQ

There are a number of learning programs for employees that can help bring about a new character and that are parts of most TQ efforts. Table 4.1 categorizes them as awareness, training, or education sessions and offers examples of each and the population that would most likely attend.

"Awareness sessions" are programs intended to make people more aware of what Total Quality is and what it can accomplish. They provide an overview of Total Quality and of the results that are possible from its components. Done well, awareness sessions whet appetites and expand horizons at the start of a TQ effort. These are typically sessions that last anywhere from one-half day to two days.

Table 4.1
Examples of Learning Programs for Total Quality Implementation

Population	Awareness	Training	Education
		Types of Programs	
Top management	Introduction to TQ for leaders Update awareness sessions as the TQ effort progresses	Common vision workshop Steering committee training Teamwork training Positive influence and negotiation	Measurement/reward systems for TQ TQ tools and techniques
Middle management	Introduction to TQ for managers Update awareness sessions	Task team training Team leader training Positive influence and negotiation Facilitator training	Structured problem solving Work flow analysis Design for excellence JIT tools for TQ
Supervisor/professional	Introduction to TQ for supervisors Introduction to TQ for nonsupervisory professionals Update awareness sessions	Task team training Team leader training Facilitator training Supervising in a TQ environment Positive influence and negotiation	Structured problem solving Work flow analysis Design for excellence JIT tools for TQ
Work force	Introduction to TQ for work force Update awareness sessions	Task team training Team leader training Facilitator training Positive influence and negotiation	Structured problem solving Work flow analysis Design for excellence JIT tools for TQ

"Training" means programs that train people in specific behavioral skills:

- interpersonal skills such as active listening or giving feedback in a helpful way;
- influence skills—particularly helpful in an environment where vertical authority means less and where getting something done well often means people from different departments and from different organizational levels working together;
- negotiation skills—because the resources of various departments will need to be shared in a company with a TQ character.

These sessions should be active, with attendants being more "participants" than "students," taking an active role in their own learning rather than just listening (as they would in awareness sessions). This means that role play, active analysis of questionnaires to diagnose management style, and various exercises are integral to the design of these training sessions.

The third type of learning event is an "education session." An example might be a seminar on statistical process control or one on the details of Just-In-Time in achieving huge reductions in time and cost. These sessions could last anywhere from a few hours to a week, depending on the topic and need. What distinguishes education sessions from awareness sessions is that education sessions present conceptual material in more depth and go beyond awareness, delving into more detail.

In addition to Table 4.1, see Appendix B for designs of a typical awareness session, for a task-team training program used for problem-solving teams working on pilot projects, and for an agenda for an education course offering an overview Statistical Process Control.

Ideal Character for Each Company Is Unique

There is no such thing as a standard TQ organization character. The ideal organization character to aim for will be adapted and tailored for individual company circumstances because we are dealing with individuals in an environment that depends in large part on who they are and how they interact. Add to this the company's unique product and market situation, then add the impact of the company's lineage and the policies and methods that developed through the years. What results from that set of ingredients is a unique character. The characteristics described previously are intended as a starting point. Their value is a function of the care and judgment with which a company's leaders decide where and how to proceed, and what they want their company to become as a result of a Total Quality effort.

Part of the task of leading a TQ effort is to become as clear as possible about the sort of organization character that is sought through Total Quality. Most common among those ways to establish a model are these three:

- Benchmarking—visiting and studying other companies that have moved well down the road to establishing a character that is admired.

- Common Vision Workshops—where top managers can learn to more clearly envision the sort of place they wish to create. The goal is not a pie-in-the-sky vision, but a picture that is fairly concrete and realistic while challenging and inspirational at the same time.

- Intra-company communications strategies—to "market" the vision of top managers (in the most positive sense of that word) through the right communication programs so that that vision is adapted, shaped, and made into a common vision that all employees can embrace.

In one case, a large financial services business did all three. Figure 4.1 depicts the sequence.

The Common Vision Workshop was split into two parts. Part I lasted three days and resulted in prioritized, draft lists of the key operational metrics for the ideal business and of the characteristics of the sort of company that would most likely achieve them. The top team was then divided into three subgroups to complete different tasks over the subsequent eight weeks. Team 1 was to find companies it could visit that had achieved or were trying to achieve such a character. Meanwhile, Team 2 was assigned the task of research by reviewing literature and interviewing TQ thought leaders to determine what it would likely take to move toward the desired character. Team

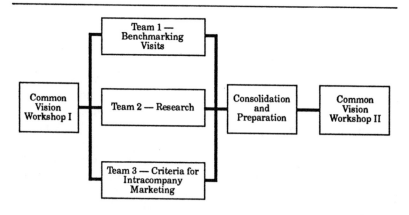

Figure 4.1
One Way to Establish a Model of Organization Character

3's task was to draft a marketing plan so that when the top team was ready, there were communication programs available to spread the word.

The three teams came together after eight weeks for another three days to describe what each team had done, discuss findings and recommendations, and decide on the next steps. Characteristics of the sort of company that could achieve what the top team wanted were hammered out at this second workshop. Among the next steps established at that workshop was to decide how to best discover the nature of the company's current character.

The Current Character

Once the process is underway of envisioning what the ideal, realistic character might be, it is time to take the temperature of the current organization, to measure the current character of the company. There are three sets of activities that can help make such a measurement: (1) ask customers, (2) ask employees, and (3) analyze both how people get ahead in that organization and the image it projects externally.

Ask Customers

One way to measure the current character is to go to customers and ask what it is like doing business with your company. This can be done through visits from leaders to their counterparts in customer companies. These so-called "top-to-top visits" offer benchmarking opportunities. They have the potential of building bonds between top-level executives. They can make one feel proud or humble (both are needed at various times) depending on what is heard. They can spur a leader on to action. There is nothing quite like looking a customer straight in the eye and hearing what is good and bad about the company that you are responsible for; it is educational and, at times, cathartic.

Another way to hear from customers is a survey. This can be in the form of a series of focus groups or a questionnaire or perhaps both. The advantage of a formal survey is that large numbers of customers can be surveyed and the data can be tabulated, analyzed, and stored to be compared with similar surveys at regular intervals.

What is right in any particular case depends on several factors: the nature of the market; the location of customers; what one wants most to discover from customers; and objectives of the survey. It is usually best, however, to do some sort of formal survey every 18 to 24 months and to conduct visits on a much more frequent basis. Regardless of the industry, if the CEO is not out in the marketplace meeting customers at least once each quarter, there is danger of losing touch with what customers are thinking and feeling and of not being able to direct the business sufficiently with the customer in mind.

Ask Employees

Another necessary way to assess the current character of the business is to conduct an employee survey. Here again, there is a range of options. Meetings can be held of employees and leaders over a brown bag lunch, focus groups, a formal survey using a questionnaire. These are just three of the ways that can be used to find out what people are thinking and feeling. The combination of these thoughts and emotions will build the mosaic that is the organizational character.

Roland Pampel, former CEO of Bull HN, said in 1990 of asking employees,

> I can't see how a leader of a large, complex organization can get a grasp of what he's running without face-to-face contact with employees on a regular basis. They're the

ones on the front lines dealing with the problems that get in the way of our customers being satisfied. If I just sat in my office or in the Board Room or even with customers without direct feedback from our hourly people, supervisors, middle managers, salesmen, customer service people, and engineers I just don't see how I could make the right decisions about the business and where it's going.

The most complicated of these options is also the one that will deliver the most rich and useful data. This is the formal survey of the organization using a questionnaire. For TQ purposes, it is best to follow rules such as these when conducting such formal surveys:

1. Make sure the questionnaire is tailored and specific to meet the particular needs of your organization. It may be easier to use a standard version without tailoring, but the results will not be as rich.

2. Survey every employee. It adds to the complexity and the time involved to complete the survey, but if the point of doing the survey is to find out what is going on as well as to give people a chance to participate, then it only makes sense to ask everyone what is on his or her mind. While there are added administrative costs, the overall cost is not that much greater when sampling is compared with surveying every employee; the cost is in establishing the right questions and feeding it back in the right way, not processing data.

3. Introduce the survey in the right way. Make sure people understand what this survey is for, how data are to be used, that all responses are confidential, and that everyone will receive feedback of some kind. Formal announcements by memo or company newspaper or magazine should be complemented by managers and supervisors discussing the survey directly with their people. For large, far-flung organizations, a videotape of the leader discussing the survey is often helpful.

4. Ensure that turnaround time is as brief as possible. If a goal of the TQ effort is reducing cycle time, what better way to make the point than to set an example by

fast turnaround with something as complicated as this sort of employee survey. To offer an idea of what is possible, one can look to Corning. One of the initial steps taken there was an employee climate survey of all 25,000 employees. The first phase involved about 15,000 U.S.-based employees. The questionnaire was tailored during August and early September of 1983. It was administered in October through early November. By the first week in December, Jamie Houghton, the CEO, received an overview of the results and his top managers had their feedback session in the first week in January. By February 1, feedback of overall results was being distributed to all employees through the company newspaper and every employee began to receive feedback from his or her manager directly.

5. Structure the data into a useful tool. Done well, an employee survey will give the big picture as a reference point and also offer employees data on issues they have some control over. It should point to the pluses and uncover the minuses of any business and will thus offer rich fuel for managerial improvement actions. The best way to ensure that happens is for the data to be broken down by unit and for the unit manager to feed back the results of the survey to his or her employees. For example, take a plant that is part of a group in a corporation embarking on a TQ effort. Under this scenario, the plant manager would feedback

   a) overall results in the corporation,
   b) overall results in the group, and
   c) results of his or her plant that are more specific and actionable.

   Comparisons can be made between this plant and others in the group. It is also particularly useful for the plant manager to carve out data from the plant management team (that is, the actual data offered in questionnaires completed by the plant manager and direct reports) to be used as part of a team-building session.

6. Use the survey as an organization improvement vehicle. The reason for doing an employee survey as part of a TQ effort is not for top management to discover what is on the minds of employees so that it can decide what action to take. If that were the objective, a simple questionnaire, untailored, and given to only a sample of people would suffice. Rather, the reason is to engage people in uncovering opportunities and to involve them intimately in the task of capturing those opportunities. Asking employees what is on their minds while maintaining individual confidentiality, and then feeding back to them an analysis of what was offered is an initial step in enlisting their commitment to improve. The data they offer are important; the fact that they are being asked to provide it is just as important.

7. As with any component of a TQ effort, make certain that it is conducted in a "Total Quality way"—that the values and principles on which the TQ effort is based are apparent in the way the survey is conducted. Doing so ranges from ensuring the right amount of organization in conducting the survey and arraying the data clearly and succinctly all the way to maintaining confidentiality and protecting individual rights.

There are options from which to choose in doing such a survey. One is to construct questions according to the following categories. They have been shown to represent characteristics of companies that have achieved excellent results with Total Quality and do not exist to the same degree in companies that have achieved average results.[6]

The following elements will each be explained briefly.

- Influence
- Responsibility
- Innovativeness
- Desire to change
- Satisfaction
- Teamwork
- Common vision

Influence The degree to which people *believe* they have influence over changing what is around them is important. Resistance to change is higher among people who have a low sense of influence because they have no sense of ownership in the process and little self-confidence about making conditions different. Many middle managers and supervisors often believe they have less influence than they should have, given their title or spot on the organization chart. Sometimes, people resist change just to exercise the little influence they believe they have.

People who perceive their own influence to be low and are forced to participate in a team activity or to accept more decision-making responsibility often acquiesce, but they are usually not energetic, persistent, or committed.

Responsibility People who have a healthy sense of influence are comfortable accepting responsibility to do the right things the right way. Companies that have a history of compartmentalization, where Engineering hardly ever talks with Manufacturing and neither department relates much with Sales or Marketing, often have a low collective sense of responsibility across the whole organization. High levels of responsibility should correlate with high levels of innovativeness, a desire to change the status quo, and teamwork. A person who is comfortable taking responsibility is willing to work with others to enhance the group's responsibility.

Innovativeness The degree to which new ideas are encouraged, listened to, and considered seriously is one measure of innovativeness. Highly innovative companies get ideas from many different locations in the organizational hierarchy. This tends to happen in organizations where four conditions exist:

1. People are encouraged to experiment with new and different ways of operating, knowing that mistakes for the right reasons will not provoke negative feedback.

2. People are accustomed to operating in small teams or task forces.

3. Those who come up with the best ideas frequently are held in high esteem and rewarded.

4. The leader encourages people to constantly innovate.

A climate of innovation will allow people to be different and to question the status quo. It exists in the company where employees believe that the leader wants to find new ways to solve problems and will support new ideas, and where the emphasis is on solving a problem, not finding a culprit.

Desire to Change A healthy level of dissatisfaction is necessary to make things better. In companies where the desire to change is low, there is typically less innovation and more difficulty developing the sense of influence and responsibility necessary for employees to take on more decision making. At the same time, if the desire to change persists without being responded to for a long time it can turn from healthy dissatisfaction to unhealthy frustration, diminishing teamwork, responsibility, and innovativeness. When employees have crossed the line from dissatisfaction to frustration, the likelihood of constructive change through employees working together and taking on more decision-making responsibility diminishes.

Satisfaction is a measure of the degree to which employees' basic needs are satisfied. In order for people to accept responsibility and exert influence, their physical, economic, and psychological needs must be met.

Among the psychological needs that must be met as the company moves to become more competitive are the individual's need to achieve and to be recognized for achievement, the need to identify with some social group (such as a work team or ad hoc task team), and the need to influence and have some control over what is affecting his or her satisfaction. When these basic needs for achievement, affiliation, and power are met, the base is established for individual motivation.

Teamwork is a measure of the working state where people trust each other enough to work together to get a job done. An atmosphere where there is teamwork is characterized by several elements:

- Issues are confronted directly, often in group meetings, and the group will stick with an issue until it reaches resolution.

- Members of the group participate in decision making, and in so doing, group members are sensitized to one another's needs.

- Feelings are freely expressed, and they are listened to and appreciated by others; motives are open and clear.

- Responsibility is distributed, and people believe they are all in it together; because of this, help is freely offered.

- Power and credit are shared. There is sufficient respect for each member's contribution that it becomes unimportant who receives the credit.

- Achieving consensus is easier because people are more of one mind about what must be done and because there is greater respect for one's contributions.

Common Vision   The image of the organization's future must be compelling and exciting enough to rally employees around it. The common vision must be not only clear and compelling, but also consistent and always presented in terms that are most relevant to all members of the organization. A big part of guaranteeing its impact is to base it on values important to employees, values to which they aspire.

Analyze How People Get Ahead and What Image the Firm Projects

A third way to diagnose the organizational character starts with a careful look at the actions taken by leaders in terms of management succession and of the image that is projected externally.[7] There are five ways to judge the character of a company in this category.

1. Understand the career path of employees. Who gets ahead? Which departments produce leaders? Which kinds of people are promoted: Who is put on the fast track? What are their individual character traits? Why did they get promoted?

2. How long do people stay in jobs—particularly middle-management jobs? The rate of moving from one job to another will indicate whether people will try to make their mark quickly so they can be promoted again. In one Fortune 100 company, moving from one job to another each 18 months is very common.

The effect is that young managers hardly ever get the chance to see, and to live with, the results of their mistakes. But the message from corporate is clear: "If you want to get ahead here, you will do what you have to do to make your mark fast and in the short term or you will be passed over for promotion."

3. Look at what is being said and written within and outside the company. What is the tone of the annual report? Line up the press clippings that have been published over the past year: What do they collectively say? What image has been created in the press?

What is communicated in memos sent from the leaders? What is reflected in those memos regarding the major priorities and questions they were concerned with? Take your In basket for a month and list the categories that are represented by the memos you receive.

Also, analyze what is said. Look at the speeches that key people deliver over a six-month period. What are the major messages they wanted to send? What tone did they actually project? What questions did they ask or imply? One of the best ways to determine the priorities of a leader is to analyze the questions he or she asks.

4. What are the anecdotes and stories that people tell most frequently? The same stories told by many different people are particularly important. Inventory these anecdotes to see how many relate to customers, to individual initiative, to core values such as fairness, control, integrity, and so forth.

5. Why do people get fired? For what reasons? What kinds of people are fired? Were they fired only for poor performance or for ethical and professional reasons? Are poor performers kept on if they are loyal?

Signs to Be Concerned About

Whatever the option or combination of options selected to diagnose the current character of the organization, the result should be a picture of where the character is strong, vibrant, and positive and, in particular, where it is weak, negative, and antithetical to Total Quality. The major signs of an organization character that is in trouble and will not support a robust TQ effort are as follows:

- The company lacks a clear vision of what it can and should become.
- The values projected by the leaders conflict, either with each other or between what is said and what is actually done.
- Disdain for customers is widespread in the firm and resistance to changing in the face of clear, understood customer demands is strong.
- Compartmentalization is so extreme that attempts to reduce barriers between departments are discouraged and the rights of individual units or departments supersede the common good.
- Top management cannot reach consensus on what the company should stand for and how it should project itself in the marketplace and community.
- Focus is so short term that it blocks any attempt to take positive action for the long term. There is no clear, coherent strategy for the long term.
- Dervishlike activity prevails as managers seem constantly to be reacting to external issues and decisions made by competitors.
- People are constantly on the defensive rather than being proactive and at least occasionally taking the high ground.
- Understanding of the basics of the business is superficial. Management is not well grounded in the market, technology, production methods, and so on. (This may seem too obvious, but it is truly and constantly amazing the degree to which companies can survive for long periods of time run by people with little understanding of the basics of their businesses.)
- Friction between units or departments is constant. Departments continually try to undermine one another. Tension is palpable.

Diagnosing and analyzing the character of the organization will provide a clear view of strengths and those things that must be retained and built upon. It will also uncover weaknesses and barriers to moving from where the organization is now to where it should be. Such insight will enable the leader to choose the correct trajectory to launch the effort to achieve Total Quality and prepare the entire organization for implementation. Launching TQ is a delicate process. Chapter 5 explores how to give implementation the best chance of succeeding.

References

1. The term *organizational character* is offered by the Reverend Tom Thomson of Bristol, Rhode Island, and Lexington, Massachusetts, to denote the sort of environment to aim for in a TQ company, a description that is more accurate than the term *Organization Culture.*

2. See E. Schein, *Organizational Culture and Leadership* (San Francisco: Jossey-Bass, 1985) for a more detailed discussion.

3. R. W. Galvin, Statement on Motorola Quality Experience, Motorola, Schaumberg, IL, November 1988.

4. "George Fisher, "Our Time Has Come: A Manufacturing Renaissance," *Executive Speeches,* 3, no. 3 (October 1988).

5. "Quality," *Nation's Business,* January 1990.

6. For more on this, see Dan Ciampa, *Manufacturing's New Mandate* (New York: Wiley, 1989).

7. A useful book on the clues to look for is A. Deal and T. Kennedy, *Corporate Culture* (Reading, MA: Addison-Wesley, 1982).

5

Implementing Total Quality

As more and more companies experiment with Total Quality, we all learn about ways to implement it to alter the character of the organization to better meet customers' needs and exceed their expectations. Here are some learnings in this regard after more than a decade spent leading, participating with, or watching some companies that have started the TQ process from scratch and succeeded, some that have been at a middle point and then called for help, and some that failed. These comparisons suggest a handful of characteristics that exist in companies that have succeeded at TQ and do not exist to the same degree in those companies that have had marginal or worse results with Total Quality.

Characteristics of companies that have succeeded at implementing total quality are as follows:

1. The leader starts with a mental picture of how the company should be and sees Total Quality as a means to get it there. The top team holds a consistent picture. Throughout, the leader is sincere, credible, and consistent.

2. Analysis is done often and becomes a natural part of decision making. This analysis relates to customer needs and expectations, and is made visible for employees.

3. Problem solving is done effectively, often, and involves every employee possible. The emphasis is on important

problems that cross department lines, and every attempt is made to get at problems as quickly as possible.

4. Learning new ways of operating is done through active, hands-on experimenting. Pilot projects often provide the perfect opportunity.

5. As learning new ways of operating progresses, the leader and the top team continue to emphasize and clarify the vision through deeds, not by a written statement.

6. At the right time, education courses are used to supplement pilot activities and to reinforce the vision being clarified by the leader. Rather than generic programs, these courses are tailored to the particular needs and people of the company.

7. The top team works at institutionalizing gains by altering the basic systems of the business, getting employees trained to help other employees, and constantly reinforcing the TQ principles.

The leader's role in Total Quality is explored in the next two sections and is dealt with in more detail in Chapter 6.

The Leader's Vision of What Could Be

One characteristic of successful TQ efforts is that their leaders positioned TQ as a means to an end. In contrast, where the effort to achieve Total Quality has had less than excellent results, it was usually positioned to become an end in and of itself, or was simply allowed to be positioned in that way. Whether purposefully or naturally, the successful leaders position Total Quality in the context of "a way to get us to be the kind of company that will dominate markets and be the place where we will always have people who want to work here lined up outside (personnel's) door wanting to get in," as one leader put it.

With these particular leaders, an image has formed in their mind's eye of what their companies can become. They have a vision of the way the organization should be. For many, the vision is not crystal clear. But it is there, and is usually there before they ever heard of Total Quality.

It is a vision of employees working together to solve problems; of customers thanking the leader for helping them or providing them something of value, of the place operating smoothly like a well-oiled machine; of employees who are satisfied but who also are never through improving and who enjoy winning and win often. It may also be a vision of a factory that is flexible, able to alter processes quickly and respond fast to changing customer demands and new technology. It may include a new-product-development process that wins the company accolades and awards for being the fastest at releasing products of the best quality in the industry. It usually includes an image of the leader reporting to the board of directors excellent financial results and basking in the feeling that comes from doing so. It also often is accompanied by a sense of the emotions that go along with creating something that wins, that is admired, or that provides satisfaction. These "future feelings of success" are real to these sorts of leaders.

When such people hear Total Quality described, they begin to see ways that its philosophy and its tools can bring about this picture. They get excited. Total Quality may be a way to bring about what they *know* can happen and, along with it, those desired personal feelings of success.

Other leaders are motivated differently and think differently. They look around and see all the problems and the things that shouldn't be happening in the first place. They don't have the ability to look at something and imagine what it could be, but only to see something as it is. If they are not given a framework and tools to formulate a picture of what could be, when they hear about Total Quality they may see it as merely another way to solve or minimize the day-to-day problems that exist, rather than a way to create something of special value. Lacking that mental picture of what the company could be will cause them to make Total Quality just another management program.

If they adhere to a traditional notion of running a business by constantly, relentlessly reducing costs to improve performance rather than adding value for customers in a cost-conscious, responsible way, Total Quality will turn into another cost-cutting program. If this happens, Total Quality will surely wither and die. What such a leader must do is put in the time and effort necessary to develop a vision by reading, visiting other leaders, and, especially, by talking with customers and with employees.

Regardless of how it happens, one of the first phases of implementing Total Quality must result in the leader becoming more clear about the sort of place that he or she wants the company to become. There are at least four steps that can be taken to form or clarify that picture.

A necessary and powerful step is listening to customers. It will be helpful to the visionary leader and essential to the leaders who do not naturally form a picture of the ideal. The customer's view can be obtained through a formal survey, visits, or focus groups. Whatever the format, it is crucial to include the voice of the customer in the early steps taken in a TQ effort.

A second way to supplement or inspire the vision is through visiting other companies to set benchmarks. The leader should find ways to contact leaders in companies that have succeeded at Total Quality and those that are in the process of implementing it. Hearing directly from someone who is in the same job and who has or is trying to do the same things is often more useful than talking to a consultant.

Another step to take is to import into the company a one-half day or one-day awareness session for the top executives. It should include the parameters of Total Quality, how TQ can be tailored to fit into the current situation, a well-reasoned approach to implement it, what to watch out for, and the requirements of the leader.

It is usually important to have a Common Vision Workshop, often lasting two to three days, where the top management team can gain consensus on what it would most like to create. Such a session can surface differences, explore alternatives, find common ground in the search for a picture of what the organization can become, and explore ways to make the leader's vision common throughout the company.

Usually, such a workshop has the following stages: Prework includes one or two readings on common vision and a questionnaire that highlights the values and priorities of the top team members. Before the workshop it is also essential for trainers (workshop leaders) to become familiar with the business strategy and its operational imperatives, opportunities, and issues. During the workshop itself, the design is specially tailored for each group. To tailor the design requires the following:

- Clarify the personal visions of the top team members, that is, the image or picture that each person carries regarding what the company could be. These images are not usually clear and have often not been articulated by the people who attend. Questionnaires, exercises, and the skill of the trainer provide the ways to clarify and articulate personal visions.

- Develop a common vision by finding the areas of overlap, commonality, and differences and crafting a picture that includes the highest priority and essential parts of various personal visions into a more common, eclectic one. Here again, the ways to do so vary depending on the group involved, but the trainer's skill and ability are crucial not only at group facilitation but also at knowing the vicissitudes and vagaries of running a business.

- Clarify the values held by the people on the top team that also form the core value system for the common image or vision the group is shaping. Values are reflected in one's behavior and are a reflection of deeply held beliefs and attitudes. Questionnaires can be helpful in collecting data on beliefs and can be analyzed and processed by the group in such a way that core beliefs and attitudes can become more clear.

- Identify the A-items, sometimes referred to as "system pullers," the few (usually no more than four) superordinate issues that have the attraction and magnetism to pull energy through the organization. These A-items should be connected with the imperatives of the business, often related to time, to customer focus, and to new product development.

A-items are the leverage points for realizing the vision. Aligning the business's strategic direction and A-items with the visions that the top team is starting to forge into a common vision is the final phase of the workshop. The result of hard work on workshop activities is the framework for a truly common vision that can be shared by all of the top team. The vision is a shared set of principles about the future that encompasses both what the organization of the future will "do" (the major outcomes it will achieve embodied in the A-items) and what it will "be" (its character and climate).

A Common Vision Workshop can be a giant step forward for a top team that is launching or wishes to invigorate a Total Quality effort. But, as much potential as it has, it will not in and of itself create a real, robust, and truly common vision. It is a start or can be a vital ingredient. It is essential that the team continue beyond the workshop by doing three things. (1) Each top team member must take on one of the A-items and study it in detail, benchmarking with the best examples of excellence in that area, writing white papers, reading, doing research, and so forth. (2) Members of the leadership team talk to others (direct reports, in particular) about the emerging common vision, test it, and get other employees to think about and challenge it. (3) Have follow-up meetings off site to continue to refine and explore the vision, especially as events challenge and test the business and its strategy and vision.

The Leader's Behavior

Another element that great TQ companies have that average TQ companies do not have is a particular kind of behavior from the leader. In addition to being able to imagine a future state and have a strong sense of how it should feel to work in the company if it were operating to its maximum, customer-oriented capacity, leaders should exhibit some other important characteristics. For example, the leaders of companies where there have been very good TQ results have convinced employees that Total Quality is important, that it is not just another program, and that they, the leaders, are serious about the company embarking on TQ and making it work. They do this by being credible, clear, consistent, and confident. There is less of a need to be a great presenter or a charismatic speaker; while these abilities may help, they are not enough.

Credibility is a function of believing in something deeply and projecting that belief. Clarity usually means that the leader has carefully considered TQ and has a well-thought-through argument as to why it makes sense to pursue a TQ effort, one that makes sense to employees. Consistency is as important an element. The lack of it will cause any new TQ effort to falter and, perhaps, never to take full flight at all. Credibility is lost if employees hear the leader give a rousing TQ speech stressing the need for perfect quality and then see him meet a quarterly shipping target by shipping a new product that is predicted to not work as advertised. Confidence means being optimistic that TQ can happen.

Analysis

Another characteristic of companies that have been successful at implementing Total Quality is that employees use data and analyze those data systematically as a natural part of making decisions. Customer-satisfaction metrics are established and traced. Customer wants are determined systematically and used in making product decisions. Failure rates, reject rates, scrap rates, and conformance to specifications are charted. There is emphasis on a systematic problem-solving and decision-making process, and expectations that it should be used are set clearly and reinforced often.

Also in companies that achieve Total Quality, such analysis is made visible. The analytical tools that are such a part of the technical facet of TQ are not new. They are decades old. They have been updated perhaps, dusted off, and made more contemporary. The new and radically different facet of using these analytical tools as part of TQ is that everyone is expected to use them and therefore they must be visible for all to see. The quality control manager in a typical factory in the 1960s or 1970s used Precontrol, $\bar{X}$ and R charts, Pareto diagrams, and fishbone diagrams (described in Appendix B). But they were usually kept in the QC department and used the way a policeman uses a radar gun to trap a speeding motorist. Preventing rather than checking is the difference.

Today, in companies as diverse as Milliken and Hutchinson Technology, the signs of TQ are hanging on the walls in the factories and the offices. It immediately strikes the visitor that these are companies that measure themselves, and do so visibly. From productivity to customer complaints to conformance to shipping plans, large multicolored charts trace trends that are used to determine success.

In great TQ companies, analysis is an integral part of the process of being customer-driven and being successful. The analysis involves tangible, product-related issues as well as less tangible things like the organization climate and whether customers are satisfied. There is also regular measurement of these tangible and less tangible elements.

These companies avoid being too enamored and paralyzed by analysis by positioning that analysis in the right way. They do so in three ways: (1) by making sure that the right analysis is aimed at the important issues of the business; (2) by analyzing the key business *processes* rather than discrete parts of a process; and (3) by making sure that action follows analysis and that decisions are made crisply, based on the analysis that has been done.

It is vital in doing analysis that opportunities be identified that Total Quality can provide the ways to capture. Improvement targets should be specified in the areas that are most important to the business. Among them might be customer satisfaction, manufacturing lead time, quality, delivery, or some portions of costs such as inventory. The strategy and the marketplace will lead to the most important categories. Effort should be put into assessing the current situation objectively and determining realistically what it is possible to achieve, quantifying each to a level that is as precise as possible.

As opportunities are quantified, the organization climate should also be assessed. A good climate survey will answer questions such as: To what degree do people here feel they can control and change what is around them? Do people accept ownership for solving problems and take responsibility to do what is required to keep them solved? Do employees know who our customers are and what they think about us? If they know, to what degree do they care? What cultural barriers to innovation exist? What is the current state of teamwork? Is there a healthy degree of dissatisfaction that will cause people to do what they have to do to change? To what degree are there common beliefs and a mental picture of what our company could become?

Both quantitative opportunities and the organization climate are important to include on the analysis agenda. Opportunity analysis should provide a base on which to judge future progress as well as targets to achieve. Climate analysis should outline the emotional context within which those opportunities are to be realized, as well as the people and the cultural barriers that stand in the way of those opportunities.

Problem Solving

Great companies know how to solve problems and keep them solved. The analysis that is done is the warm-up for these companies. The real satisfaction comes from using the analysis to solve problems.

Companies that achieve excellent TQ results solve problems in a particular way; they use cross-functional teams. They emphasize those problems that cross department lines, and people get involved who not only know something about the issue at hand but also can apply solutions to similar problems or symptoms with the same root causes.

Cross-functional teams consider the entire process rather than just the immediate problem, so that when adjustments are made, it is clearer what the impact will be on the whole process. It could be new-product development, customer service, or distribution that needs to be improved, but in a company that does an excellent job of implementing Total Quality, you'll hear people talking about identifying the "process variables" and when one problem in a part of the process gets solved you won't see a celebration until the process itself is made to operate the way it must.

A hallmark of companies that have thrived at implementing Total Quality is that they arrive at this kind of problem solving as quickly as possible. While average companies are taking time and spending money to educate every employee in quality terminology or in the use of SPC charts before they are asked to use them, the excellent TQ companies are forming teams to attack problems.

Getting to process-focused problem-solving teams quickly has two other advantages. First, it is a most effective way to get people involved in the TQ process in an active and meaningful manner. It simply stands to reason that motivation and involvement are greater if someone is actively working on solving an important problem rather than sitting in a classroom hearing about concepts that they are then expected to go use. The key words here are *important problem*. The analysis should point to the issues that have the most impact and that are most crucial to satisfying customers.

The second advantage is that cross-functional teams focusing on a common problem bring the potential of team building and reducing barriers between departments. Some of the most effective teamwork takes place when a group of people come together and solve important problems by applying new techniques. Problem-solving teams should always have team-building training to aid them in their tasks. Usually, team building done in this context will pay rich dividends and will cause teamwork to last longer than team building that is not done as part of a problem-solving process.

Third, cross-functional teams working on solving important problems provide the best forum for training employees in new, better problem-solving methods. Working as part of a team to solve an actual problem is a much more effective and efficient way to learn, and to learn to use, new problem-solving approaches than sitting in a seminar hearing about them. This sort of learning lends itself to pilot projects, which are the key to learning new ways of operating.

Learning New Ways of Operating

A few options are available to help people learn to use new problem-solving approaches effectively. One is to teach people by lecturing to them. They can also supplement lectures by analyzing case studies of real situations. Even better, however, is to combine these teaching methods with simulations. Whatever combination of teaching methods is used, the point to the learners is that they will hear about something and then they will be expected to go find places to apply this new knowledge. This approach can be of some help in exposing the learner to concepts and models. It will fulfill the purpose of education—to close gaps in knowledge.

Most consulting firms offering TQ services reinforce this notion by recommending that large-scale education be one of the very first steps taken by the client. They suggest a two- to three-day course for all employees at all levels on the principles of Total Quality and a treatment of the various SPC tools it encompasses. The idea is that in order for employees to do something differently they must know *about* it. This is solid, traditional pedagogical thinking. The problem is that when it comes to behavior and organization change, it doesn't apply. These suggestions often come from consulting firms with education or training programs to sell or from those who have little practical experience at comprehensive organization change.

More is required to become a customer-focused, satisfying, and always-improving company. Employees must not only become more knowledgeable, but they must also learn to apply that new knowledge in ways that lead to fundamental change in behavior and attitude. Such change cannot come about through education; more is required than closing gaps in knowledge. One requirement is a concrete experience that can be a real-time case study. A related requirement is the chance to reflect on that concrete experience. A mechanism that meets both requirements is the pilot project.

A Pilot Project

In one case, a company's leader decided that the process of introducing new products was vital to its competitive strength. He appointed analysis teams to map the current process for creating and introducing new products. The teams also visited companies known for their skill in this area or who were also trying to improve. Based on the recommendations of these teams, the leaders decided that the time from conception to completion of the first prototype had to be cut in half in order to regain lost market share. They came to recognize two other things: 1) what happens in that conception-to-prototype portion of the process is the determining factor in how easily and how quickly the product is manufactured, and 2) the performance and reliability of the product for the customer is by and large a function of that conception-to-prototype portion of the process as well.

The next step was to form a cross-functional pilot team with the right representatives from the marketing, research, design engineering, manufacturing engineering, production, finance, and human resource departments. The leaders gave to this team the charter of determining the key barriers to reducing this part of the process to one-half the time it then took, and after approval from the leaders, to take steps to reduce or eliminate those barriers and realize a 50% reduction. Another aspect of the charter directed the pilot team to complete its task so that the product, once in production, could be made faster and its appearance and performance for the customer enhanced.

The pilot team started with a two-day off-site meeting to plan its approach. It reviewed the results of the analysis team (members of the pilot team were also on this predecessor group), and went through a situation analysis. It identified the major categories of problem symptoms to be addressed. Following the off-site meeting, it delved deeper into the process outlined by the analysis team and analyzed more carefully what actually happened. It learned from an outside consultant how to do a flow analysis to separate value-added tasks from non-value-added tasks. It also learned how to construct a histogram that displays instances and frequency of certain kinds of events. It learned that through Pareto analysis it can determine which vital few steps or actions cause or contribute to over three-quarters of the barriers to reducing time. Two members of the team attended a seminar on the techniques to determine whether a production process was in control (within tolerable control limits); they then came back and conducted a seminar for the others and together they figured out how to apply those techniques to the task at hand.

During their work on the pilot, jealousy and turf-guarding surfaced on the part of the representatives from Production and Manufacturing Engineering, both of whom worked for the vice president of manufacturing, who seemed always at odds with both the vice president of engineering and the vice president of marketing, bosses of other pilot-team members. Accusations and tension threatened to slow the team's work, or even to cause it to not agree on recommendations. An outside facilitator was brought in by the representative from Human Resources and the team went through a two-day team development off site. Some differences were resolved and others that could not be resolved were surfaced and discussed openly. The session helped and the representative from Human Resources took on the role of team facilitator to ensure that other relationship issues did not get in the way of the pilot team's task. The experience also caused the team to recognize that upper-management relationship and teamwork problems were part of the reason that the current product introduction did not work as it could and should.

The team used a fishbone (cause-and-effect) analysis to separate symptoms from the things that caused those symptoms. It identified that faulty information, lack of collaboration and information sharing at the top, a not-invented-here attitude, and inadequate information from marketing to R&D underlay some of the surface issues. It went further as team members asked why these conditions existed in their company, and then asked "Why?" once again, finally arriving at what it believed to be root causes.

A problem-solving/decision-making model was suggested by one of the team's members, and a working seminar followed to move from the analysis to deciding what steps to take to actually extract time from the conception-to-prototype part of the process. Once this step had gone far enough, the team met with the company's leaders for an update. The most tense part of the meeting occurred when the pilot team described its cause-and-effect analysis—in particular, the part about lack of enough collaboration at the top. Fortunately, the team previewed its analysis with the CEO, who supported the analysis and headed off attempts to divert or cover up the airing of such a delicate subject.

The team then proceeded to begin changing a few parts of the process. It experimented here or there, trying new techniques and involving the people who lived day in and day out in this process.

The experience of this team is an example of an effective way to change attitudes and behavior. This team learned what it needed to know on the job. The new tools and techniques were applied to a real and important problem. The progress made while this team was learning a new way to operate has had enormous payback. These people were more motivated to learn because of the relevance of these new techniques to the task they were asked to address. Because of the way they learned, they are in an ideal position to teach other employees how to do the same things. Pilot efforts have proliferated on a variety of problems in this company. The experiments to reduce non-value-added time produced some gains right away. Once the pilot team had done its job, it was disbanded, and the responsibility for continuing to reduce time up to and beyond the 50% target was transferred to the line managers of the departments involved;

the top management team took on the responsibility for monitoring, encouraging, and/or forcing progress.

The analysis and time-reduction techniques the team learned about were the easier part of making substantive changes to the way new products were introduced. While they required new ways of operating that were more data-driven and more disciplined than what had been required in the past, changes were procedural and once it became apparent that working in this way would make their jobs more rewarding and satisfying, those involved in the process embraced these new techniques and continue to refine and tailor them. The more difficult issues were relationships within the top team—in particular, the relationships of the vice presidents of manufacturing, engineering, and marketing. The president avoided confronting this issue for some time, unsure of his own ability to resolve it, not sure it was resolvable, and afraid that one of the three would leave if the conflict came out into the open, something that the president believed the company would suffer from greatly because of the knowledge and ability that each brought to his or her job.

At this writing the president is moving gingerly to surface and finally confront the issue. He has spoken to each vice president separately (a facet of this particular leader's style in that he is very much of a one-on-one manager; in fact until the TQ effort began, he rarely had had a staff meeting) and is considering a session where all four will be brought together to discuss common objectives and the impact the vice presidents' relationships are having on those objectives. Perhaps the most powerful motivators to resolve this issue are the embarrassment the vice presidents feel at how successfully those under them are working together, and also the fear felt by the president that at some point one of the VPs will receive job offers in less contentious environments and will leave.

Two points are of note here. First, problems can be solved and progress toward Total Quality made even if the relationships of key people are less than ideal. It may be ideal that relationships are team oriented and mature, and certainly the most progress will be made if that is the case. If such problems do occur, though, and cannot be resolved, TQ can still be effective. Second, Total Quality, while potentially powerful and pervasive, cannot solve every problem, in particular not those that require the top person to exhibit leadership rather than avoid confronting a festering problem. TQ, like Organization Development or any other model for organization excellence, may support and improve it, but it will not take the place of effective leadership.

On the Art of the Pilot

Pilot projects should be encouraged as soon as possible after the analysis phase. How many pilots should be launched is a matter that must be decided given each company's situation. The important things to remember are these:

Focus of Pilot   Pilot projects must be focused on issues or problems that are important to the competitiveness of the business. They should be related somehow to the customer and to meeting customers' needs and exceeding their expectations. It will provide more meaning to the task if employees can relate what they are doing to the impact it will have on the real, live person who buys the product they make and who, ultimately, pays their salaries.

Pilot Team Membership   The people chosen to work on the pilots, especially the initial ones, should be employees who have their own constituencies, who are influencers among their peer group. This will create ambassadors for Total Quality (assuming the pilots are satisfying experiences) and the chances will be greater that other employees will wish to be on a pilot team. All-volunteer pilot teams have obvious advantages, but are neither essential nor practical. It is important to have the right people on the pilot team rather than the wrong people no matter how enthusiastic. If the initial pilot teams succeed and are satisfying experiences, placing people on pilot teams will not be a problem.

Adequate Resources   Pilot teams need to have resources made available so that they have what is required to complete their tasks. Training resources are particularly important.

Guidance   The pilot teams must have a sufficient amount of guidance and mentoring from a senior manager who will help break log jams, provide political "air cover," ensure access to other senior people, and so forth.

Freedom There must be sufficient freedom to experiment and, in particular, to challenge the sacred cows of the business. A pilot team without appropriate and sufficient license to experiment will result in missed opportunity and frustration.

Task: Realism Versus Challenge The task given the pilot team should be realistic. It is both unfair and unwise to attempt through a pilot to solve a difficult, complex issue people have been trying to improve unsuccessfully for years. At the same time, there must be some challenge and some degree of difficulty to achieving the task. A task that is too easy will not provide the richness of learning of one that is difficult but resolvable. The task should be achievable in the short term; interest will wane if the task takes longer than four to six months to complete.

Significant Payoff The payoff from the work of the pilot team should be dramatic and impressive. A 10% reduction in, say, the time it takes to change over a press from one mold to another is not a dramatic difference and will not raise many eyebrows. A 75% reduction, however, is another story. The outcome of pilots should be reflected on the bottom line. Pilots should pay for themselves, and then some.

Celebrating Success Successes should be celebrated, but only real successes. Celebration before anything is really accomplished (common in many companies) is hype, not a motivating, satisfying experience.

Feedback It is vital to provide feedback to the pilot teams as they perform their work. Leaders should ensure that mechanisms are created so that the pilot teams know where they stand in relation to their goal and also that they know what the leaders think about their work.

Capturing Commitment Pilot projects offer an opportunity to capture the imagination and the commitment of employees to a new way of operating. Leaders must do everything possible to enable employees to enlist. One way to do so is for the leader to be visible to the pilot teams, to meet with them, encourage them, give feedback, and offer guidance.

Conveying the Vision of What Could Be

The outcome of creating a vision, the activity outlined at the start of this chapter, is a picture of the sort of place that Total Quality can be used to create. The leader, in particular, and the rest of the top team should be able to describe that picture to employees through both word and deed. This is an ongoing activity for senior managers. It is never complete in the sense that there is a final picture. With each TQ-inspired step taken, the vision becomes sharper.

It is important during pilots for upper managers to grasp the opportunity to do two things. The first is to talk with pilot-team members and, through the questions they ask and the points they make, to stress the themes of the vision. Comments such as these from the leader will go a long way to stressing a particular theme: "That sounds like a logical plan of attack, but explain to me how taking those steps to address this issue will help our customers," or "Before we get into the results you've gotten so far, let's talk about the process you've used to get them," or "We're just as interested in how you people have worked together as a team, so start by characterizing your level of teamwork before we talk about anything else." Most people discover what a boss wants and really cares about through the questions the boss asks. A declarative statement only requires the listener to listen patiently. A written directive requires even less. But a question requires the listener to go active as he or she readies a response.

A second opportunity that pilot efforts afford leaders is to sharpen and clarify the vision of what could be. Pilots are to the TQ effort what exhibition games are to the professional sports team. It is one thing to talk about the team's strategy or even to hold intrateam scrimmages, but a coach cannot really assess the overall strategy until the team is in a game situation, playing an exhibition against another team. How employees take to new techniques while working on a real and important issue in a safe-to-experiment situation will say a lot to the leader about the image of what the company could become on which the top team is working.

The way the vision is communicated is almost as important as the vision itself. How it is communicated will convey to employees the true level of top team commitment. The best way to get across the vision is not in writing. A one-page description is for mission statements, not for a meaningful picture of what the company can look like and what it should feel like to work there. It is also not in a rousing speech. Communicating an image of what the leader is trying to create is much subtler. It must happen over time, and the leader must get to the point where the vision is not exclusively "owned" by him or her but employees can see it, taste it, touch it, and, in general, make it their own as well. Conveying such ownership is a function of how the leader acts, the questions asked, the consistency of what the leader says and what other top managers say and do, and of the decisions made regarding strategy, promotions, and other visible reflections of the leader's beliefs.

Education

At the appropriate time, it is essential to provide education courses to participants in pilot teams to reinforce learnings. Such courses fill in the gaps and provide the underlying concepts for the techniques and the tools that have been tried in the pilots.

Let's go back to the example of a pilot team working on reducing the lead time of a portion of the new-product-introduction process and see where education fits in. As that team was working, others were tackling other issues. Three teams were reducing setup time in the factory. Two were working on improving the process to deal with customers' complaints. One was looking at the way information was gathered and transmitted from the field sales force and from service/installation groups back to the people who designed and made the products. Six pilot projects going on simultaneously involved about fifty people. Because each situation was somewhat different, each team moved at a slightly different pace. The top-management team stayed on top of pilot activity through biweekly review meetings. When it appeared that all teams were close to completion of their tasks, or at least nearing that point, the top group made two decisions. First, they set aside two 2-day periods one month apart and told all the teams to be prepared to review their progress in front of the top management group, selected midlevel managers, and the other pilot teams. They expected at least three of the pilot teams to have completed their tasks by the second of these two-day sessions based on what these teams had reported. These sessions established a deadline for a final report for these three teams and also set the expectation for all the teams that they were to review what they had done and what they had learned in front of their bosses and their peers.

The second decision made by the top team was to begin looking at education courses. Information had been shared with the employee population through a newsletter devoted to the progress in implementing Total Quality, and through discussions at various staff meetings and other events such as roundtable discussions of employees and the CEO. Also, the people chosen to work on the pilots were visible employees who were seen as high-potential leaders for the future and/or as having a good deal of influence with peers. Word about the pilots spread in this way as well. Everyone knew something about the pilots. It was now time to take the next step and start thinking about education. At a top team staff meeting recommendations were collected and discussed for the kinds of education programs that might have the most impact and benefit. The recommendations agreed to are described in the following paragraphs.

Overview Course An overview course will present the basic analytical and problem-solving tools of Total Quality. Some of these tools would have already been used by the pilot teams who had been exposed to them through focused training sessions. Where possible, it was decided to take advantage of this fact by having cases developed using the actual experience of these teams at applying those tools. Also, it was decided that three of the employees from pilot teams who had taken to one or two of these tools particularly well would be asked to teach other employees to use those tools during this course. Among the topics that were to be covered were Pareto analysis, cause-and-effect analysis, value-added flow analysis, control charts, scatter diagrams, and histograms. The purposes of these tools would be reviewed and examples offered of their application during the pilots.

This course's purpose would be largely transferring information to employees through lectures from an outside consultant/trainer and descriptions and case histories from employees. Forms of various kinds were to be prepared for employees to take away with them, along with two books that supplemented the information presented. Eventually, all employees would go through this course. It would be designed in three half-day modules. Some would attend all three in a $1\frac{1}{2}$-day program, others would attend one-half day at a time.

A Basic Problem-Solving/Decision-Making Training Program There was clearly a need for a common language and a common methodology by which to solve problems. Experience during the pilot projects had reinforced this need. As people from different departments came together to work on a particular issue, it quickly became apparent that each had had different training on (or, at least, each had a different idea of) how to solve a problem. Some were analytical and others intuitive. Some wanted to get all the known and assumed data listed first and then structure and prioritize, while others wanted to home in on what they knew to be the case and hold off on any assumptions. Some defined a problem as a deviation from the way things should be and a decision as a choice between options, while others defined problems and decisions differently. Some had had a good deal of sophisticated experience with decision trees and planning models, while others found it difficult to plan a vacation trip.

It was decided to purchase a training program that would be required for all managers, supervisors, and those who would be part of future pilot teams. A criterion for selection set by the management team was that the program be tailored to meet the particular situation of the company rather than a generic, off-the-shelf design.

One-Day Overview A one-day overview of Total Quality as it was seen by and as it was being applied by this particular company. Topics would include its history and how it developed, the connection between statistical/analytical tools from quality assurance and Just-In-Time, the reason Total Quality was right and important for this company (a videotape of the CEO would be made for this segment), expectations of employees and the overall strategy to implement Total Quality. Throughout the session, it would be emphasized that the purpose and the prime measure of success of Total Quality would be the customer and constantly sharpening the company's ability to understand what the customer wants and expects and then meeting those needs in a way that exceeds the customer's expectations. This overview would be delivered to all employees.

A Training Program on Influence and Negotiation Skills The TQ environment would result in more interaction between employees from various departments. Emphasis would be placed on employees providing information better and faster to other employees, and in so doing they would ask for and provide services to one another, all aimed at improving overall service to the customer. As decision-making power was pushed down to mid and lower levels of the organization, the task of influencing other employees to do something to help one get his or her job done would increase in importance and frequency. This requires sharp influence skills. Here again it was decided to search for an outside program. Managers, supervisors, and all employees on pilot teams would go through the training.

Meeting Management Since Total Quality encourages the formation of problem-solving teams and since coordination is often done through steering committees, the number of and importance of meetings increases. Getting the most out of a meeting is an art. Keeping the conversation on track, establishing and sticking to desired outcomes, ensuring full participation, ensuring everyone has the chance to participate, and making decisions as a group while gaining consensus are all required of the person responsible for the meeting. There are a variety of programs and materials available for this purpose (as with all learning programs, care should be taken to ensure the program chosen fits the needs and demands of the TQ effort) and here again it was decided to purchase an outside program and train employees to deliver it.

It was anticipated that as these courses and training programs took place, pilots would continue to be chartered and pilot teams would be formed or be disbanded as work was completed. Eventually, most employees would be part of a pilot team, but at any given education session it was likely that some people would be on or have been on a pilot while others would not. The top team instructed the vice president of human resources to find a way to deal with this education task taking into consideration the likelihood of a mixed population attending most programs; it was also the vice president's responsibility to locate outside training programs.

Making Gains Permanent

What has happened up to this point is akin to an overweight person shedding pounds and getting into shape. The person realizes that eating habits and lack of exercise must be changed and, during the initial period, makes progress. The person is satisfied with what has happened and feels some pride in having achieved a healthier and more attractive body. But now, a different kind of work is called for. What will make all the sacrifice pay off is remaining healthy and in shape permanently. In order to do so, life-style changes are necessary.

Similarly, up to this point in implementing Total Quality, some problems have been solved. Attitudes have begun to change. New behavior has been tested. People have been exposed to new ways of thinking and of approaching problems. The task now is to put in place ways to make those gains permanent, to institutionalize change, and to make those attitude and behavior changes a way of life. There are several ways to do so.

The first has to do with the three systems that combine to make up the central nervous system of the business—the information system, the measurement system, and the reward system. As more experiments take place and more pilot projects solve more problems the image of what Total Quality can mean for any particular organization and the sort of company that TQ can lead to become more clear. A question top management must ask is: "Does our current information system provide people the data needed for that new company?" Another is: "Does our information system support the conversion of those data into useful information?" A third question must be: "Are we measuring the right things, do we have the right metrics, and is our measurement system consistent with the customer-focused, continuously improving company we want to be and are becoming?" A fourth key question is: "Are we rewarding the right behavior and does our reward system send the appropriate messages about how people must behave in the sort of company we are creating?"

Changes in these three areas are not easy to make and, often, substantive change does not happen quickly. It took six years to launch the first pilot to change the measurement system at one well-known Fortune 100 company that has won the Baldrige Award. But it doesn't necessarily have to take that long.

One of the first applications of Total Quality on a large scale at Hewlett-Packard was at the Greeley, Colorado, plant in the late 1970s. Gary Flack was the plant manager; he had also been a division controller. As he became more aware of Total Quality and what it could do, he recognized that the measurement system that was in place was inconsistent. He instituted a new one as one of the first steps taken in his TQ effort. In investigating this, he found that more money was spent on measuring labor cost than was spent on labor. Basically, he eliminated labor variances as a metric and focused on cycle time and yield measurement. His hypothesis was that if cycle time improved, yield would improve and if yield improved so would cycle time.

Another facet of making gains permanent is establishing internal capability to educate and to train. It is not common to find within companies training and development capability that is already up to speed on the principles and the tools and techniques necessary for Total Quality. (This is a sad commentary on human resource departments that is explored in another chapter.) Even if outside consultants are needed to launch a TQ effort and help it become ingrained into the fabric of the company, there must be ways created to transfer those capabilities to the company's employees.

The work done by these newly trained employees is fairly focused. There will be need for people to facilitate meetings of pilot teams. There will also be a need for instructors for education and training programs. It is both motivating and reinforcing to be trained to be an instructor or a trainer of a management-skills program. It also benefits the company, since being trained to deliver learning programs is in effect a management-development program. It exposes people to aspects of the company they otherwise may not touch, and it sharpens or develops their ability to communicate and to get across complex ideas.

A third area that will lead to institutionalizing positive changes is ensuring that both strategic planning and annual budgeting are done in a way reflective of Total Quality, and so that the TQ ethic is furthered. Most strategy and budgeting is done without the word "customer" ever being uttered. Often, current financial ratios and performance measures are extrapolated and extended, thereby reinforcing the current measurement system. Especially when economic conditions are foreboding, training and development costs are viewed as an expendable expense, often the first ones to be cut, rather than an essential investment. In many companies, planning processes are inefficient, cumbersome, and not satisfying; a hallmark of a company that is serious about Total Quality is that the planning process is the subject of improvement activities to reduce time, improve connection with the customer, and increase participation.

Another way to institutionalize progress is the most obvious. The leaders of the organization must visibly reinforce Total Quality. This can be done by integrating the language of Total Quality into the vocabulary of the top managers. Continuing to ask questions that stress TQ themes (the customer, creating a TQ climate, measuring and documenting, and so on) is another. Taking advantage of forums such as speeches, text for the annual report, visits to management development courses, and round table discussions with hourly workers are other ways. Also important is who gets promoted and for what. This is a part of the reward system that is in direct control of top managers. If people who are supportive of Total Quality and identified with its progress are promoted to important, visible positions, the message will be sent that those who make Total Quality a reality here will get ahead.

Summary

Figure 5.1 charts the steps required to implement Total Quality. The elapsed time needed should be 18 to 30 months. It is important to point out once again that there is no single best way to implement Total Quality. These are principles that have been shown to produce positive results.

Figure 5.2 shows how one company moved toward a TQ environment. This is a Fortune 100 company that is made up of a corporate unit and 13 operating divisions. This chart spans 22 months and major phases in the process are shown horizontally. Those phases that were driven by and the responsibility of the corporate office are on the upper portion of the page and those

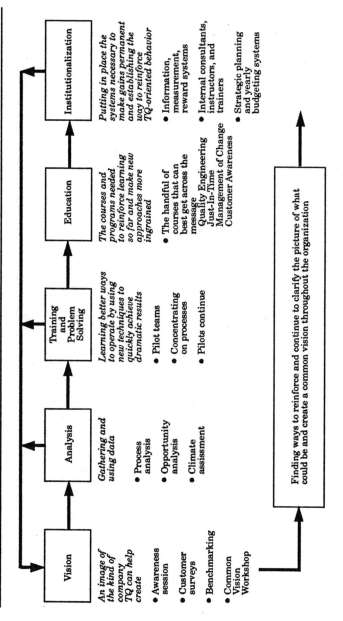

Figure 5.1
Implementing Total Quality

The figure contains the following flow (left to right):

Vision

An image of the kind of company TQ can help create

- Awareness session
- Customer surveys
- Benchmarking
- Common Vision Workshop

Analysis

Gathering and using data

- Process analysis
- Opportunity analysis
- Climate assessment

Training and Problem Solving

Learning better ways to operate by using new techniques to quickly achieve dramatic results

- Pilot teams
- Concentrating on processes
- Pilots continue

Education

The courses and programs needed to reinforce learning so far and make new approaches more ingrained

- The handful of courses that can best get across the message
  Quality Engineering
  Just-In-Time
  Management of Change
  Customer Awareness

Institutionalization

Putting in place the systems necessary to make gains permanent and establishing the way to reinforce TQ-oriented behavior

- Information, measurement, reward systems
- Internal consultants, instructors, and trainers
- Strategic planning and yearly budgeting systems

Finding ways to reinforce and continue to clarify the picture of what could be and create a common vision throughout the organization

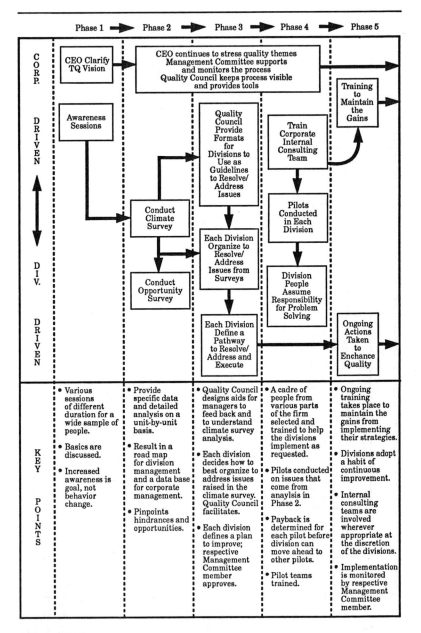

Figure 5.2
One Company's Total Quality Map

driven by and the responsibility of the divisions are on the lower part of the chart.

Key points for each major phase are listed below.

1. Go to customers early and find out what they want and why, and listen hard and well.

2. Measure and document what happens today and set quantitative, specific, realistic, and measurable targets.

3. Get to the point of launching pilots as soon as possible. Not only can they solve current problems and pay for themselves but, equally important, they can capture the imaginations of employees and result in their enlistment.

4. Education is important, but it will help only if it happens at the right time and includes programs focused on the right needs.

5. The task of sharpening and clarifying the picture of what could be is one that is never entirely done. It will progress throughout this process.

6. Institutionalizing Total Quality involves the basic systems of the business, getting internal resources trained and up to speed, and constantly reinforcing the TQ principles and way of operating.

Total Quality is not something that ends. Rather these phases over a period of one and one-half to two and one-half years can establish Total Quality as the way to operate effectively.

Part III

Roles to Lead or Support Total Quality Implementation

6

Common Vision Leadership— The Leader's Mandate

Most companies that have implemented Total Quality company-wide have devoted a good deal of time and effort to training and educating their employees. Many have experienced significant savings of time and cost through pilot efforts. However, the organizations that have come the farthest and done the most are the ones where something else has happened in addition to these visible steps. These are the organizations where the leader has actively taken charge of the TQ effort and used it as a way to create more overall value for customers and a more satisfying environment for employees. This chapter discusses the leader's role in shaping and implementing Total Quality and institutionalizing it.*

Leading Versus Managing

Leading a change effort is different from managing it. While managing is systematic planning, execution, and follow-up, leading involves creating and clearly articulating a vision of the future that is bright and compelling.

Leadership depends on capacities that are nonrational and nonanalytical. Rather, leaders respond to and bring out powerful emotions that can spur people on to accomplish things

---

*The ideas, research, teaching, and experience of Dave Berlew have for some time influenced my position on leadership, and therefore, what is in this chapter on the role of the leader in altering the character of the business organization. The concept of "push" and "pull" energy was developed in the 1970s by Dave and Roger Harrison.

they didn't think they were capable of doing. Managing, on the other hand, is mostly rational and depends on systematic and logical tools such as goal setting, problem solving, analysis, and effective ways to communicate or to process information.

To make the point for yourself, take a minute and complete this exercise:

1. In the space below, list the words that come to mind when you think of leadership. In particular, describe what you *see* or *experience* when there is effective leadership. Try to describe what you see or experience in one- or two-word phrases. List as many as you wish, but in each case, make them as descriptive as possible.

2. In the space below, write the words that describe what you *see* or *experience* when it comes to management. Be as brief and as descriptive as possible.

3. Now, think of a person with whom you have first-hand experience and whom you have admired as a great leader. In the space below describe how you felt or feel being a follower of this leader.

Most people responding to item 2 list words like "the job gets done," "efficient," "things operate like clockwork," "control," "predictable," "the most done in the least amount of time," "organized," and "no mistakes, everything works smoothly." For items 1 and 3, on the other hand, there appear words like "inspiration," "excitement," "commitment," "all headed in the same direction," "all wanting to head in the same direction," "see people do things that no one ever imagined they would do, including them—extraordinary things," "people dig down deep inside themselves, challenge themselves . . . the motivation to change comes from inside them, but the leader causes it to happen," and "lots of teamwork, people cooperating and working together to get something done."

There are many elements of Total Quality that require management; where efficiency is crucial; where events must be organized; and where a number of variables must be balanced. While the leader should ensure that these sorts of things happen, there is another, more important challenge for the leader of an organization going through a TQ effort focused on the customer. The mandate is to inspire, to invoke commitment, to enable employees to form a different concept of the organization in which they believe deeply, and to change without being threatened.

Usually, Total Quality and becoming totally focused on the customer requires people both to act differently and to undergo a fundamental change in attitude and mindset about the business. In order to see this sort of change happen, the leader must lead rather than manage. It's really not unlike aligning an energy field, as shown in Figure 6.1. The essence of energy alignment is that everyone knows where the organization should be heading, why it should be heading in that direction, what the organization will look like when it gets there, and how it will be better than what exists today.

There are two ways the leader can do this. The first is to put in place policies, procedures, rules, and systems that direct energy of employees. The second is to create a picture of what could be that is compelling and inspiring. The first is to push while the second is to pull.

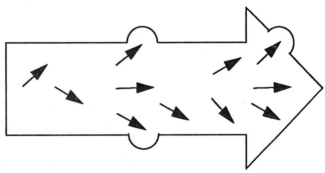

Figure 6.1
Elements of the Organization (Whether Departments, Divisions, Improvement Efforts, or People) Usually Head in the Same Direction.

Push and Pull Energy

One example of a tool that aligns energy through pushing is a mission statement, which establishes what business the organization is in or will engage in. Another example is a set of policies that aim behavior in a particular direction. The strategic-planning process and the yearly budgeting process are other examples. Push tools set guidelines and seek to ensure consistency and predictability. They organize, synthesize, reward, and inform.

Pull tools, on the other hand, respond to a different need. Rather than aligning through establishing limits and rules, they create a future state that people can be drawn toward; and do so in a way that sparks people's imagination, that causes anticipation. One such tool is a common vision. Figure 6.2 shows the effects of push and pull tools.

Push tools rein in, setting parameters and limits; pull tools enable people to establish their own boundaries. Push tools are often imposed on people in the organization by a small number of other employees, usually bosses; pull tools enable people to drive themselves from within to a greater degree.

Both push tools and pull tools are necessary to create alignment. However, most organizations and the leaders who run them rely exclusively on push tools. They do not have in their

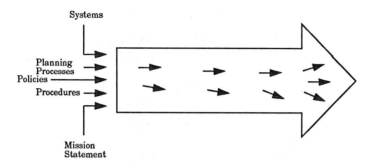

Push Tools That Bring Predictability and Efficiency

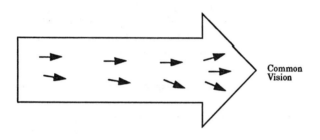

Pull Tools That Cause Inspiration and Motivation

Figure 6.2

tool kit tools to bring about the inspiration and motivation necessary to cause people to want to alter their attitudes and behavior.

A Personal Vision

At the core of the pull tool kit is the creation of a common vision, a picture of the future that is both inspiring as well as shared and consistent among employees. The first step in the creation of a common vision for the organization is a personal vision for the leader; that is, an image in the mind's eye of the leader of a future state that he or she wants most to see created. That future state may not seem practical at the present time or may not closely resemble what currently exists, and the distance between what is and what is desired may well seem daunting.

This vision is not a mission statement; nor is it a list of goals. It is quite literally a picture of what an ideal state will look like and what it will feel like to work there. What is desired as an outcome is different from the sort of place that enables that outcome to be achieved.

When formulating a personal vision, it is not uncommon for leaders to first say that they want a company that is focused on the customer, or one that responds fast and where time is a competitive weapon. But these desires do not pass the test of depicting the future. The leader must go farther and ask why it is desirable and what good will come of having achieved these sorts of things. But the leader can't stop there, either. He or she must then go to the next level of vision clarification and determine how to know when those things have been achieved. This leads to the next level, where the leader must clarify what will actually be seen, what will be heard in the company that is focused on the customer and responds fast, and how it will feel to be a part of such an organization.

Even the answers to these questions will be inadequate unless they are based on a foundation that has meaning to the leader. Building this foundation entails extraordinary effort. But it is key to providing motivation and drive. It also is the stuff of commitment.

We have all experienced the boss or the professor or the seminar leader who, though talking about an important topic, doesn't seem to be into it. The words are the right ones but there is something missing. We have also all experienced people who speak or teach or train and seem to do it effortlessly; time passes quickly and the session, program, class, or conversation ends leaving us wanting more. Sometimes the speaker is not as polished or as erudite as in the first case. But it's *better*. It clicks. It has impact. Why? Probably because in the latter case, the speaker is talking about something that has meaning to him, that he cares about deeply, that he's thought about, that is important to him.

M. L. Carr is a former professional basketball player and now a successful businessman. As an athlete, he was considered a good player who knew the basics of the sport, but not an outstanding athlete who dominated the game or had remarkable skills compared to his peers. His peers and coaches, however, considered him one of the most important members of the team.

Why? Because he had passion. Because he loved to play basketball, and it showed. Because the team and winning were so important to him that it exuded from his personality and his playing style in every way. This passion is the reason he has two world championship rings.

Carr is now very active in the Boston community and speaks widely to youth groups about not using drugs, staying in school, and overcoming deprivation and poverty. He doesn't use notes in his talks but inevitably receives standing ovations. What comes across in his speeches is the same passion that showed when he played basketball. He believes in and has strong feelings about what he says.

Meaning provides us with the motivation, while vision offers a picture of where that motivation will take us. Peter Senge puts it this way: "Vision is different from purpose. Purpose is similar to a direction, a general heading. Vision is a specific destination, a picture of a desired future. Purpose is abstract. Vision is concrete. Purpose is 'advancing man's capability to explore the heavens'. Vision is 'a man (walking on) the moon by the end of the 1960s'."[1]

Most of the time things happen and get done without a vision. But rarely do things that matter, that cause substantial and positive change, happen without a motivating purpose or meaning. When there is a strong purpose and meaning but no vision, there is often directionless passion. Many private not-for-profit organizations, start-up businesses, or government initiatives suffer from this weakness. There are certainly meaning and passion and people who are truly committed and working tirelessly to bring about something good and worthwhile. But they don't last or don't go far enough and fall short of their potential.

This was a common dilemma in some of the U.S. government antipoverty programs of the 1960s. Committed people were involved in programs in Appalachia and elsewhere in the United States; whether they worked for the federal government, for consulting firms, or were volunteers they shared a desire to help the poor and the underprivileged. Extensive efforts to build a self-sustaining infrastructure were funded by the Office of Economic Opportunity, the Small Business Administration, and the National Institutes of Health in places like Olive Hill, Kentucky, the Delmarva Peninsula, McAlester, Oklahoma, and the inner city areas of Washington, D.C. The success rate was mixed for several reasons; among the most important was the fact that while there were passion and meaning, there was not a clear and commonly held vision of the sort of community that these development efforts were attempting to create.

A vision based on meaning can provide passionate direction. The way this sort of meaning is brought about is by the management team responsible for a unit or company embarking on TQ being clear about their core values. Discussing values is uncomfortable for many business people. To some it is too personal. To others it is a topic they haven't thought through very carefully and are uncomfortable exploring it. There is no getting away from the fact, though, that our basic beliefs, or core values, drive our attitudes about work, about our role in the organization, and about how we wish to relate to people. These are attitudes that are inextricably tied to our mental picture of the kind of company we wish to create.

For groups of people who do not naturally think about or wish to discuss values, it is often best to get them talking about the sort of company they envision, making certain they become very specific and descriptive, then for a consultant, trainer, or group facilitator to suggest the underlying values from which those descriptors seem to emanate. In the years that Dave Berlew has been conducting Common Vision Workshops, a set of values have emerged as categories which form the basis for most visions. Once the top team in a Common Vision Workshop gets as far as it can on its vision, it uses a score sheet to tally the comments from its discussion that fall into one or more of the categories. Table 6.1 is the tally sheet; it briefly describes each value category.

Think of creating the vision as analogous to building a skyscraper, as shown in Figure 6.3. An effective vision will encompass each of the building's three segments.

First, it will be based on a set of core values that provide meaning and a sense of purpose. This forms the foundation. It will not stop there, though. A visioning effort that does not go beyond the clarification of core values will not lead to a vision. It might be a useful way to highlight important values such as pride or integrity or serving the common good, but more is needed. It may be a solid base, but it won't be a skyscraper.

That brings us to the second facet—a handful of the enterprise's most vital imperatives or A-items. Going from raw stock

Table 6.1
Value Message Coding Sheet

Definition of Value Category	Priority	Key Phrases
Achievement (Excellence, Quality Phrases reflecting commitment to: • doing well, better, or best • excellence, quality, unique accomplishment • providing challenging, personally rewarding work		
Power and Influence Phrases reflecting interest in: • becoming large, influential, dominating, or powerful • having impact, power, or control • recognition or status		
Affiliation and Loyalty Phrases reflecting commitment to: • warm, authentic personal relationships • team spirit • loyalty		
Service and Contribution Phrases reflecting commitment to: • service or contribution to customers(internal or external) • creating a better community, society, country, or planet • eliminating poverty, pollution, disease, injustice, suffering		

(continued)

Table 6.1 *(continued)*

Definition of Value Category	Priority	Key Phrases
Individual Worth and Human Dignity Phrases reflecting commitment to: • respect and consideration for the individual • equal opportunity, decency, good working conditions • eliminating exploitative or patronizing policies/practices		
Ethical Behavior Phrases reflecting commitment to: • honesty and fairness • respect for the spirit as well as the letter of the law		
Material Rewards and Assets Phrases reflecting interest in: • individual rewards: pay, bonuses, perquisites, equity • organizational rewards: for example,revenues, profits, return-on-investment		

Source: ©1989 Situation Management Systems, Inc., Hanover, MA, 7/89-D

to a finished product in 24 hours (when the norm is two weeks) is an example. A-items are superordinate priorities, the imperatives most crucial to the business. They could have to do with time, with response, with quality of product or service, or with employee involvement. Most often they originate in the marketplace; it is the customer who can best point the way to A-items. It is usually best to generate a list of all the possible A-items and then winnow down that list to the vital few by answering the question, "Why do I want to realize that item, what value or meaning does it have?" Answers to this question will cause some items to be eliminated and others to be combined. It will further help to determine how it will be known that the A-item has been realized. What are the metrics? What will be the indicators?

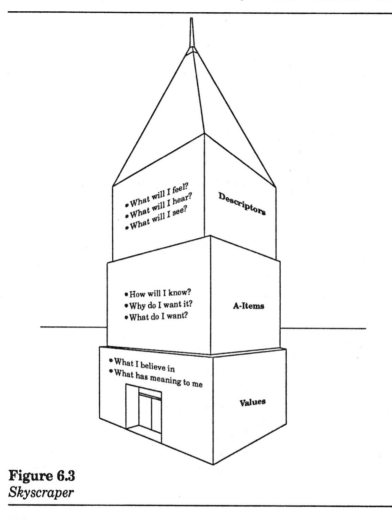

Figure 6.3
Skyscraper

Also, answers here will be a direct reflection of core values, and a useful way to reaffirm those values.

In the third segment of our skyscraper are the descriptors, statements that describe what the company of the future will look like, what one will hear in that place and what it will feel like to work there. Often, managers will say, "I see a lot of team-work." Not good enough. In order to be helpful, what one would actually see or hear must be described. "I see a place that responds in one-third the time that we do now" is also not helpful until it turns into a description of what would be seen, heard, and/or felt in a place that responds in one-third of the time; such as, "I see people running to get the job done fast," "I see groups of workers huddled over a table looking at drawings, with engineers there, too, working together to solve a problem fast," "I see a product distribution pipeline where the product goes on a truck from the shipping dock direct to the customers' receiving dock."

A Common Vision

It's one thing for the leader to feel passion about a particular image of what the company could become; but that is only part of what is needed. The other part is to build on that foundation to create a vision that key people throughout the company can become equally passionate about—a common vision. Especially when the task is to change the way an organization operates and to alter its character, there must be a shared vision of what is being sought that is commonly held throughout the business. Unless shared and committed to by most employees (and certainly the key people), a personal vision will not lead to organizational change.

A vision is shared when the motivating picture in the minds of most employees is more or less the same. It will not be exactly the same in each case, and should not be. Just as the leader must have a personal vision that has meaning and purpose, each employee must have that picture in his or her mind as well. It may be the leader who gets it started; indeed, it is there that the responsibility rests for strategy and for managing the climate of the organization. But the leader must then enable as many other employees as possible, especially those who are key to the firm's success, to have their own mental picture that they carry with them. If those pictures are not consistent, there will not be alignment and it is not likely that all will be moving in the same direction.

Openness and freedom must exist in order for there to be a common vision. The character and the culture of the organization must encourage open dialogue and exploration of ideas. Common vision will not result when people are not encouraged to think on their own and to express what is important to them. Suspicion and insufficient trust to say what is on one's mind are the enemies of a common vision. Employees must believe that they have enough freedom to create something that is of value. Ensuring that such conditions exist is an initial task for the leader.

But agreement can be quite different from commitment. The CEO of a large, global, high-technology company puts it this way.

> One of the most frustrating things for me is when people don't take personal responsibility for making this company what it can be. Here's an example. We've cut back quite a bit over the last several years here and there are a lot fewer employees. That's helped our bottom line, but we're trying to handle the work load in the same way as before, only with many fewer people. People are stressed and stretched.
>
> Take purchasing. We have people in our field sales offices and field service offices who always go through central purchasing here at corporate for MRO (maintenance, repair, and office) supplies. We figured a central unit could get a better price. But the time and the paperwork that system required were actually costing us more than if we just let the local people purchase from local suppliers and gave them Just-In-Time purchasing help to negotiate. My purchasing people here at corporate made a presentation to the management committee saying they needed to hire more people. I asked them why we couldn't think differently about this, that more people was not the answer. I told them to think about this other option so that central purchasing could help people in the field offices rather than being the ones to do all the purchasing. So they're going off and doing that now.
>
> But what's frustrating is that there are all sorts of opportunities like that around here and rather than people always thinking of better ways to do something, different ways to go about work, they'll take an idea like this one in purchasing and go implement it and they'll do it well, but then they won't keep looking for other opportunities. They'll take an idea from a senior manager and implement it, but then they'll stop—sort of unfreeze and move forward, but then they'll refreeze again.

This story and the frustration behind it is a common tale to anyone who has led and tried to change the character of an organization. These aren't cases where employees are intransigent or negative. Nor are these cases where employees are incompetent or not at all prepared to compete in today's world; when these situations exist, the next steps are often much easier to determine. It often has nothing to do with employees not being willing to assume personal responsibility, as this CEO believed. They are often cases where the leaders have a mental picture that employees do not have. The concept is different of how work is to be done and how the organization should operate. When a different way to operate is suggested and if it makes sense to employees, they will implement it, as the purchasing department did in this case. But it will not become a habit unless they embrace a picture in their mind's eye of a company where non-value-added tasks are eliminated, where speed of response is relentlessly pursued, and where innovative, set-breaking ideas are highly valued.

For this to happen, enough of the key people in the organization must believe they have influence over changing what is around them. The people who traditionally hold decision-making power must relinquish some of it so that others can make local decisions. This is, literally, what empowerment means; to give power to, to allow to influence. It does not mean to allow someone to have input. Nor does it mean to allow someone to say what is on his or her mind. It does not mean that employees are trained to make decisions. All three are what too often occur when companies launch "employee empowerment programs."

Unfortunately, the word *empowerment* has become popular and is used to refer to any attempt to increase participation. Too often, programs from the past are dusted off and given a new name. What is needed for TQ to take hold is the redistribution of decision-making power. For that to happen, more is needed than simply employee participation or employee training. There must also be decisions made at local levels where basic work is done so that problems can be solved fast or, better, avoided. Not strategic decisions or those involving the direction or operation of the whole business or decisions affecting the organization's culture (the leader cannot delegate these), but local operating decisions that are close to the customer and involve the meeting of his needs and exceeding of his expectations.

Ways Common Visions Form

The content of a vision that becomes common can come from many places. Below are three cases that describe different pathways to forming common visions.

Case 1

In one large consumer products company, the new head of engineering and asset planning (in charge of the strategy, building, maintenance, and renovation of all of this company's manufacturing and distribution facilities) had been handed a strategy from predecessors to continue the building of a distribution network based on large, automated central warehouse and distribution centers. The cost of these regional facilities and the software and hardware to manage and keep them linked together was extremely high, more than any other building program in the company's history. The analysis done by the company's own industrial engineers and distribution people, as well as by outside experts, showed that economies of scale and down-the-road efficiencies made this economical in the long run. Still, it didn't seem quite right to "Chet" (all names in this case history are disguised). The dollar cost was enormous. Some of the automated equipment that had been planned for was untested. The task of linking and communicating between these megadistribution centers was daunting. It all caused Chet to rethink the whole idea. He benchmarked other companies. He read. He questioned. Time was running out. His bosses were pressuring him to stay with the schedule and move ahead.

At a convention of his company's dealers, he heard a presentation on Just-In-Time, the philosophy of speed, flexibility, and eliminating the steps in manufacturing processes that do not add value. "Storing something doesn't add value. Counting it doesn't, either. Inventory is merely potentially useful product waiting to add value," he heard. He also heard of hard-to-believe cost savings that had resulted in other companies by thinking small and avoiding automation's inflexibility.

The germ of an idea began to form. If this could work in a plant, why not in a distribution center? In a network of distribution centers? What is our business anyway, he reasoned, but, really, a local business. It is the drug store manager and grocery store manager who are our customers and it is they who determine our shelf space, in large part. How are megadistribution centers going to better serve them? Can we do better by having our product closer to customers rather than in larger warehouses hundreds of miles away? Where's the added value of that to the customer? Why not a system where the product goes right from our plants to the customer's back door? Why not small warehouses right near the customer when we need to have inventory?

He began talking about this emerging image with division presidents and high-ranking staff people. He was asked to make presentations. He used only two slides for much of these sessions.

The first showed the current system and the path the product took. In the upper right-hand corner was a sketch of a manufacturing plant. From it a line led to the sketch of a tractor-trailer truck. From that, a line led to a warehouse. Then another truck, and a line to a larger warehouse. Another truck. And so on, until the product eventually arrived at a point on the lower left-hand corner at a sketch of a customer's store. He then showed his second slide. It was the same as the first except that several of the lines connecting the sketches and two of the trucks and three of the warehouses had black crosses drawn over them. It was the best way Chet knew of conveying his picture and getting others to understand it, as well.

What emerged from this line of reasoning over time is a distribution strategy made up of small, low-cost, local warehouses geared to fast response. Interim warehouses and the transportation and communication costs that come with large, centralized systems are largely eliminated under Chet's strategy.

While Chet was coming up with a new picture of a distribution system, John, one of the division presidents, became committed to establishing an employee involvement effort. He had become convinced that getting employees involved and pushing responsibility to lower levels was a big part of revitalizing his division, which had slipped in volume and profit in recent years. John had brought in outside educators to "teach" employee involvement. He wasn't satisfied with the results. He began talking about it himself. Still, he felt there was something missing. Something was needed to give the employee involvement effort life that he had become so committed to.

He attended one of Chet's presentations and became intrigued by the vast potential for cost savings that could come from such a distribution scheme. He began testing Chet and his countercultural scheme. Was it merely a pie-in-the-sky dream or was there really something to it? The more he delved into the idea of a dramatically shortened product-distribution pipeline, the more viable it seemed. The savings were real.

John also realized, though, that this sort of system required a change in the mindset of managers and employees and in the way that they went about doing their work. But, making it happen could mean the difference between getting his division back on track financially and being behind budget for the next fiscal year.

Kevin had assumed the CEO role in this corporation a year before Chet began formulating the new product-pipeline strategy. He had risen quickly through the managerial ranks and, with each managerial assignment, been known for increasing market share, repairing relationships with customers when necessary, and generating strong customer loyalty. He had been dismayed at the lack of attention to the customer of other divisions when he assumed the CEO role; he was also disturbed at the lack of connection with the customer on the part of staff directors and managers at the corporate office. He began talking about the customer constantly, asking questions at staff meetings and middle managers' presentations about what impact the proposed new program would have on the customer. He began asking what value to the customer was provided by some of the staff departments that existed at the corporate office. He began to be thought of by employees as a customer-oriented leader. His questions and the obvious intensity of his conviction regarding the customer's importance began to have an effect. But Kevin wasn't satisfied. More had to be done.

At a staff meeting of his division presidents and senior staff, the topic of the new distribution system was discussed in detail. All the senior staff had heard Chet's presentation, and the two slides he used were by now well known throughout the company. John, the division president, endorsed it. The only challenge, he said, was how to change the current thinking of employees so that it would work. Kevin had been thinking about the new distribution system, too. A decision had to be made to go one way or the other. The first and more traditional strategy with its promised economies of scale or the new, more radical one. He liked the new one. He liked its simplicity and Chet's argument that if large chunks of activity were eliminated, cost would be eliminated as well. But each time he thought about Chet's idea, what excited Kevin the most was its potential for fast response to a customer, much faster, at least theoretically, than the current one or the one proposed for large megadistribution sites. That sort of speed could be a decided competitive advantage and boost market share. He knew from customer surveys and meetings with customers that what mattered to them was getting the right product when they needed it, not later, and not before so that they had to carry the inventory. Local warehouses could make that easier. He also recognized the potential for the corporate staff groups to be part of this program and through that involvement, to become more in tune with customers and their needs.

Kevin recognized the danger of taking a stand one way or the other at this point. He was a persuasive enough leader that his subordinates might go along and not be committed. By encouraging conversation and the formation of two different positions, they could also perhaps emerge with a better and more well-thought-through solution. He encouraged John to talk more about this; and he probed to find out how deeply committed to this new system John really was. As John talked, things began to gel in Kevin's mind. He knew of John's frustration at not being able to get a real and robust employee involvement effort off the ground. He also began to see how a pilot program in John's area could answer several questions.

"John, hold on a minute," Kevin said. "You've talked about the cost savings and simplicity of this new system and Chet is certainly convincing, but we don't have any real evidence this will happen."

After reciting some of Chet's analysis and adding some of his own on the potential impact in his division, John said, "And, Kevin, I *believe* in this thing."

"But how can it be implemented? In order for this to work it will require people working differently than they do now. Getting the people in the field committed to it is the key."

John sat up and leaned forward in his chair. "The way to make that happen is to give them responsibility for thinking it through. If we have small, local warehouses we won't need another layer of managers. They can be run by self-managed teams. The responsibility can be the clerk's or the route-truck driver's to make this a success. That will save cost as well as get people involved. Let's let the people who will be affected the most get at this idea. Let's push it down to them. If they get committed to it they'll implement it!"

The more John talked the more convincing he became. "There's no question this is going to have a positive impact on our share in the market, too. I have store chains in my division that get out of stock frequently. Others that sell out on some of our products and not others. Others stock out at odd times."

"Bingo," Kevin thought, "the customer connection."

"So, John, let me go a step farther. This distribution system can gain us share if we can use it to respond faster than (our competition). It will also be less expensive to operate. The way to make it happen is to get people at the local levels involved in really thinking this through, get them to tell us if this really makes sense and how to make it happen. Is that what we're saying?"

The entire group talked through the pluses and minuses of this notion for the rest of that meeting and over the next couple of weeks. At their next meeting, two weeks later, Kevin started off by saying,

> I've been thinking a lot about our discussion of the pipeline concept and market share over the last couple of weeks, as I know each of you have. It has made me step back and ask more fundamental questions. 'What kind of place do we want to create around here? Is it a place where decisions get pushed down that are as important as our distribution strategy or where we make all the decisions in this room? Is it one where our decisions are based on the impact on a grocery store manager? Is it one that really wants to listen to our customers? Is it one that is willing to step out and do something different?' We have to get clear on that first. When we are all in the same spot about the kind of place we want this company to be, then these important, strategic decisions are going to be easier to make, and they'll make a lot more sense to our employees. Once we do this we should come back to this decision

about a distribution system and see which option most helps us get to where we want to be.

Another spirited discussion followed. An off-site meeting took place soon after to focus on Kevin's core question, "What kind of place do we want to create . . .?"

The group decided the firm should be one where the customer comes first, where employee loyalty and commitment and teamwork are high, and where success is a function of providing the best and fastest service and a product that the customer can depend on. But they didn't stop there. They took the next steps and determined the metrics that would indicate they were becoming this sort of company. Then, they addressed the question of what such a company would be like, how decisions would be made, what would happen in a monthly business review, what the local clerk and route truck driver would do and say, what they would hear from a customer six months from now. Table 6.2 shows examples of vision categories and questions that were used during this off-site meeting.

This is a case where the vision of the organization came from a few different places. Each was born of dissatisfaction with what currently existed. Commitment was high because there was widespread involvement and much conversation among the top team in shaping the vision. Also, because the vision that emerged met specific objectives of several people. John, for example, found a way to give life to an employee involvement effort as well as to cut costs in his division. The key was Kevin. He kept people thinking about the issue and avoided taking a strong public stand regarding either of the options being discussed. Also, he brought the group up above the issue at the critical decision point by raising strategic questions. Then, he brought the group to a level of practicality and detail by ensuring it spent time clarifying what the organization would look like and how it would act. It is very much in keeping with his style to get his group to talk through an issue and to have a lot of one-on-one discussions before deciding which way to go. But not every leader can do what Kevin can accomplish in this regard, which in turn affects how visions are formed.

Table 6.2
On Clarifying a Vision

Two Facets of a Vision
Physical: What will our company/unit look like and what will be the flow of work?
• Structure
• Information flow
• Decision-making process
• Physical environment
• Equipment

The primary indicators of the physical facet must be defined through metrics such as time and customer satisfaction.

Behavioral: What will it feel like to work here and how will people act?
• Needs that will be met
• Satisfaction defined
• Behavior
• What will be seen and heard

Indicators are more difficult to define for this facet but must be based on values that are strongly felt and compelling.

Questions to Form Vision in Each Facet

Physical	Behavioral
How will we be structured?	What styles of managers and what supervisors are needed?
What type of information will be shared?	How will the company be managed?
How will products be developed?	How will coordination take place?
How will products be distributed?	How will problems be addressed?
How will production flow in plants?	How will employees be involved?
How will distribution flow?	What form will it take?
How many suppliers will we need and where located?	What will be the nature of relationships with customers and suppliers?
	What style of teamwork should we have?
	What will be the organization climate?

Case 2

At times the vision of what the company could be comes from the leader rather than as part of a collaborative process. Here's an example:

A large sector of a Fortune 100 corporation made up of 10 companies had grown rapidly, largely through acquisition. Its president had shepherded its growth over a 10-year period. He understood that the businesses that had been acquired had changed and matured over time and their markets had changed as well. As these companies had grown, the need for specific R&D or legal or strategic or financial help was significant, but the cost of such specialized help couldn't be justified on the division profit-and-loss statements. There were also demands from the corporate office on this sector as there were on other sectors in the corporation. A sector headquarters group had grown as the way to centralize costs and ensure that the growing divisions had the help needed, and to be a central point of information for corporate requests.

As the businesses grew and were encouraged to survive and thrive on their own and to become independent entities, their top managers sought to develop their own sources of staff capabilities rather than depending on the staff support from the sector headquarters' office. Predictably, role conflict resulted, with the tension and turf protection that often accompanies it.

Over time, it became unclear which group had responsibility for certain aspects of product development and for assuring product quality. Some costly and embarrassing product failures resulted. New-product-development targets were missed. Market share of some businesses began to slip. The shining star of the corporation, growing at a rate faster than other sectors, began to tarnish. The president could predict a slowdown in growth, and he also knew that product-quality problems was the road that would most certainly lead to disaster. He looked to the creation of a Total Quality effort as one answer.

He set benchmarks by talking to peers in other companies. He read. He brought in outside experts. He became intrigued by what he heard of the experience of companies such as 3M, Motorola, and Milliken, and how they had linked the solving of product problems with impressive new-product-development efforts. He invited executives from such companies to speak before his managers. He did not explain why these other executives were visiting, or what he had in mind regarding Total Quality.

Over time, he became committed to establishing a TQ effort throughout his sector. The tricky part of doing so had to do with a central tenet of the sector, as well as of this particular executive's management style: maintaining the integrity and independence of individual divisions and allowing the division manager to be in charge of and to control his or her own destiny. How could he ensure that Total Quality was helping to create products of high quality in every division? Ordering the division heads to adopt Total Quality was not the answer, he knew, and was foreign to his leadership style.

First, this leader became more clear in his own mind about what he wished to create. Once he completed his benchmarking, he followed his usual process when an important decision needs to be made. He thought about it on his own.

Others come to a position or decision by talking about it, encouraging discussions and absorbing the various perspectives of other people, and using it as a way to clarify their own thinking. The archives of President John F. Kennedy and comments of his advisors show evidence of this style.

Others establish poles of thought about them through strongwilled advisors and position themselves in the center to be the arbiter, deciding on the veracity of individual positions and then piecing together a position or strategy. Franklin D. Roosevelt as president in the 1930s and 1940s displayed the ability to foster competition between strong, independent advisors, setting himself as the final decision maker.

Still others, like this leader, have a one-alone modus operandi. In a more private, don't-show-your-hand style, they gather data, listen, perhaps read and come to a position. Ronald Reagan showed some of this decision-making style, at least as governor of California in the 1970s, by his now-famous solitary rides on horseback (sometimes overnight) to think through options and make a decision.[2]

Not one of these styles is necessarily best. Each has benefits and shortcomings. They are simply different. The sector president happened to be most comfortable with a one-alone style.

A personal note: When I began consulting as an undergraduate in the late 1960s, my belief was that there was one best way and one best style by which one should manage and lead, and I happened to know what it was! It was an open, confrontive, democratic style where things were dealt with openly and where everyone had the chance to participate in the formulation of policy. I was fortunate enough to have participated in some of the early employee-involvement experiments and organization-change programs of the time, some quite significant. Group dynamics played a major role in such efforts and the "excellent" leaders were the ones who had good group skills.

As I continued to consult, and performed more consulting than small-group training, I was exposed to equally effective styles, and also saw the limitations of the open and confrontive style. When I became a manager myself in the mid 1970s and then eventually a leader, it became painfully and embarrassingly obvious what I had missed in those earlier days. There is no one best style that is appropriate for everyone who leads. Rather, the need is to match one's style, personality, and preferences to the task at hand. By the time a person becomes a leader, his or her style is established. It has worked and brought success and promotion. It is unlikely to change significantly, short of some dramatic, personal crisis or trauma.

Style will, and in some cases should, be altered to meet the needs of the situation; no one should sit still and fail to develop and change style, but a person who has learned to work in a formal or competitive way and done so for years is unlikely to change to become a participative leader. The leader's style should be accepted for what it is and, as long as the values and intent are the correct ones, ways built around the leader through people or systems to compensate for or shore up the inevitable shortcomings of that style.

Back to the tale of the sector president. He emerged from his period of contemplation convinced that Total Quality was necessary, but that the division presidents and their staffs had to drive TQ in their particular units. He also was convinced of something else. From his benchmarking he had learned that even a decentralized operation like the one he led could maximize the effectiveness if the TQ effort in each unit was based on a common set of principles. Not to stifle, but rather to help to avoid redundancies and ensure at least some commonality.

He worked hard at deciding what he wished to have happen and what he needed to create. He spoke to outside experts as well as a few of his most trusted advisors but still did not announce his intentions. The picture began to become more clear. He then did something very uncharacteristic of him, something that captured the attention of employees—he scheduled an off-site meeting of his senior advisors to try to shape a common vision among the top team.

Prework questions asked what each senior manager believed would be the optimum sector. How would it look? How would it operate? What would it be known for? They were then asked to speculate on the factors that currently existed that could move the organization toward that optimum state, and those currently existing that could block it. This prework set the tone for a three-day off-site meeting where the following decisions were made.

1. Total Quality had the potential to help the entire sector, and there would be a TQ effort in each of the divisions as well as in the staff groups in the sector's headquarters.

2. There were principles, "stakes-in-the-ground" that would shape implementation of TQ efforts in the sector. One principle states that it is up to the individual division exactly what the TQ effort will look like, but that the effort will at least include (a) some way to clarify an image of what the division should become; (b) a formal process to gather and analyze data, showing where there are quantitative opportunities and a way to measure the division's climate; and (c) a method to involve employees in solving problems. Another states that the customer is the reason for the TQ effort and that the entire sector (divisions and headquarters) will redouble efforts to understand the needs of and to satisfy the external customer.

3. The off-site meeting produced a new and different image of a sector. Rather than a sector with a number of very independent units that never came in contact, the leaders envisioned one where units helped each other, where the strength of one could be used to shore up the weakness of another, where the president of one division was in contact with the president of another division and was a sounding board and someone to help offer advice, where relationships with the headquarters staff were positive, and where divisions saw headquarters staff as

helpful and performing value-added work. The opposite had been the case historically.

4. The group went further and outlined several categories where it expected to see the divisions as well as the headquarters staff groups make progress. One example was to ensure that employees were involved in decision making. Another was to ensure that new-product-development efforts are launched and managed so that development time was shorter than it ever had been. A third had to do with the way decisions should be made in the divisions and, in general, how things should work. For each of these categories, the top team listed what they would see, hear, or perceive were it being acted out. As the group worked on these A-items, these TQ imperatives, they had to continually stretch their thinking, get beyond merely listing what they wanted, and get to a level of specificity that answered the question, "What would it look like, what would I hear or feel were that actually the case?"

Table 6.3 shows examples of this group's work.

The task of devising a vision for a decentralized company or, in this case, sector of a larger corporation is different from the task of devising a vision for an operating company or division. It is by nature less specific. The decentralized sector does not produce a product. Rather it is the divisions that make up the sector that produce products and actually interact with customers on a daily basis. Also, the people on the top team of a decentralized sector or corporation wear two hats. On one hand, they are part of the sector's leadership group and must take into account the needs of the whole sector. At the same time, though, those that have divisions reporting to them must also wear another hat—that of the operating head, and he or she must have the needs of the divisions in mind.

A second difference has to do with the style of this particular leader. The leader formulated an image of what he believed would be a better and a more successful sector. Then, through one-on-one discussions and the common-vision off-site meeting, the key people on his staff embraced a similar picture. It was not done by way of threats, there was no implication that people who did not get on board would lose their jobs. Also, the leader stopped short of laying out a picture that was so specific that there was no room for others to adapt it or find a way to make it their own.

But the leader did make it clear that there were major components of a picture in which he believed. While he also made it clear that he could and would be influenced, it was apparent that the basic ingredients of the picture were ones to which he was committed. Because of this leader's style, he had to do more convincing than was necessary with the CEO in the previous example. This sector leader emphasized his commitment through one-on-one meetings and also through a common-vision off-site meeting, an unusual step for him. He is wise enough to recognize that his key managers must want to make his vision a reality as much as the leader himself and encouraged them to do their own benchmarking, reading, and other groundwork.

As mentioned before, the sector president knew before going into the off-site meeting what he wanted to see happen in his sector and what shape a TQ effort should take. He participated actively in the off-site session, and did so in such a way that the picture he had formulated was the one the group endorsed. When polled at the end of the session, the other top managers on the president's staff voiced strong support for the vision. What had happened was that the president had convinced his staff to adopt what he had in mind. He succeeded because loyalty to this leader is high and there is respect for his abilities and standing in the corporation.

This approach is different from that used in the previous example by the leader I've called Kevin; but it is not necessarily worse or less effective. The key difference is that because the vision truly did evolve in the first case there is a greater likelihood that each vice president will be committed to it. In the second case, the sector president must continue to stress the vision and emphasize its precepts in every way. In the first case there is a greater likelihood that the vision will be truly shared. In the second case it is a common vision but may, over-time, prove to not be truly shared.

One point of this example is for those consultants, internal or external, who face the task of helping to clarify a common vision. There is no one, best way to do so that can be used in

Table 6.3
Common Vision Categories

Faster Response

People would concentrate on reducing time everywhere and would talk about it constantly.

Product-development system would be broken down and understood. It would be charted out and everyone would be able to describe it.

Fifty percent reduction in development time would be a typical goal committed to by division management team.

Division presidents talk of TQ often. Total Quality is a key responsibility and presidents constantly stress it.

Measures and goals on time reduction are apparent. . . . I'd see them and hear people talking about them.

. . . intuitive sense that everyone is oriented to doing the right things in the best way and doing them fast.

Sector headquarters would analyze processes and work at streamlining in an aggressive relentless way.

Customer Focus

Evidence of constant interaction with customers . . . charts, surveys, comments about customers

Voice of the customer would be communicated throughout the company . . . in-house newsletters and other vehicles would reflect it.

Engineers will be in the field talking with customers

Data on customer response and satisfaction would be posted on the walls.

Division presidents would ask about impact on the customer and about customer satisfaction on regular visits by senior staff.

Customer complaints would be acknowledged immediately and 90% resolved in 90 days.

Each division has a customer service standard and constantly measures performance against it.

Employees everywhere would be able to relate their jobs to the customer and could describe who customers are and what they want/need/expect.

People Driving Change and Taking Responsibility

People would regularly come forward with new ideas and be willing to fight for them.

Things wouldn't fall through the cracks, with problems lost over time and no one picking up the ball.

We'd come to grips more quickly with a project that is going to fail.

Upward delegation—people in the middle and lower levels would push those at the top.

We'd challenge Corporate more on non-value-added tasks.

Employee Involvement

There'd be more evidence of decisions made at lower levels.

Lots of ideas . . . they are recognized and action is taken on the best.

People at all levels talking about pilots . . . excited . . . proud.

Lower level people making presentations on key projects showing pride and commitment.

A middle manager would be facilitating employee involvement activities . . . would be leading task forces . . . involved.

A climate survey that says people are hungry, energized, winning, and want more.

Lots of task forces working on the vital few issues.

How the Business Should Operate

Key headquarters people constantly on the road, constantly talking of TQ.

General emphasis on streamlining processes.

Constant attention on measuring how we're doing.

Would not see turf battles.

Look at performance in different way—not use old ways to judge it . . . measure performance based on merit.

People in training programs would learn new ways to operate and get excited about them, such as
- tools and techniques to diagnose and display problems;
- JIT tools to reduce time and cost;
- Techniques to improve teamwork and the organization climate.

Every employee would go through at least a minimum number of hours of training/year.

every situation. The best approach depends on the situation, especially the style and proclivities of the leader. At the same time, there are tools that can be used whatever the approach; the way those tools are employed and at what time will depend on the leader's style. Does he learn best by reading or by face to face dialogue or by observation? Is she better in a group or one-on-one? Does she tend to make decisions by choosing from alternatives? Is he deliberate or intuitive? How does he utilize the people around him? Are they people who test and challenge the leader or tend to follow what she says? How much dissent is there on the top team and how able is the leader in managing that dissent? The answers to these sorts of questions will determine how to use the vision clarification tools of reading, benchmarking, visits to and from leaders who are farther ahead in the process, and an off-site common-vision workshop.

This case raises a question at the core of TQ success, and one often asked by midlevel managers: Is it possible to have a successful TQ effort if the top person is not in favor of it? The answer, as with most questions like this is, it depends. There have been cases where VPs of manufacturing, for example, have embraced TQ, made it work for the manufacturing and related areas over which they had control, and learned how to extend it to include product development and engineering and/or marketing. The vice presidents have made it work in these cases and convinced their boss to support it because of the impressive results TQ had caused to happen. This requires strength, perseverance, and some courage on the part of vice presidents.

On the other hand, if the impetus for TQ is at lower levels in the organization and vice presidents, or others with legitimate, formal power and/or leverage do not support it, it will not happen.

Rolling Out a Vision

Part of the task of forming a common vision is for the leaders to agree on what they wish to see, hear, and perceive. The other part is for them to manage the rollout of that vision so that there is widespread commitment. There are at least three components to doing so. First is a plan that communicates the top leaders' vision. Then, ways must be found to crystallize their own pictures of what the organization should become in a way that it becomes motivating and has deeply felt meaning. Finally, the systems and policies that guide day-to-day activities must be made consistent with the vision. Throughout, the behavior of those most visible to the organization must be scrupulously consistent with the sort of behavior that is implied in the vision.

The rollout plan must, if nothing else, engage the minds and the imaginations of employees. One company decided to do so in a tiered fashion. Once the top 12 people were clear on what they wanted to create, they brought together the next group of managers, a group of 70, in a three-day off site meeting. The vision was outlined by the top team in ways the group of 70 had never seen them act.

Senior managers who traditionally had been known to not always agree, shared the podium and also shared a conviction on a set of common parameters. They heard the leader speak with a sense of purpose that was rare. The total group of 70 was divided into subgroups to discuss and explore what they had heard. Reports and plenary discussions followed. Subgroups met again to determine the vital few areas where progress had to be made. After combining and synthesizing, 10 areas emerged—five where more data had to be gathered and five where action could be taken.

The meeting ended with the leader forming 10 teams of seven people each, each team chaired by a member of the senior staff. He also charged the entire group with a challenging assignment: in addition to their regular job assignments, devote 50% of their time to one of these teams over the next 90 days. He said he realized that this would be a demanding task, that people were probably wondering where they would find the time. He replied to his own rhetorical question by saying that each of them simply must find the time, that this effort was perhaps the most important one in the history of the company. They must delegate or stop doing work that is not as value-added.

The groups worked on their tasks for the next three months. Pressure and stress increased, especially on those who couldn't or wouldn't delegate. At the end of 90 days another offsite meeting was held. Each team reported to the entire group what it had done. Some had completed their tasks and were disbanded. Others were at a midpoint and laid out what they had to do to fulfill their charters.

Thirty days later another off-site session was held. This time the top 12 and the next 70 were joined by the next level in the structure—a group of 400. By this time, the group of 400 had heard about this effort and its interest and curiosity were high. The story was laid out first by the top 12, but for the most part by the group of 70, who were the bosses of the next layer of 400.

Commitment to the vision grew among the group of 12 and the group of 70 step by step. The original off-site meeting was step 1. Step 2 was the task of standing up and discussing the vision. This caused these senior people to think it through to a greater degree than they ever would have had the leader written a vision statement, or worse, delegated to an outsider the task of writing it. The commitment was deepened further during step 3, when they chaired task forces and had to defend what had emerged from the off site. The next 70 people went through a similar process with the subsequent 400 employees.

The stakes in the ground, the principles that would guide the TQ effort, were established and reinforced. (For example, there had to be a formal process to identify the needs and expectations of internal clients, the TQ effort would be driven by what customers wanted; pilot efforts would attack problems and train people in new techniques; all improvement efforts had to be consistent with the TQ principles the top team had defined.)

Case 3

It is one thing to communicate a vision formulated by a top team, even in as involving a way as the preceding example. But it's quite another to enable groups throughout the business to formulate their own vision that is consistent with that of the leader.

In one case, a $450 million electronics manufacturer decided to follow the top team's common-vision workshop with a series of similar sessions in cascading fashion down the organization chart. Each of the eight vice presidents gathered his or her staff together for $1\frac{1}{2}$ days off-site. At the start of each session, the vice president outlined what had taken place at the top team's vision session and laid out the vital few imperatives that the top team had identified: teamwork, fast response, local decision making, customer satisfaction that was the best in the industry, and a new product set that would catapult this company into new markets and far ahead of the competition. Each VP, however, stopped short of outlining the vision of the sort of company that could achieve these sorts of things. Instead, they led their groups in a discussion of what these imperatives might mean for their departments, that is, what it would look like, act like, and feel like if people took these imperatives to heart and acted on that basis in their own areas of the organization.

Each session resulted in a series of statements for each of the four categories that indicated what would be observed, heard, or perceived. In all, there were eight sets of statements, one for each department. The top team met to review what had resulted. It was surprising to its members that the statements were so similar. Differences were discussed and new input explored. The statements representing what the groups decided they envisioned were compared with what the top team had said in its original off-site meeting. The original list of the top team was adjusted to reflect this new input.

A two-day off-site meeting was held with the top team and the eight sets of department leaders, 64 participants in all, where the statements from each group were presented, and the top team's revised set of descriptive statements were presented as well. Through small group meetings over the two days, they were discussed, debated, and, eventually, brought together into a set of descriptors that the entire group voiced commitment to and agreed could form the basis for a different, better company.

Three steps followed.

1. Meetings were held to communicate to the next layer down in the organization chart what the top two layers (the group of 64) had done

2. The top team continued to meet periodically off site on the topic of the vision. It also instituted as a permanent part of its biweekly staff meetings an agenda item called "Vision Update," when it discussed progress made and barriers to the vision

3. The group of 64 met once more, six months after it had met the first time, to reaffirm its commitment to the vision, discuss problems, and share ideas on how to overcome them.

Throughout this process the leader was more active and visible than he had ever been. He met with employees at brown-bag sessions in the cafeteria, visited field-sales and field-service operations, and spoke at management development conferences for the company's managers. Whenever he had the chance, it seemed, he asked questions about customers and whether managers knew how satisfied employees were, or the degree that they received prompt replies to questions. He "suggested" that a field office which had had notorious customer-service problems begin charting the number of customers who called, when they called, the speed of response, and the mean time that it took from the customer's original call or correspondence until the problem, or issue, had been resolved to the customer's satisfaction. Before long every sales and service office had adopted the same report card.

As has been said previously, the behavior of the leader is perhaps the single most important ingredient and indicator of success of Total Quality. In the case outlined above, the leader's behavior once the TQ effort took shape was more demonstrative than employees had ever seen it in the past. It was not that he tried to become someone else. He was not acting. Rather, he chose this as the time when he would become dedicated to the success of a company-wide thrust. He had seen them come and go. The productivity programs of the early 70s. Material Requirements Planning in the late 1970s. Computer Integrated Manufacturing programs of the early 1980s. But this, he reasoned, was an effort that was strategic in nature and broad enough so that it could both be the umbrella for improvement efforts and also provide the criteria for those efforts at the same time. Even though he had not so apparently embraced other improvement efforts, this one was one he could become truly enthusiastic about and it showed. As a result, he came across in a sincere, unfeigned manner that got people's attention and added significantly to the credibility of the entire effort.

Principles for a Common Vision

The elements necessary for a common vision suggested so far are these:

- The leaders' personal image of the sort of company they want to create shapes the common vision.

- Openness and freedom prevail.
- Top management agree and are committed to the vision.
- Employees see, hear, and experience the top team as being of one mind regarding a vision.
- Leader and top managers speak of the vision with a sense of purpose.
- Meetings and workshops (more than most companies normally hold), for example:
  —Common Vision Workshops
  —Communication meetings
- Vision is integrated into normal meetings, such as regular staff meetings.
- A-items point to the company's imperatives and descriptive statements define the vision.

While the task of making a vision truly common and ensuring its precepts are widely shared is largely dependent on specific circumstances there are some principles the leader can employ as the basis for a strategy.

First, the leader must take the same medicine that he has suggested others take. Full involvement cannot be expected unless the leader lives by the same rules. This means attending awareness sessions. If the leader attends a course or seminar as a learner along with other employees, the leader as well as the TQ effort will gain in credibility. Another example of taking the same medicine is for the leader to use the TQ tools that have been prescribed for others. When delivery problems become so severe that they reach the senior level, chart them to show trends and facilitate analysis; or, if the senior staff needs to improve its meetings conduct the same training sessions for it as task teams and steering committees use to ensure their meetings are adding value.

Second, the leader should be a model for the rest of the organization. Part of the task here is to be consistent, since the surest way to lose people's enthusiasm is for the leader to say one thing and do another. The majority of employees will judge how serious a TQ effort is based on what the leader and other senior people do, not on what they say. If the leader makes a point about being customer-focused, but does not increase the contact he or she has with customers and does not visibly reflect the new knowledge that results, credibility will be lost.

All departments must participate fully in the creation of a TQ organization. There has been a tendency to begin TQ efforts in manufacturing; indeed, sometimes it is the manufacturing vice president who drives TQ, as we see with Jim Litts at Johnson and Johnson, who discusses his efforts in a later chapter. The success of the TQ effort, however, is a function of the degree to which each department embraces it and pulls in the same direction using a common language.

Most people will plan for the future from the present moment when thinking of how best to rollout a vision; that is, they will consider the current position and list steps into the future. It is the wrong way to think about this task. They must reverse their planning schematic. Rather than thinking about this task sequentially starting with today, they must first clarify what they would see and hear if employees had embraced a TQ vision, and work backward from there.

Use a time frame of 18 to 36 months when devising a plan. Anything less will not allow enough time and anything more pushes the time horizon out farther than most companies will find practical—the pace of change in many companies is such that people and market conditions can be altered dramatically over a four- or five-year time span. It is often the case, though, that the conditions under which the business operates stay more or less consistent for one-and-one-half to three years.

There is a tendency to form ad hoc groups as the vision is being clarified. Task forces and steering committees are examples of such groups and they can be extremely helpful. They present a danger, however. They can subtly absolve the line organization of the responsibility to make the vision real. Any *ad hoc* group should conform to the literal, Latin translation, "to this"—that is, a group focusing on a specific task and only that task. It should not go on forever. If it becomes permanent, the line organization will be less likely to assume responsibility and ownership.

It is important for as many people as possible to be involved in clarifying the vision. This can be done through on-site and off-site meetings such as those mentioned above. It should be noted, though, that the leader should avoid the urge to define a vision and tell others what the vision for the organization should be. Rather, the leader has the responsibility to get the process started and certainly to be clear personally regarding his or her vision of the future, but at the same time, to enable each employee to have a personalized vision as well. Even the sector head who came to a personal vision that was well developed stopped short of telling his senior managers the entire vision. Utilizing one of his strengths in one-on-one meetings and a Common Vision Workshop, he talked extensively about what he believed was necessary in such a way that his direct reports did not feel as though their boss's image was being imposed on them. He laid out the framework and principles and instructed them to set benchmarks, to read, and so forth, in other words, to fill in their own images. The vision will have meaning to the degree that the employee can personalize it, can see himself or herself in the picture that is taking shape and represents something that is important. The leader must ensure that the pictures are consistent.

Finally, the question is often asked, "Shouldn't we write a vision statement in a few words or at least write something?" The answer is both no and yes. A vision statement written in a "few words" is really most often a mission statement that describes the business or wants of the top people. It also often has meaning only for those who participated in its crafting. Too often, the leader will delegate the task to staff people or, worse, to outside consultants. This is a double negative. Not only is an attempt being made to write in a sentence or two what cannot be made that succinct, but the wrong people are doing the writing.

One danger of trying to reduce the vision to a pithy statement is that its meaning is sacrificed to brevity. Another danger is that it is too complete, too wrapped up in a neat package and not malleable enough for people to make their own or at least have some input into. Another danger is that once done it tends to be framed and mounted or put on a shelf and forgotten.

Realistically, though, something has to be put on paper. Especially in large organizations, there is a need to communicate over vast distances the collective picture of the future that has been formulated by the company's leaders. There is also the need to leave a record, a trail, of the process by which the vision took shape. It is usually best for those most involved to discuss their vision to the point that categories of behavior are defined and agreed upon. Then, for each category, descriptive statements of what would be seen, heard, or felt can be listed. An example is shown as Table 6.3.

The vision is what each person thinks of as the picture of the place they are attempting to create. The written descriptors are a necessary manifestation of that mental image. The vision will become more clear as time goes on and as people have experiences together that are based on a new idea of the enterprise and how it can become more competitive. It is a dynamic thing that will continue to become more and more refined as new people participate in giving it shape and as events take place which were unanticipated at the time the process of creating a common vision began.

A supplement (not a substitute) for a written set of statements might be a videotape. The leader and the key managers on a videotape describing their image of how the organization could be and the meaning it holds for them can be quite powerful. It can also lend a more personal touch that can be used for new employees' orientation and remote locations. It must be done in a way that is natural and does not appear staged, however. The senior managers talking in their own manner will have more impact and credibility than if they look as though they are giving a formal speech or reading from a TelePrompter.

The preceding are guidelines for getting a vision known in a way that maximizes the chance that it provides sufficient room for employees to make it their own. Let's return to the leader and end this chapter by summarizing the sorts of behavior that can bring about a commonly held vision and fuel a TQ effort.

Consistency, Credibility, Clarity, and Confidence

There is a thread that runs through the behavior of each of the leaders who have successfully guided their company's TQ efforts. It is made up of four parts.

The first is that these leaders have stuck to the course they established. They set the tone and acted consistently over time, hammering the nails of the themes of Total Quality over and over again at every opportunity. Employees become used to hearing the leader stress these themes. After awhile they can anticipate what the leader would think about a particular event or thrust or problem.

Then comes credibility. The leader's message is credible when the leader comes across as being sincere. This does not mean that he or she has to be an electrifying public speaker; just that the leader speak from the heart, speak as though the words and the message have meaning. Leaders who try to treat the TQ message as if it were an acceptance speech at an association meeting will come across as less than sincere, and credibility will suffer. One example of a leader who lost a great deal of credibility is the vice president who prepared to make a speech to new employees on Total Quality by asking a summer intern, an MBA student, to write the speech for him.

The third part is clarity. The effective leader is clear about what he or she wants to see created. Whether eloquently or not, these leaders paint a picture verbally to which employees can relate. This is often done most effectively through analogies and metaphors. The effect these analogies and metaphors should have is to spark the imaginations of employees so that they can form their own pictures. The descriptor statements, while more specific than an analogy or a metaphor, should do the same. The balance the leader must strike is to be clear without being so specific that there is not room for other employees to personalize it and to see how they fit into the vision.

The three criteria of consistency, credibility, and clarity can take on even more potency when they are wrapped in confidence, much as a rope becomes stronger when another strand is added to make it thicker (Figure 6.4). There are some who contend that CEO stands not for chief executive officer, but for chief eternal optimist. While the leader hopes to be on the correct side of the line that separates challenging but realistic thinking from

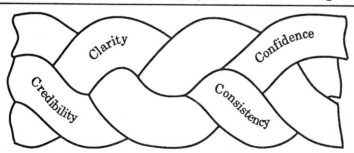

Figure 6.4
Criteria for Successful Leadership of a TQ Effort

wishful thinking, there is no doubt that a requirement of the leader who is leading a TQ effort is to project a level of confidence and optimism that his vision can indeed become a reality, and will.

References

1. P. Senge, *The Fifth Discipline* (Garden City, NY: Doubleday, 1990).

2. For more on policymaking styles of U.S. presidents see Alex George, *Presidential Decision Making in Foreign Policy* (Boulder, CO: Westview Press, 1980).

7

The Total Quality Driver

Now that the various elements needed to achieve Total Quality have been discussed, this chapter reviews how a few such efforts have played out in practice, and, in particular, the attributes of the person who is called on to make it happen. This person might be called the Vice President for Quality, the vice president for Total Quality, or Director, Quality and Continuous Improvement. Regardless of the exact title, this person's job is to shepherd the TQ effort; to do more than merely administer it, but to *drive* it. For our purposes, this person will be referred to as the "TQ driver."

In this chapter, TQ drivers from three companies where TQ efforts have been underway for at least three years will describe what they have experienced and what they have learned. Two are the administrators of the TQ efforts in their companies and facilitate the day-to-day activities of Total Quality. The third is a head of operations who is the spearhead of the TQ effort.

Attributes and Tasks

Before we hear from these people, let me outline briefly the general attributes that must be present in the TQ driver, the major tasks he or she must perform, and when this person should enter the process. Attributes and tasks are summarized in the following list.

Attributes

- Has a broad experience in how the business operates
- Thinks like a staff person as well as a line person
- Gets things done without creating a new bureaucracy
- Organizes separate elements into a single, forceful effort
- Finds common ground on which TQ participants can meet

Tasks

- To gain access to and the trust of the leader
- To get broad-based support from the leadership team
- To create a plan (and sell it) for the deployment of TQ
- To find ways to articulate and to spread a new set of values defined by the leaders
- To construct and manage organization change efforts that move the company's character to one which carries out those new values
- To influence department heads to ensure TQ initiatives stay out front
- To influence line managers responsible for annual plans and budgets, with staff people responsible for measurement, reward, and information systems, and with all employees

These characteristics should be taken as guidelines, not to be enforced rigidly. As you will hear from these people themselves, the process of becoming a TQ organization is not a systematic and ordered one; it is full of experimentation. What works for one company will not necessarily work for another. Who fits the role of day-to-day TQ driver will depend on the size, structure, and culture of the particular organization. The individual may come from any area: operations, marketing, human resources, or finance, and in some cases may even be a senior line manager.

Whatever this person's background, the ideal TQ driver will be someone who has broad experience in how a business operates and has earned a certain level of respect. Even a person who has spent most or all of a career in line management should, when wearing the TQ hat, be able to think like a staff person as well as like a line person, to get things done without creating a new bureaucracy, and to seek to accomplish things for the good of the company and not for the personal credit success will bring. He or she must be able to organize disparate elements of the company and find common ground on which participants can meet and work together.

This person must be able to gain access to and the trust of the leader and the leadership team. The TQ driver must be able to get broad-based support from the leadership team not only for the concepts of TQ, but for the implementation plan and its timetable. The driver must create a plan and a way to market it in the company that the leadership team buys into wholeheartedly so there are no mixed messages to other employees.

The TQ driver plays a role along with the leader in articulating values. One element that separates excellent TQ efforts from average ones is that the excellent ones are based on and personify values for which the organization stands that are attractive and motivating to employees. Often, this has meant that the leaders take advantage of the opportunity afforded by the TQ effort to redefine or clarify the values they intend to use as the foundation for a new, reinvigorated company. The articulation and spreading of such values becomes a primary ingredient of the TQ effort and the TQ driver should play an important part in making it happen. This means the TQ driver must believe deeply in the values established by the company's leaders. Then, he or she must be able to construct organization-change efforts that can move the character of the company more toward one that can carry out those values and ensure that these efforts proceed on track.

In addition, it is to the TQ driver that the task falls of ensuring that the TQ effort is visible and is kept out in front of every department head and manager. This is another example where the TQ driver shares responsibility with the CEO or the unit head.*

The leader will keep the TQ effort visible in at least four ways:

- at events such as meetings with the upper levels of managers;

---

*Hereafter in this chapter the top manager of the company, group , or division implementing a TQ effort will be referred to as "the leader" to avoid interrupting the flow of the text each time it refers to the top manager.

- with the top team during its day-to-day interactions;
- by ensuring that the systems and the building blocks of the business (the strategy process; the information, measurement, and reward systems; the yearly planning process; and so forth) are both responsive to customers and satisfying to employees; and
- by the comments and, especially, the questions posed to employees during day-to-day interaction.

There is no question that these sorts of tasks are significant and important to the TQ effort. Without the leader performing them, the effort will be directionless and interest will soon fade, making success more difficult to achieve. At the same time there is another set of tasks to be carried out that is less strategic and more tactical in nature. This set of tasks is as important as those of the leader. If leaders set the tone in ways only they can because of their visibility and position, but these more tactical tasks are not carried out, the TQ effort will lack movement. Day-to-day events will not happen as planned. There will be "disconnects" between expectations set by the leader and events taking place day to day.

To keep the TQ effort moving and visible the TQ driver can

- develop a communication mechanism to publicize successes and experiments and make sure people learned from them.
- influence line managers, especially those responsible for annual budgets and plans, to reinforce the TQ message and to balance the inevitable trade-offs between short-term action and longer-term development.
- work with the people responsible for developing and maintaining the measurement, reward, and information systems so that they can be adapted to a TQ environment.
- get out on the shop floor, into the field, and in the offices to learn what people are thinking and feeling and to spread the word in person about TQ and about the leader's vision of the sort of place TQ can help create.

- schedule events that reinforce and spread the word about TQ and the sort of place it is meant to create.

Selection—Timing and Process

The right point at which to select a TQ driver varies by company and situation. Below are some general guidelines that can be used based on what has been witnessed over the past ten years from excellent, average, and not-so-successful TQ efforts.

Choosing Too Soon   There is a tendency on the part of many leaders to choose the TQ driver as soon as a decision is made to launch a TQ effort. This is something like throwing darts at the New York Stock Exchange listings to pick the common stocks for a personal portfolio. Until it is clear what one wants TQ to create and what the TQ implementation strategy is, there is simply not enough data to choose the right sort of person. Would you hire a new executive vice president of marketing and sales without thinking through carefully the nature of the job and the challenges the person who takes it will have to meet? This is why executive search firms begin a search with a complete list of specifications.

It is usually best before deciding on a TQ driver to decide on the strategy of the TQ effort as well as having taken steps to crystallize a vision of what the company will become as a result of TQ initiatives. In this way, the shape of the TQ effort will be clearer and the type of person who will be best at driving it will be clarified as well.

Different Phases   Different types of people are needed to fill the role of the TQ driver depending not only on the strategy and vision, but also on the phase of the TQ change effort itself. The type of person who will be best when the effort is accepted by employees and must be ingrained more deeply into the fabric of the company will not necessarily be the right person when a new TQ effort is about to be launched.

At Corning, the first head of Total Quality was someone who was well known and widely respected as a senior line manager throughout the corporation. He had enormous credibility. He had decided to retire and Jamie Houghton, Corning's chairman, convinced him to stay for 18 months to handle this new assignment. He could get access to anyone, and everyone knew that he had Jamie's trust and could get to him at any time. These attributes were vitally important at the start of the TQ effort at Corning; more important than what might have been used as criteria had the decision been made quickly or casually. Most top managers selecting a TQ driver will look first for someone with characteristics such as enthusiasm, polished presentation skills, good staff-work abilities, and, perhaps, some background in using the tools and techniques of Total Quality. Depending on the phase of the TQ effort, though, the more important need is for a mature, steady style, credibility, and knowledge of the company, its culture, and its people.

Competency Model The leader can draw a lesson from good management development strategy in selecting the right TQ driver by devising a competency model. Competencies are characteristics that separate excellent from average performance. The best management-training programs start with determining the competencies necessary to do a particular job and then design training that will specifically help people develop those competencies. The same can be done in choosing a TQ driver. Determine the most important things that must happen at the particular phase of the TQ effort. Then, decide what kind of person can best drive toward making those things happen. What must that person know, what skills must he or she have, what attitudes, and how should that person come across to other people?

At R. J. Reynolds, where the TQ effort started in 1984, examples of competencies for the TQ driver were to understand the production process as well as know the R&D process well; to have the skills to influence people at the lower ends of the organization chart (supervisors, in particular); to believe deeply that old habits acquired over years could be altered rather than resorting to bringing new supervisory and management people in from other companies; and to be equally credible at stand-up presentations in front of upper managers as with research chemists as with shop floor people.

Hiring from Outside Sometimes it may seem the right way to go is to hire a person who has made Total Quality a reality in another company, to short circuit the getting-up-to-speed process. It may be an appropriate strategy, but there is also a cost to doing so. The culture of every company is unique and because TQ is at its core an effort to alter behavior and attitudes and to cause work to be done differently, it may well be a handicap for someone to come on as TQ driver who does not know the company and how it works.

At Johnson and Johnson's McNeil Consumer Products unit, the person who became the TQ driver was the vice president of operations, who kept that line job in addition to taking on the TQ task. It was decided that doing so would better ensure that Total Quality would catch hold and work more quickly and effectively. Similarly, at Milliken, when a companywide initiative is decided on, a general manager of one of the businesses takes on the task of being the owner of that effort in addition to continuing current responsibilities. This ensures the appropriate clout and visibility. Another example is GCA, the manufacturer of wafer processing equipment for the integrated circuit industry, where the TQ driver is the vice president of manufacturing. Actions such as these at J&J, Milliken, and GCA have the added benefit of forcing line managers in key positions to understand completely Total Quality and what implementing it entails.

To summarize, there are some general attributes and tasks that are needed to implement Total Quality. The tasks involved alter the character of the company, how it behaves and responds, and the attributes are those of a person who must drive programs to achieve this new state by getting others to change their behavior. The TQ driver is often held responsible for the success of the TQ effort, but has little real power; he or she must be able to effectively influence those who do have legitimate power, however, and those who are successful at this job will thrive rather than be frustrated in such a position.

Comments from Three TQ Drivers

In the accounts that follow, the TQ drivers were asked to explain the basic components of their companies' TQ efforts; the role of leadership; the notion of the customer and the role the customer plays in driving the TQ process; the role they as TQ drivers play; how the effort has extended or changed basic company values;

the way TQ messages are conveyed, both inside and outside the company; what successes have been achieved and what the goals are for the next couple of years (the interviews were conducted in the fall of 1990).

David Luther—Corning

Dave Luther joined Corning in 1962 as an accountant. He's had a number of jobs in finance, was a production superintendent, was director of the company's information services, and has held several positions in Corning's human resources department, culminating as vice president of personnel. In 1983, at the beginning of Corning's quality effort, he was named head of quality for one of the company's major sectors, then in 1986 became vice president of quality for the corporation. He was a judge for the 1988 and 1989 Malcolm Baldrige National Quality Awards and continues to serve on the judges' panel. He is a widely recognized speaker on the topic of quality. Below he describes Corning's TQ effort.

> *There are six main pieces to our TQ effort. Start with leadership. The second piece is the focus on customer results. The third is training everyone in the organization. The fourth concerns employee involvement and recognition. The fifth is communications, both internally and externally. And the sixth talks about total quality processes, tools, and measures.*
>
> *If you put those six dimensions down the vertical axis of a matrix and on the horizontal axis create three phases, you can see how our emphasis has changed over time.*
>
> *In the first phase, introducing the whole TQ pie, the emphasis was on training and leadership; the leadership was making what I would call "opening statements." This phase started in 1983 and went until about 1985.*
>
> *During this first phase, the focus on the customer was zip. But we trained 30,000 people. There was minimal employee involvement, mostly a carryover from previous efforts. Communication was strictly internal. And in the final bucket, processes and tools, we introduced our basic 10-step quality methodology.*
>
> *The second phase went from 1986 through the end of 1988 or the beginning of 1989. A lot of things started happening.*

Leadership became more assertive in actually doing things, setting examples, reviewing results, and planning. We introduced the idea of customers, first focusing on internal customers and then moving that focus toward external customers. We had focus groups, did surveying, customer partnerships, etc.

In the third phase, we're getting back to training, and we're moving from awareness and basic knowledge to quality—skills training, communication, group dynamics, problem solving and statistical process control—the kinds of things that allow people to really do the job. The amount of training is going right off the charts. We have a 1991 goal of 5% of work time on training—that translates into about 70 hours—for everyone worldwide.

During the second phase we had maybe 40% of our people on teams, about 1500 teams. Today we have 3000 teams and participation is still picking up. The messages have shifted from internal to external.

The place we're at now is world-class quality. From the leadership standpoint, it can be characterized as achieving real integration of quality into the business processes and with the way the company does business. Quality is no longer a separate agenda item; it is the agenda. When you submit your business plan, the quality chunk is there, it's not a supplement. We set up our management goals for our bonus targets and our MBOs based on quality.

We now have high participation, new work forms, high-performance work systems, new organizational systems, spreading to virtually every North American unit. You are seeing fewer layers of management.

We are constantly coming up with new process tools and measures. We are currently moving toward a Six Sigma-like system to measure results.

---

*Six Sigma is a term made popular by Motorola. It is Motorola's quality/customer responsiveness target and means, generally, almost perfect quality—specifically, 3.4 defects per million opportunities. Sigma is a statistical term that refers to the number of standard deviations from the mean in any process. The mean is an arithmetic average and the standard deviation is the indication of how what is measured varies from that average.

If I were going to do it again and do it differently I would make customer satisfaction a more explicit part of the basic system from the start. When we designed this thing back in 1983, we said that one measures quality by the cost of quality. Now we know that's not a very good measure.

Cost of quality measures basically how effective and efficient you are at allocating resources to produce something for the customer. But that's not the issue at all. The issue is whether or not the customer likes it. If I were to do this over I would find some way to make happy customers the thing you're really after.

In education, when we went through it the first time we did it layer by layer through the entire worldwide organization. That's not really smart, because within a given unit by the time the last person has heard it, the first person has forgot what it's about. I would do it vertically rather than horizontally; I'd carve out a unit and say, "Let's storm this group and let's get ready to go within a month."

I would insist on specific problem-solving algorithms from the start. I would say, "Here's how we solve problems, guys," and lay out the steps. "So, when you come in and tell me you've got a problem, also tell me what step of the problem-solving process you're in now, data gathering, brainstorming, etc."

We spent about three years talking about internal customers before we focused on external customers. Now, the notion of internal customers is a necessary precondition to understanding external customers, especially in an organization like ours where 90% of our people never interact with an external customer. The whole quality process caves in on itself unless there's some sort of customer–supplier relationship, so we need people to think of internal customers.

But you need to be careful that the focus on internal customers doesn't occur at the expense of taking care of the external customers.

In terms of leadership, our chairman is identified as Mr. Quality. His position has been very explicit since about eight minutes into the process. The problem really is, how do you get leadership down through the organization? A big problem is getting leadership from that second layer beneath the chairman to be perceived as leaders and not followers. That took a while.

From the start, union leadership got out in front of this effort and demonstrated leadership. At every level of leadership, from the head of optical fibers, with a time horizon of 10 or 15 years, to a shift foreman, who may legitimately have a time horizon of Friday afternoon, people are expected to know where their unit is going, to have a vision of the future and how to make things better, and to be able to convey that.

The chairman did a superb job in describing his vision of the company as a whole. He did it in 1983, and again in 1986. We're now working on redoing that vision for 1991–1995. The chairman's vision was remarkably free of structure, remarkably free of barriers. We called the original statement his Martin Luther King speech. He said: "I see a Corning where we do not inspect incoming vendor supplies. I see a world where employees are free to stop the process if they see that it's not producing quality products, goods and services."

As part of the reworking process, I asked him to go through and comment on the five-year-old statement, to say, "This is okay, we're getting there, but that is a disappointment; this sounded good at the time but as it turns out it's not the right direction."

That vision has to be translated and communicated, to make it as applicable in Brazil as in the United States, as applicable in fiber optics as it is in laboratory glass. We elected to do it by having three goals for the company. They're generically stated, but they provide the umbrella for the organization.

The first is 5% of time worked devoted to training to improve the skills required to do a quality job. The second is to have 90% error reduction. The third one is first-day quality: on the first day a product is introduced it will be better or equal to the competition and better than the product it is replacing. No more shipping first attempts to customers, no more using customers for beta test sites. These goals say we're interested in all employees developing themselves; that we're going to have to find new ways to work to *create better product, to get 90% reduction in errors; and that we're going to take care of our customers first.*

In terms of values, what happened was that assumptions were made explicit. Total Quality allowed a lot of things to happen that may not have happened before, not because it was said that you couldn't do something, but because it was assumed that you couldn't. It made it acceptable for a subordinate to stand up and say, "Look, I can't do what you're asking me to do because I don't have the management, I don't have the time, or the money, or the expertise."

We have a number of locations where the number of players in the organization has been cut in half; where the employee teams are actually running the place; where people are paid based on their training and certification, and not on seniority or on what they are doing; where you can't wear a tie and you can't distinguish anybody's rank by the way they dress; where spouses and families of employees have to come to orientation so they understand what the family member who is working with us is doing.

Who should be in charge of this effort depends a lot on the company and on where in the process you are. I've seen a lot of these jobs before: I've been in manufacturing; I was assistant controller for the corporation; I created the information services in the divisions; I ran corporate planning; I was vice president of human resources.

I was not the first person at Corning to do this. The first guy was a former member of the board of directors; he was a well-known and well-respected guy. I think in the beginning you could argue that the person you need just has to be covered with respect throughout the organization.

Richard Bovender—R. J. Reynolds

In his discussion, Bovender focused on the packaging operations of RJR, formerly the Archer division, where a Total Quality effort has been underway since 1985. Like Dave Luther at Corning, Richard Bovender has had a varied career in management at RJR. He began his career at Archer in R&D, moved into sales, then customer service, where he spent four years as the department manager. He spent time as a manager in production planning, then went back into customer service for two consolidated divisions. He has also been a division systems manager and a production manager. When the company began its TQ effort, it was decided that the day-to-day driver should be someone from an operating division, but who had had broad experience in support staff functions as well.

Recently, Bovender has moved from the packaging operations into the company's tobacco operations, where he will try to replicate the Total Quality effort on a much larger scale over the next half decade.

As Bovender explains, within the packaging division the initial focus was on technical improvement. The vision was one of process enhancement, in fact, the effort was called "resource management" when it got underway. Issues of customer focus and internal organizational enhancement were secondary. But the division leaders realized quickly that the process is holistic, that while you might talk about quantitative goals, or even a vision of the company, in terms of technical improvement, people make the process happen and the customer is the reason it must happen.

In 1985 our vice president of technology and packaging became concerned because we were seeing products come in from Europe, South America, and Japan that were high-quality materials. We didn't want to be like the automotive or electronics industry, with competitors upon us before we know it, and with our sales quickly in trouble. Also we had learned to live with a lot of scrap; even though the customer eventually got what he wanted, there was a high cost for doing it.

At a conference some senior people heard about Just-In-Time and its impact on quality. But management was looking for a technical formula. They were committed, and willing to spend the time and money to have me do research and to do some training, but they were not considering the human resources part of it.

It was the consulting firm we selected to help us that made us understand that we couldn't make technical improvements last without working on the people side at the same time. That made us realize that getting a real quality process was going to be more complicated than just going through steps 1 through 10.

Going to conferences and talking to people in electronics and automotive industries, we were only able to get bits and pieces. I ended up with a group of about eight people (not from my company) in Japan for a two-week trip, where we visited 12 or 13 companies. Then when we got home, I probably visited another 25 or 30 companies in this country.

As with anything, there were some that were very successful, and some that were struggling. I noticed that the ones that were struggling were basically missing two components. They didn't have that strong support from top management. And they hadn't understood the need for the people side and so hadn't made a big investment in training.

We built a four-day training program, and eventually trained the entire packaging division, from the top person down to the entry-level person on the shop floor.

Because of the kind of operation we are—basically a job shop with large equipment—it was nearly impossible to move equipment around to form centers, so we had to make our changes in the way we managed our operations. We assigned a manufacturing manager to each product line and gave him complete responsibility from the time it started to the time it finished the process.

We realized we needed to do a lot more than training. You can say to people that after this four days of training you will have the ability to do things, and the accountability and responsibility. Then they will go off and still wait for someone to tell them what to do. Changing mindsets is really a lot harder than just training for four days. We got people involved early in projects like setup reduction and quality problem solving and we did a lot of team building as part of each of the projects.

As I've said, we had top management commitment from the beginning, and the leader didn't drop the ball even when our sales dropped.

The leader worked at crystallizing a vision, then handed it off to senior managers and let them do the implementation. Even after he handed off the implementation process, he remained very much aware of what was going on and let people know he was aware so they knew this was not a program with a beginning, a middle, and an end, but a continual improvement process.

With regard to customers, we had a real change in our attitude toward customers. As I said, we lived with a lot of scrap so that our customers would not be hurt by our internal changes in processes and in the way we managed. But as a result of Total Quality we also developed a new relationship with customers.

We used to have a philosophy of not letting the external customer become involved with the operations, because they may find out things we didn't want them to know. What we came to realize was that by working with our customers to find out what their needs were, and even designing things with them we could streamline our internal processes and get less run on our equipment. And we could take successes with some of our bigger customers and share those successes with all of our customers. Many times we got customers to change their specifications after they saw what our process was, what our controls were, and that we could produce what they needed.

This kind of more honest relationship also happened inside. We never had a concept of an internal customer and internal vendor. The feeling was, "If I'm running something and it's not bad, let the next guy worry about catching something that isn't in spec." But some out-of-spec product was getting through everybody to the paying customer because people along the way decided it wasn't their job.

If you talk to many of our folks now, they not only recommend changes directly to outside customers as a way of helping our process while still giving the customer what is needed, but they also have an understanding of their internal customer and his problems. That's a real change in mindset.

We've been at this for five or six years and we're still making progress each day. Looking back, there are a lot of things I would like to change if I were starting the process today, but I think a lot of this just takes time. You're asking people to change their attitudes and behaviors, and that takes time. If you try to force it, it won't work, because people have to learn at their own pace.

You can't make a tree grow any faster than it's going to grow. You can cultivate around it, and fertilize it. That's basically what I try to do. But it's still going to take time. You need goals to shoot for, but if you say, "Alright, in one year there will be a process," you can end up doing more harm than good. You have to find ways to allow people to buy into it, to take ownership. If they don't have ownership, you've got a problem.

Jim Litts—Johnson and Johnson

Beginning in 1988, Jim Litts led a TQ effort at McNeil Consumer Products, the J&J company best known as the maker of Tylenol. He has been at J&J for 21 years in manufacturing, distribution, planning, transportation, and purchasing. Beginning in the summer of 1990, he was given the task of replicating his success at McNeil in a new, larger J&J company, Johnson and Johnson Consumer Products, a merging of three divisions. In this conversation, Litts discussed his work at McNeil and how he is approaching his new task. He did this as vice president of operations at McNeil, which is the same title he holds at Johnson and Johnson Consumer Products. In both situations Jim has been the TQ driver. You'll notice throughout his description that an objective of his was to make TQ work in the operations areas, and in so doing to increase the strategic value of operations.

In moving to another company, Litts will try to shorten the TQ process, by trying to implement successes from the first effort more quickly in the second company and to avoid mistakes made the first time around. He has created a future vision for his responsibilities at Johnson and Johnson Consumer Products to help the company gain advantage in the competitive health and beauty aids marketplace. The vision includes converting raw materials to finished goods in 24 hours, eliminating all non-value-added costs, having total conformance to requirements and developing the best operations people in the industry. The cornerstone of this vision is a quality process that mandates job, project, or process requirements between people, departments, or organizations before business commences and problem resolution predicated on analyzing facts not assessing opinions.

I believe there is a philosophy on how to do work that forms the basis for TQ. It's a four-part philosophy.

At the top is something I call business enhancement; it is every employee's job every day to try to enhance the business. This philosophy is predicated on a certain way of working. Managers should spend time thinking of new approaches to business problems, encouraging people to think about providing services, and then introducing some kind of idea that will increase the strategic value of each part of the operation, which is unique in a marketing-driven company.

The second part is good business plans. Enhancement is a great idea, but you have to have a plan on how you're going to do that.

The third part is priority-setting mechanisms and measurements.

Finally, you have got to have communication and management development.

In order to make all this fit together, you need a vision, an idea of where you need to go. We tried to hammer out where we wanted to go in some short, succinct phrases and then worked on imagining how the company would look and how it would operate if it were doing those things.

One was 24-hour conversion; that meant we would convert raw materials into finished goods in one day from the time they hit our dock. The second piece was to become the low-cost producer in the over-the-counter pharmaceutical business. The third was to have zero nonconformance. The fourth was to attract, hire, and develop the best operations talent we could find in North America.

We set these goals at McNeil in the fall of 1988. Here at J&J Consumer we began working just a few weeks ago [in September 1990]. I've taken the top people here through this model in a two-day session. Over the next couple of months we need to formulate our vision of what this company wants to be like in five years.

Here at J&J Consumer I hope not to get caught in some of the problems we had at McNeil. I'll have some special problems here, like the turf problems that naturally come after a restructuring of three companies into one, and the fact that the management team has not worked together before.

One thing I'll do here is get R&D and Marketing involved earlier than I did at McNeil. At McNeil, about a year and a half into the process, R&D came to the manufacturing floor with one of those "throw it over the wall" new products that didn't meet the basic tenet of 24-hour conversion and low cost. The operations guys threw them off the floor. They said, "I'm not working on this because it doesn't meet these very basic criteria." R&D was still working under the old philosophy, get it out to the market quickly—even if it's the wrong formulation, has high reject rates, or whatever—and we'll fix it later on. But the operations guys literally would not do it.

That started a big philosophical debate at the senior management level about whether new product ideas were needed to meet the 24-hour conversion low-cost zero nonconformance guidelines. The answer was "yes!" because that was strategically important to the company. That took a lot of time to battle out, and I could have saved time and grief had I involved R&D and Marketing earlier, not just concentrated on Operations.

But the first year and a half, no one cared, because the TQ effort literally improved gross profit by 2.5%. We measurably reduced cycle times, about 80%. We got nothing but accolades.

We did better with Marketing. A couple of months into the process I put together a presentation called "the Cost of Complexity." The cost of complexity is not just "Here's what it costs, and here's what you sell it for." There are tremendous hidden costs—design changes, rejections and waste, slow moving and obsolete products. I argued for as much standardization of certain product designs as possible. The marketing guys were convinced. They would not think of violating standardized parts unless there was an incredible amount of research to prove that a different package would greatly improve sales and profit.

You've got to remember, McNeil Consumer Products is an immensely successful company, by any index you want to use as a measure. But my philosophy is that unless you attend to the "platforms of business" someone, in time, will eat your lunch. That's what happened to the three companies that were merged into J&J Consumer Products. They let the basics get away from them, paid no attention to cost or conforming to some set of formal requirements, and the next thing they knew they had problems.

Someone has got to carry the banner for maintaining diligence around the construction of products, the way they're costed, the way business is conducted, and the contribution at all levels of management. In my experience so far, the operations guy should be that person.

So, to get back to the process of TQ, you translate this vision into day-to-day action through your own actions. At McNeil I made two or three speeches every week. The person driving the process needs to have the energy and tenacity to continue to move the process—to preach, motivate, reward, applaud, cheerlead, supply resources where they're needed, and constantly ask how he or she can help. If you don't maintain that focus, people will gravitate toward their own area of interest.

People have told me, "I believe I'm working harder than I ever worked before. But I feel better because I know why I'm doing it, I know what we're trying to accomplish." When people come to work they need to understand why they're doing what they're doing. It's management's role to define that direction. Then you have to convince people that they are valuable and their ideas are valuable. You have to provide them ammunition to get their ideas going. You need to provide them an atmosphere in which they can be supported, provide them with actual support when they want it, and then recognize them when they accomplish something.

You don't have to do much. You do need to be consistent, because people pick up on inconsistency real quickly.

You need to continuously run through the loop, go back again and reenergize the process. I used to tell my staff people, "You need to carry three things around with you, a bag of fertilizer, a jug of water, and a nice warm environment to help your people grow. That's your job as a boss."

When we started this only one plant had a formal employee involvement program. The program was floundering, because it was not really tied to anything. I sat down with the plant manager and said, "You've got to tie these efforts to outcomes. The outcomes we get have to sup-

port the four parts of the vision we have." When we got all these things aligned it went very well.

Another thing, everybody in Operations was successful or failed because of the totality of Operations. If one plant did well on one index, and another plant not well, Operations did poorly. Same for individuals and groups within plants. The notion soon got around that if you were doing well and the guy next door was doing poorly, you better get over and help that guy out.

Summary

The TQ drivers, and others like them, share some common elements of their job descriptions.

- They keep the TQ effort alive through constantly establishing forums for people to learn, to discuss, and to share with others what they have done.
- They spend time with the leader discussing the TQ effort, the programs that make it up, their results, and, in particular, "staffing" the leader and ensuring he or she is prepared to continue to spread the TQ message.
- They report directly to the top leader, are members of the top management group, and on the leader's staff.
- Each is in constant contact with programs and ongoing efforts to alter their organization's character. They visit them (each spends a lot of time on airplanes), offer encouragement, share information about what is going on in other parts of the company, and often work to secure money or other resources needed to complete tasks.
- Each is constantly thinking about TQ, is single-minded about this way of doing business.
- Each has established some sort of mechanism to communicate what is happening throughout the organization. It could be a newsletter devoted just to TQ or segments on TQ in existing house organs, or round-table discussion sessions.

- Most important, they do not try to be a substitute for the leader, but rather, they supplement what the leader must do. They understand the leader has a unique, critically important role in TQ and see their job as helping in a way that is significant and of great consequence.

8

Total Quality and Employee Involvement

There is certainly nothing new about programs to help get employees more involved with their jobs and to take on more responsibility for problem solving. The rationale and benefits have been well documented.[1] What is new is the degree of acceptance enjoyed today for the concept of employee involvement (EI) and the willingness of managers to support EI efforts. It is greater than at any other time. There seem to be at least three reasons for this increased acceptance.

First, workers are more willing to accept and to push for increased responsibility than has been the case with past generations. Second, compared to just 10 or 15 years ago, leaders and leadership expectations have changed. For one thing, a baton has been passed to a generation of leaders for whom participation and getting things done through people is a more natural style than it was for many in the generation that preceded it. Third, in Japanese manufacturing methods, American businessmen saw the widespread use of EI methods that in the United States had been largely experiments rather than accepted ways of operating.

The Total Quality movement has provided a larger and more substantial playing field than ever before for EI efforts. It has put employee involvement up front as a vitally important ingredient for TQ success. The message has been clear from a number of people who have spoken and written about TQ—the potential benefits in profit and market-share improvement are enormous, but only if employees throughout the company are committed to improvement and are involved in the TQ process.

Total Quality offers employee involvement the ingredient for wider acceptance that has heretofore been missing: an intimate connection with business results. A major reason that methods to involve employees did not take hold in the past is that most people saw them as extracurricular and unconnected to business results. A nice-to-have for stable and profitable times but usually one of the first things to be cut when times were tough. Total Quality has changed that. As more companies launch EI efforts under the Total Quality banner, those efforts must be geared to mesh smoothly with other facets of TQ.

This chapter offers a view of employee involvement from the TQ perspective. Lessons learned are offered and thoughts are posed on the ingredients for success of EI as a driving force for Total Quality.[2]

Why EI Efforts Often Fail

Not long ago we heard a worker complain, "When I punch in my time card at this place, I also check in my brain." This worker felt she had little control over her environment. She knew the solutions to many of the problems around her, but nobody asked her opinion.

While some companies have reported good results with their employee involvement efforts, many have had unsatisfactory experiences. Many people in those companies with less than positive experiences doubt that it is actually possible to change work-force behavior patterns that go back many years. When we examine the failures, we find a common thread. The managers from these companies start EI programs with no clear objectives in mind. The general attitude is "EI will make things better around here."

Successful organizations, on the other hand, have very clear expectations and goals, and they use EI as a process to realize them. Before beginning, they ask themselves, "Why do we want to have employee involvement?" Where there have been EI successes, the management team has usually planned the process and become clear about the outcomes it wants.

Most companies that fail with EI use some kind of approach that tries to get employees to participate, but they simply do not go far enough. Typically, groups are formed from a few to as many as a dozen employees. They are trained in some basic problem-solving techniques and then told to "look for a project." Membership is usually voluntary. The group often needs to obtain permission from a steering committee or other management group before implementing any solutions, and they generally do not have a budget or any spending authority. The groups stay together following a project and seek another problem to solve. There is no clear point in time when the group is to disband.

Interviews of people from various organizational levels of companies whose EI efforts failed reveal some interesting conclusions.

1. Top managers expect miracles in cost reduction and quality improvement from these groups. They are frustrated when the groups choose trivial projects, such as moving drinking fountains or repainting parking lot spots.

2. Middle managers are angry and confused. They are not actively involved in the process and they believe many projects infringe on their job responsibilities. They have to spend precious time trying to implement someone else's (the group's) ideas.

3. Members of the teams are unhappy. They have no real power or authority. Many feel that the time spent is wasted because conditions are unchanged when they return to their regular jobs.

4. Employees who are not on a team do not understand the process that the teams have gone through and, as a result, do not value it. They believe team members are receiving preferential treatment and they resent it. This sometimes causes hard feelings when members of the task forces return to their regular jobs.

The general manager of one of these companies describes his company's EI program as "a solution in search of a problem." He is particularly unhappy with the self-directed nature of the teams. He wants these groups to work on problems he believes are most important, but has been told that such a process would destroy the organization's morale. The general manager wonders how it could get any worse.

When we examine the lessons learned from successful and not so successful EI efforts, we discover some common denominators for success. The main lesson comes through loud and clear: Unless EI focuses directly on making the organization more competitive in the marketplace, it will wither and not reach its potential. Employees must understand how increasing their involvement and the hard work this entails will make a difference to their company and how it will improve the conditions immediately around them. If EI does not pass this test—being an important and meaningful activity—employees will not buy in. It cannot be thought of as a separate activity from regular daily work or from the competitiveness of the company.

Beyond Simple Participation

Beginning after the Second World War, the management literature focused on the role of the manager in making business organizations responsive to changing markets and more satisfying places to work. The emphasis was on being systematic, on controlling the variables of one's unit or department, on analyzing and planning. The message was clear: control the physical, technical, and financial facets of your unit if you want to be seen as a success and get ahead.

Simultaneously, another branch of the literature advocated democratic values in the workplace and greater involvement of employees. The problem was that they weren't connected. Involvement wasn't usually connected with financial results, and for this reason participation perennially received second billing. As a result, while pushing responsibility for decision making down to lower organizational levels was advocated by some visionaries and experiments did take place, they were the exception to the rule and generally were not accepted.

Today, on the other hand, not only is acceptance growing for the idea of employee participation in making decisions, but companies are rapidly moving to the next step of truly involving employees. The question for many leaders is not whether it makes sense to push responsibility down the hierarchy. The question today is how to do it fast so that employees who face problems day in and day out can solve them when they occur or, better, can anticipate and prevent them.

One primary rationale for employee involvement is to speed up decision making so that problems can be solved faster. To do so, the responsibility for taking action must be placed at the source, not dependent on relayed directions from someone more remote. This means employees must assume more authority and exert a degree of influence over their surroundings. It means they must exercise the power of decision making. In effect, they must become their own managers.

The challenge for those who are in positions of management is how to best ensure that this sense of power pervades those in his or her charge. This is important to do because it makes good business sense. Doing the right things in the right way the first time leads to problems being anticipated and avoided or, at least, solved quickly. The result is less interruption in the flow of steps that provide the customer with something of value. The key success factor for making such action a reality is that the person on the job assumes responsibility and takes the initiative to do the right things in the right way the first time.

This cannot be forced on workers. They must want to do it. EI efforts, done in the right way, will lead to such a sense of ownership of results.

There is another equally important reason, one that is more altruistic and gets to the role played by the individual in places of work. As we go through the last decade of the twentieth century, it is more important than ever that man's timeless quest to express himself and establish his individuality be furthered in the face of a world that is becoming both more complex and more dependent on technology.

While banding together into mega-trading blocks as the European Economic Community will do in 1993 can obviously benefit the producer and the consumer through easier trade, the homogeneity that can result carries the risk that the essence and culture of individual countries will be lost. Individuals are facing a similar risk. As electronics enables us to communicate and analyze much faster and easier, we must take advantage of these benefits without diminishing the individual. The individual must be able to use technology as his servant to express creativity and a unique perspective; never must the roles be reversed and technology become the master of the individual. Never must the microchip take the place of thinking and never must we rely on a voice message system when we can communicate directly.

Neither can the organization take the place of the individual. Policies and procedures must only be stepping stones toward greater individual expressions. The employee-involvement part of a Total Quality effort can provide the balance needed. EI efforts that hold the greatest promise are those that are aimed at supporting and furthering the sense of self-worth and the personal expression of each employee, not promoting the power of the group at the expense of individual expression.

In one sense, increased involvement of employees will help the organizations to which they belong to succeed. This is one of the compelling reasons for EI. The other compelling reason for EI is that it provides the platform for greater self-expression and individual meaning for the employee.

The New Business Environment

While our grandchildren will probably see our rate of change as slow compared to the rate they experience, we certainly face major changes in today's business climate. The most substantial ones have been brought about by the internationalization of the market and, in particular, of competition. The emphasis on quality and the emphasis on gaining market share through customer satisfaction have resulted from these changes and have ushered in a new way of thinking about producing and delivering goods and services. The extent of these changes is even more significant than their rapidity.

In implementing Total Quality, we are doing more than just developing faster or less expensive ways to do the same things. We are beginning to change the way we do the technical elements of work and, at the same time, we are seeking to change the work climate in companies so that people relate to each other differently: more collaboration, more communication, and more commitment to carry through what is decided upon. The most significant factor in the kind of change we face today is that it is multidisciplinary, crossing from the quantitative, technical, and physical to the qualitative and behavioral, and back again.

In today's complex marketplace, competitive cost and quality acceptable to the customer are givens. Without these two, a company cannot even get on the playing field. The way to be a viable player is to add delivery and service to the competitive puzzle. The way to win the game is to excel on all fronts, to be demonstrably better than the other players in a way that truly thrills customers.

There are available today technical and physical elements that go into achieving such a state, that change the nature of the work itself and offer more complete ways to view the work. These innovations come from the disciplines of Just-In-Time and quality/reliability engineering and are outlined in other sections of this book. Benefits can be achieved from them without employee involvement, but those benefits will not be as great as when EI is included, and they certainly will not be as long lasting. Just adopting these modern practices is not enough. What must be added is for all employees to operate in a single-minded way, focused on improving the ability of their company to meet the customers' needs and to exceed their expectations. To do this requires behavior not normally found in many businesses today:

- A high degree of teamwork
- A penchant for people going out of their way to solve problems
- An acceptance of new ideas, new ways of operating, and a willingness to experiment
- A commitment to do the best possible job

If people are given freedom to make decisions on issues affecting them and feel as though they are involved in the business in general so that there is a sense of ownership for results, there is a much greater likelihood that these needed changes will come about.

All this says that because of the new business environment and the realities it brings, employee involvement can be of significant benefit when used in conjunction with other sorts of improvement approaches. It also says a lot about the role of the manager in making EI a reality.

The "Administrator" and "Strong Man" Are Managers of the Past

Until fairly recently, many people believed managers had the sole responsibility to change how work was accomplished in a department or company. Employees looked to the boss for answers. The job of a manager was to manage. That meant to take the lead and tell people what to do. One tongue-in-cheek description of bosses put it this way:

> For one thing, to be a real boss there were few restrictions to contend with: you hired whomever you chose, you told these people what they were to do, you paid them a nominal wage to do it, and you fired them if they didn't do it correctly.[3]

Michael Maccoby described managers as strong men or administrators:

> The administrator is the traditional expert engineer, accountant, or lawyer . . . he expects organizations to run by the book . . . construct the right structure, provide proper incentive and the industrial machine will run efficiently. . . . the strong man (. . . like a jungle fighter) . . . believes he can overpower distrust and gain accord by bearing down on subordinates.[4]

What is coming to be realized is that both the administrator model and the strong man model are not good enough to take control of change in today's environment.

Economic incentives, structure, or the comfort of a strict order of things—the main tools of the administrator—are not the powerful motivational tools they once were. The achievement-oriented worker today wants the freedom to establish goals and a sense of personal influence to attain them. He or she wants to have input and involvement.

Similarly, the strong man misses the mark by sacrificing a sense of teamwork for his own dominance. Today's worker sees two satisfiers equally important to personal influence and input: 1) relationships of trust with co-workers and 2) a sense of a team composed of different but interdependent parts, all moving in the same direction to achieve common goals. These satisfiers are often missing under the strong-man manager.

Influence as the Motivator

We are seeing the emergence of a new set of assumptions about managing today in which those in charge must care about developing the people under them by inviting input and sharing power. Management presents as an incentive the chance to influence operations rather than using the old piecework-oriented incentive that said to workers, "Do what I want you to do, and I will give you more money."

It is not that people today believe money is not important; but they are less likely to be motivated by money at the expense of influence over the things around them and over input into the issues that concern them.

All this means that the boss must act differently. He or she must allow subordinates to be influential and find a way to ensure they take responsibility for solving problems. The boss must see that positive relationships are built, relationships created on the basis of trust and common belief in a vision of the future. The boss must be persuasive in a way that does not diminish trust. The result should be a work environment or climate where there is continuous improvement and sharpening of the skills necessary to compete against ever-better opponents.

Not only managers must act differently. Employees, too, must become agents of change. They must welcome a new level of responsibility and fulfill its mandate. The simple fact is that people in the middle and lower strata of the organizational chart are being called on to solve problems and make decisions. In some organizations today, it is less an issue of top managers not wanting to share power than of creating the sort of climate where people can exercise the decision-making power available.

A vehicle by which decisions are being pushed to lower levels is the task team or pilot team. (See Chapter 5 for more on successful pilot teams and projects.) A common building block of a Total Quality effort is project-by-project improvement.[5] For each project, a team of workers is formed to discover the root cause of a problem affecting them, and it is asked to find and implement a solution. Detailed analysis to pinpoint root causes and determine quantitative opportunities is always a part of the task. Responsibility for making decisions is passed from managers through such teams at the appropriate juncture in the implementation of the TQ process. For several years, large companies such as Hewlett-Packard, Apple Computer, Xerox, Ford, and IBM have adopted this style. Some medium-sized companies have also moved in this direction because their leaders have found this operating style attractive.

This team-oriented, push-the-responsibility-down style has picked up more steam as large corporations have demanded that their suppliers adopt methods requiring it. Zero defects and just-in-time delivery are becoming the norm as large companies work to build more collaborative relationships with their suppliers. Along the way, those companies are training suppliers to operate in the way they themselves have learned to operate.

Operating in this fashion has impact on employees other than the hourly employee, clerk, secretary, or technician. The midlevel manager is often caught in the middle.

Caught in the Middle

Along with the delegation of more decision-making power to employees at the lower end of the organization chart, an unfreezing of the power structure inevitably takes place. In this sense, decision-making authority and latitude is of a zero-sum nature. The power offered to an hourly employee or clerk or technician is not added to that in the rest of the organization. Rather, the expectation is that the hourly employee, clerk, or technician will make decisions heretofore made by someone else. That someone else is typically the midlevel manager, that is, the first-line supervisor, the department head, and the staff person from quality assurance, production control, or other support functions. The middle manager is in the middle figuratively as well as literally. Often this means that while the top managers and lower-level workers are excited about employee involvement (after all, it doesn't affect people at the top that much in terms of power and benefits people at lower levels), the middle manager is the person with the most to lose.

This plight of the middle manager does not necessarily need to hinder employee involvement efforts from marching forward. What must happen is that the role of the middle manager in a new work environment must be defined, and as much care must be placed on this topic as on any other as the character of the business changes. When this is not done, this issue will certainly become a problem and will cast a pall over the entire change effort and may well block it in substantial ways. There should be opportunities for more involvement of middle managers as for any other employee—that is why it's called employee involvement and not hourly employee involvement. But, doing so requires changes that are perhaps more substantial for the middle manager than for others.

The new role of the middle manager in a TQ environment must be one of a facilitator and team leader rather than of a boss who directs. Rather than telling people who report to him or her what to do and controlling their actions, the new middle manager must lead problem-solving teams, must develop the problem-solving skills of workers, and must, in general, ensure that decision-making authority is pushed down effectively and that that authority is accepted by those to whom it is offered. These are new competencies for many and, too often, the middle manager has had no preparation (or, often, no warning) to play this role. It is common for someone to be promoted to a supervisor position because he or she was the best drill press operator or the best secretary or the best service technician or the best cost accountant, not because of their managerial skills. Often, through the years, less money has been devoted to training and education of midlevel people than to other employees.

In order for EI to succeed, and it must succeed for TQ to take hold, this middle manager issue must be resolved. Often this means something as relatively simple as involving the middle managers early in the process, establishing competency models for new behaviors, building those new competencies into the performance appraisal system and offering training to help people move in those new directions. Sometimes, it becomes apparent that the shift is too great for some to make. In these cases, companies have used early retirement programs and attrition programs to reduce the middle management work force. One large, well-known company simply eliminated the first-line supervisor position when its leaders decided that the resistance to change and to give up some power at that level was too great to alter in any other way.

Whatever solution is best for each company, the fact is that a TQ effort will alter the traditional balance of power and paying particular attention to the middle manager early in the process will make implementation much smoother.

What all this means is that as much of a change of style, perhaps more, is being asked of the employees in the lower and middle levels of the organization chart as of the leaders. Such new ways of operating require commitment. That sort of commitment is affected greatly by the environment within which one works.

Organization Climate and Commitment

But how can that new level of commitment come about? Telling people to act differently will not make it happen and last. Simply offering to pay people more money will not work, either. There is no one leverage point, no one answer. A number of things must be done simultaneously. Depending on the situation, what is called for might include training of managers and of supervisors, altering the measurement system and/or the reward system, changing people or the organization structure, offering special coaching to supervisors, or promoting people who contribute the most to creating a TQ environment. The key to the success of any of these sorts of initiatives is the organization climate. A certain climate or environment to provide the foundation for those simultaneous activities must be created in the company in order for a new level of commitment to take hold.

There are seven key factors in the climate of an organization that foster employee commitment to new ways of operating and to accepting new levels of responsibility. These characteristics are essential for organizations to succeed at implementing TQ. They are listed in Table 8.1 and explained in more detail in Chapter 4.

Something necessary to bring about such a state is the knowledge and belief of employees that by taking on responsibility and exerting influence they will be rewarded. One type of reward is personal and takes the form of something tangible (a bonus, a raise, or some other benefit). Another type is less tangible but can be as or more powerful: it is recognition for their efforts and positive feedback. A third type of reward is the realization from their effort of a better, more satisfying place to work.

Another ingredient that will help bring about an environment where participation can thrive is that mistakes made while trying to improve should not cause someone to be punished. This doesn't mean that failure should be rewarded; rather, when a new way of operating is being learned, there must be experimentation and with experimenting comes mistakes. Encouragement must take the place of ridicule and helpful feedback must take the place of harsh actions.

Table 8.1
Climate Factors to Support New Ways of Operating

Influence
People believe they have influence over changing what is around them.

Responsibility
People assume ownership for improvement and regularly and naturally go out of their way to make something better.

Innovativeness
New ideas are encouraged, listened to, and helped along to become reality and people are allowed to be different and encouraged to change the status quo.

Desire to change
A healthy level of dissatisfaction with the status quo leads to the willingness to do what must be done to change.

Satisfaction
Employees are pleased with the way their basic physical, emotional, motivational, and financial needs are met. If such factors are not taken care of there will not be the foundation for improvements that are interpersonal or that involve whole departments or entire work processes.

Teamwork
People are operating in harmony sufficiently to achieve the goals that require that each person play a part and require that those individual efforts be combined and made interdependent.

Common vision
A clear picture has been created of the sort of company that Total Quality will enable and, this picture of how things could be is commonly shared throughout the organization.

A third ingredient is consistent action. Once the tone is set by the TQ effort and the employee involvement ball begins to roll, the day-to-day decisions and actions of managers must be consistent and nonsupervisory employees must continue to be patient with the pace of change and continue to move the process forward in their own areas.

Lessons from Successful EI Efforts

From investigating EI efforts that were by all accounts successful and contrasting them with those that had mediocre results, at least five lessons become clear; think of them as common denominators for effective employee involvement. The lessons are

1. Create a common understanding.
2. Make the involvement genuine.
3. Provide the right conditions for people to become empowered.
4. Reward success.
5. Implement EI in a truly involving way.

Each one carries some important messages. Organizations that are implementing Total Quality can use these lessons to ensure the EI component goes smoothly. Companies that are having problems with their current EI process can use them as a repair manual.

Lesson 1. Create a Common Understanding

There must be a common understanding of the business imperatives and how EI can help realize them. Total Quality demands that everyone in the company know not only the strategic direction of the business but also the current imperatives and current performance, and that everyone understand where they fit in working toward those imperatives and achieving that performance. They should understand that the overall task of the entire company is to supply the customer with the correct product or service, excellent quality, and fast delivery in a way that is truly satisfying to the customer. This overall objective must then be reduced to specific imperatives that are realistic, time-phased, and measurable, such as:

- We must respond to what our marketplace wants and develop a new product with these characteristics within two years to gain a 25% increase in our market share.

- We must introduce new products in half the time of our best efforts in the past.

- Our customers cannot tolerate more than one defect per million going out the door, and we have to get to that point within two years.

- Over the next year, we must drop our manufacturing cost by 25% and reinvest those savings to chop our prices in order to gain market share and maintain or create more jobs.

- We must be able to fill every order within eight days.

In particular, it must be made clear how involving employees and pushing down decision making fits in with such market and customer-oriented imperatives. If the imperative implies faster product introduction, the link to EI might be that through greater involvement employees will identify the blocks to product introduction and if they believe they can influence those blocks and have the power to take action, problems can be solved much faster. If the issue is cost reduction, the link to EI might be that employees grouped in analysis-and-problem-solving teams are given the charge of finding non-value-added tasks and recommending ways to minimize or eliminate them, then implementing those recommendations.

The point of this first lesson is to make the link clear between employee involvement and the sorts of business opportunities that TQ seeks to create in any particular case.

Lesson 2. Make Involvement Genuine

The involvement must aim at improving what is close at hand and meaningful. Simply bringing employees together once a month and exhorting them to work harder to achieve the business's objectives is not enough. A process is needed that enables them to make significant improvements in their own work area that help meet the business imperatives in a way that will satisfy the needs of the individual employee. If employees do not sense that their efforts are going to improve their own job as well as meet the competitive needs of the business, two important ingredients may be missing. First, by applying improvements to their own work area successfully, important feedback and close-at-hand rewards are offered; the employee can see and benefit from the improvement. Second, by employees making improvements that positively affect how they carry out their jobs, they can feel pride in what they have achieved and increase self-confidence.

The key issue in Lesson 2 is the willingness of top or middle management to encourage workers to make their own decisions about changing what is around them. If there is such freedom, there will be more emotional ownership of results and that sense of ownership will in turn lead to commitment.

Does this mean that management abdicates responsibility for strategic decisions? Of course not; nor does it mean that midlevel mangers will become redundant because decision making is being pushed down. It does mean that the role of supervisors and middle managers will change. They will need to facilitate decision-making processes and manage a climate where their subordinates can make more decisions.

It is not uncommon for midlevel managers to be accused of being a prime block to change, in general, and implementing Total Quality, in particular. Sometimes it is true. Usually, when it is true, the middle managers have been left out of the TQ process in significant ways and the EI effort was aimed at hourly and nonexempt employees rather than including the managers and supervisors to whom those employees report. Compounding this, the job of the middle manager and supervisor was not redefined to reflect new tasks such as facilitating decision making and managing the climate. The point here is that improving what is close at hand and meaningful to employees must also involve the supervisor or middle manager, making them important parts of the TQ effort.

Lesson 3   Provide the Right Conditions for People to Become Empowered

The dictionary defines "empower" as "to enable or give authority." Unfortunately, it has become a buzzword today, and what gets lost in its overusage are the practical steps to bring about empowerment. There are at least three: skill building, changing the organization, and providing a no-strings budget.

Skill Building   Because different behavior is called for in an environment where people feel empowered, employees need the correct skills to succeed. There are two kinds of skills: analytical/technical and behavioral/organizational.

Analytical/technical skills come from quality and reliability engineering and from the Just-In-Time philosophy of manufacturing. They are physical, statistical, and/or mechanical in nature. They enable employees to know more about why problems occur. They result in large-scale reconfigurations of the workplace or dramatically different ways to distribute a product. These skills should reduce significant amounts of time, thereby setting the stage for reducing costs and improving customer service. They require an analytical mindset and a certain degree of organized thought in the way data are collected and approached.

Behavioral/organizational skills are those having to do with working more effectively in a team; with building lasting relationships with other people (customers, vendors, or co-workers); with decision making, especially under stress; with planning complex change efforts; and with motivating people. They also have to do with how to best thrive in and get satisfaction from being part of an organization, especially the influence and negotiation skills needed. If one did not have to work with other people to accomplish something, there would be little need for these behavioral/organizational abilities. The fact is, however, that nothing can change and nothing can be accomplished without people interacting, and EI demands more, and more complex, skills to do so than a more authoritarian system.

Unfortunately, many EI efforts do not include analytical/technical skills and assume that getting people together or training them to work as a team is enough. But enabling people to make decisions without both sets of skills is at least naive and at worst damaging.

While each can be powerful in its own right, these two sets of skills work together in an important way. Analytical/technical skills can achieve gains in the short term on their own. They will improve the processes that produce goods and services and reduce costs. But whether those tangible gains will last over time is a function of the second set of skills. It is this second set that builds teamwork and contributes to a climate where continuous improvement can thrive.

Changing the Organization Structure Offering new concepts and the training to make them work is one way of empowering people. Another may be changing the structure. Often, EI is best supported through a flat organization structure. If the goal of the process is to push decision making down to the people doing the work, the ideal organization is one that is not bureaucratic and encumbered by many requirements for decision-making approval. The rationale for this is provided by one of the true pioneers of employee involvement, Jim Richard, who in the mid 1950s was president of the Red Jacket Manufacturing Company in Davenport, Iowa. He wrote:

> The more centralized and dominant the leadership pattern of an organization, the more rigid the organization structure. The more rigid the . . . structure, the more imposing must be the control. When dominance and rigidity are enforced, acquiescence is required. Acquiescence spawns dependence. To the degree that people are required to be dependent, their freedom to apply ingenuity and creativity to their work is reduced. Therefore, a centralized, dominant, controlling leadership and organizational pattern tends to reduce the usefulness of employees as living, thinking, creative people.[6]

A No-Strings Budget   Another way to support empowering people is to have a no-strings budget. It allows a task team or department to make its own decisions rapidly without going through bureaucratic channels about low-cost improvements. One company's EI team recently worked hard to redesign its entire department. After implementing the new layout, the team discovered that a simple assembly hook was needed to eliminate three non-value-added tasks. When the team requested the hook, it was told by purchasing that it would take two and one-half months. A budget for such items and the freedom to buy them would have allowed the team to buy the hook from an industrial supply house across the street.

Lesson 4: Reward Success

Rewards can be intrinsic or extrinsic. Intrinsic rewards come from recognition and feedback. They result in the good feeling one gets for being recognized by the rest of the organization for superior performance. Extrinsic rewards are more concrete, such as money, promotion, or special privileges.

Historically, managers have used extrinsic rewards when attempting to motivate employees. Intrinsic rewards can also provide a powerful stimulus for work group improvement efforts.

Extensive research funded by AT&T found that a formal celebration following success brought about very positive feelings among team members.[7] During such recognition, the rest of the organization can acknowledge and show sympathy for difficulties the team encountered and can also applaud successes. The study concluded that such intrinsic rewards are often more meaningful and lead to higher motivation than standard, extrinsic rewards such as cash pay outs.

When giving extrinsic rewards, quicker is better. Profit-sharing plans that are paid out once a year are not fully effective in stimulating the sort of behavior called for in an EI environment—fast decision making in a supportive climate where people are moving in the same direction. This sort of environment is best supported by giving extrinsic rewards at the completion of a task or at least quarterly or semi-annually.

Some EI efforts do not distinguish between individual initiative and empowerment, on one hand, and department or unit empowerment on the other. The goal of such efforts is to push down decision making, often not being particularly concerned if it is to an individual employee or a group. This is not good enough for EI in a TQ effort. Achieving the goals of Total Quality requires collective effort and teamwork. One-alone effort can be self-serving and work against the development of the necessary organizational character. The rewards offered for EI success (and, as important, the measures on which those rewards are based) must stress results gained from team-oriented initiative and acceptance of ownership.

Choosing which type and method of reward is best is an opportunity for top management to do what the reward system itself is intended to encourage—involve employees. Posing the issue and asking those who will be most affected by the choice is often the route that will lead to the best results. This leads to Lesson 5.

Lesson 5. Implement EI in an Involving Way

Some of the failures we see are cases of EI being designed and implemented in a way that does not involve the employees whom the EI effort is supposed to empower. It is not uncommon for some managers to decide that EI would be good for the organization. Then, they alone learn about it and one day announce there will be an EI effort.

There is a delicate balance to be struck here. On one hand, it is management's decision to launch such an effort, there is no doubt about that. On the other hand, if it is to be successful, the people most affected must be committed to it; for this to happen those employees should have the chance to be a part of its inception. This could mean starting with a companywide survey as a way to ask people what they believe to be the blocks to greater involvement and the faster decision making that it brings, or it could be as simple as the leader chartering a task force to look at what has worked and failed in EI efforts of other companies and to recommend a sequence for their own organization.

These are ways to get lower-level employees involved; what about middle managers? As mentioned above in Lesson 2, it is common in unsuccessful EI efforts for middle managers or supervisors to have sour feelings about EI because they are not a part of it.

Top managers and hourly employees quickly see the benefits of pushing down decision-making authority. For those at the top, it means faster decisions and less cost by cutting out bureaucracy. To those at the lower ends of the organization chart, it means more influence. But in many cases, to people in the middle, EI only results in feeling threatened.

As was pointed out earlier, in many cases people have become supervisors for their technical skills, not because they were judged to have management capabilities. This, combined with a general lack of supervisory training when they assumed new duties, left these people unprepared in the management and behavioral parts of their task. In many cases, midlevel managers in support departments were encouraged to focus narrowly on their specific task and worry neither about the big picture nor about how to help other departments. The ones who lasted kept their heads down and did the job that was asked of them.

Then with all the best intentions, the leader sends out a memo or a videotape saying that all employees need to change the way the work gets done. Instead of showing by doing, the supervisor must become a "facilitator" so that hourly people can be involved in decision making; decisions heretofore made by support groups such as quality control or materials management will be made by people on the line. Then the leader says: "We're all in this together and by working as a team, we will scale even greater heights." The result is confusion and resentment rather than motivation for middle managers who experience the rules changing.

Some people will feel threatened regardless of whether the organization takes positive steps to establish the appropriate expectations. The fact is that EI does dramatically change the role of people in the middle. Jobs will change and so will what it takes to succeed. However, with some forethought and by considering the perspectives and feelings of middle managers, these sorts of reactions can be minimized through the right sort of involvement at the right time. Some possible steps to do so are:

- Letting midlevel people know that top management is planning an EI effort before it is announced and asking for their input.
- Offering the right training programs for building the skills needed for change.
- Making clear what role employees will play and what will be expected of supervisors.

TQ: An Effective Umbrella for Employee Participation Many companies that report positive employee involvement results place the EI effort under the banner of Total Quality. These companies use the five lessons well. The workers understand what needs to be done: satisfy customer requirements (Lesson 1). They learn the requirements through face-to-face discussions with customers. Often, this is the first time employees have ever interacted with the people who buy their products. They had worked in isolation, not knowing who received the output of their work or how satisfied they were.

The teams participate in a very real sense (Lesson 2). The improvements they implement not only make their customers happy but also improve the workplace environment. The teams feel empowered (Lesson 3), because they are given the skills to improve their workplace and receive the support of the rest of the organization. They feel connected to their customers and feel good about meeting customer needs.

Employees receive both intrinsic and extrinsic rewards (Lesson 4). The self-satisfaction and recognition for meeting customer needs provide intrinsic payback. Pay raises and promotions for high achievers provide the extrinsic rewards.

Early on in the process, employees at lower and middle levels of the organization chart are involved in determining the direction of the efforts through surveys, visits to customers, and membership on task forces (Lesson 5).

Tasks for the Leader

As with Total Quality as a whole, ultimately, it is the leader who must ensure the success of an effort such as companywide employee involvement. In doing so, there are five "don'ts" of leading a companywide employee involvement effort that must be kept in mind.

1. When implementing EI as part of a Total Quality effort, don't believe that yesterday's answers are appropriate for today's questions. The "participative management program" that was used in 1975, for example, might not succeed today. History can provide valuable lessons only after the leader has formulated a new way to proceed. Being tied to the past often leads to replicating actions taken in a different environment for different reasons by different people—actions that may not suit today's realities.

2. Don't assume that people who have done things one way for years will change their behavior easily. For some it may take time and effort that simply are not available. For many companies, EI requires significant reorientation in how people act and react to one another. For many, it is a frightening change. Many will choose (often without even realizing a choice has been made) to keep things as they are rather than act differently.

Wise leaders will become dissatisfied with the status quo before subordinates do. They will think about it, worry about it, ask questions about it, and formulate a way to address it. Some subordinates will be slow to grasp the significance. When it is time to act, these leaders must be realistic in the way they pull the organization along, giving people enough time to get to the point of urgency. At the same time, they must not hesitate to replace people, especially high-level people, who will never embrace the sense of urgency enough to change their behavior.

3. Don't believe you can do it all yourself. There is a fine line between confidence and megalomania. The changes needed in most companies are too enormous, and the problems too deeply rooted, to be resolved by one person. Everyone has a role

to play in bringing about EI. The wise leader will find a way to have those roles defined and make sure people fulfill the requirements.

The most effective leaders understand what they do well and do it, but find others to do the things they do not do as well. The industrial graveyard is filled with epitaphs of companies that had a better mouse trap but also had a leader who could not, or would not, involve people in the change, people who were necessary to help him or her make the firm a bigger, better competitor.

4. In trying to make EI a reality, do not assume that you can anticipate everything or that you don't need a game plan at all. As has been suggested, successful EI is a function of changing people's attitudes and then their behavior. Attitude change is something that cannot be systematic. The comforting sequence of the scientific method can get in the way rather than ensure success. Changing attitudes is iterative at best. Not only must one often take a step back to repeat the one just taken, but one must take a step sideways, as well.

At the same time, a game plan is essential. The right level of planning here is more like a basketball game than a football game. A basketball team only has a handful of basic plays. The point guard calls a play as he brings the ball down court, but what actually happens depends on how the defense looks, who is overplaying, who gets double teamed, and so forth. A football team has a playbook three inches thick; the players memorize the spot to go to. When a quarterback overthrows a receiver by 10 yards, it is usually because he is throwing to a spot and one or the other has the wrong play in mind. Organizational change is a basketball game, not a football game.

5. Don't believe the old adage, "If it ain't broke, don't fix it!" This flies in the face of every principle of preventive maintenance—from yearly physicals, to getting one's teeth cleaned, to a 5000-mile check-up on your car. A better guideline is, "If you care about it, improve it before it breaks!"

The wise leader is always looking for opportunities to make things better before they break. The cost of repairing a broken organization is enormous compared to the fine tuning and constructive change required to keep it sharp. If a company's climate has deteriorated to the point of no teamwork, very bad management–labor relationships, and extreme lack of trust, just instituting an EI effort will (at least) take enormous energy and (at most) simply not be enough. The best route is to not let the situation get to that point in the first place.

Table 8.2 summarizes this view of employee involvement from the Total Quality perspective.

Views of EI from TQ Drivers

Here are comments on the way some companies incorporate employee involvement efforts into their quest for Total Quality.

Dave Luther, Corning

Like most things in a quality effort, employee involvement is a matter of degree, not of time. Involvement moves from sharing of information at a basic level up the scale towards "let me tell you what's going on and get some feedback." The next stage is where you start to solicit input from people. At the fourth stage, management isn't involved because people are doing things themselves because they know what needs to be done to meet the company's goals.

We've got several locations where the number of players in the organization has been cut in half, where employee teams are literally running the place; where people are paid based on their training, certification, and skills rather than on their seniority or on what they do; where you can't tell a person's rank by the way he dresses because ties aren't allowed; where spouses and families come to orientation so they understand what it is the family member who works with us does.

Richard Bovender, RJR

It takes time for people to change their attitudes and behaviors. They have to be involved and take ownership. People have got to buy in in order to have ownership. And they have to break through cultural barriers.

In our company, people are very used to working for a supervisor. So up until just a short while ago, supervisors were leaders of our teams. That's not the way the theory says its supposed to go, but for us it worked very well ·

Table 8.2
Employee Involvement from a Total Quality Perspective

1. The primary reasons for EI are (a) to improve the business's ability to compete by passing power to make decisions to the people who encounter those decision-making situations day in and day out, and (b) to further man's quest for individual expression and creativity.

2. This requires employees to assume more authority and exert greater decision-making power over their surroundings. Each person must, in other words, become his or her own manager. This means both that authority must be offered and that employees must take it; they must welcome this new level of responsibility and fulfill its mandate.

3. We exist in a business environment today that supports employee involvement. In fact, that makes EI essential to compete effectively and it is a perfect platform for EI.

4. The middle manager's or supervisor's role must change in a TQ environment and for EI to take hold smoothly. That role must be one of facilitation rather than authoritarian direction. Defining new competencies for middle managers or supervisors, involving people in those jobs in the change effort, and training all play a part in success.

5. The Total Quality movement provides an ideal umbrella under which EI efforts can thrive. Its customer focus, its extensive use of problem-solving teams, and its emphasis on developing new skills have offered an ideal context for EI to flourish.

6. To do all this requires a level of commitment not usually required in today's businesses. We have found that such commitment tends to thrive in a certain organization climate, one where employees feel in control and take ownership for getting things done, where motivation and teamwork are encouraged, where

(continued)

Table 8.2 *(continued)*

worthwhile basic needs are met, where there is a healthy degree of dissatisfaction, and where a common view of the future is shared.

7. By investigating employee efforts that were not successful and contrasting them with those that were more so, several lessons can be drawn:

   a. A common understanding of how EI can help achieve the business imperatives is needed.

   b. Involvement must be aimed at improving what is close at hand and meaningful.

   c. Certain conditions must be in place for empowerment to take hold.

   d. Success is rewarded both intrinsically and extrinsically.

   e. EI is implemented in an involving way.

8. It is the leader who must ensure success of an EI effort. Five rules for doing so are these:

   a. Do not believe old answers are appropriate for new questions.

   b. Do not assume people will change habits easily.

   c. Do not believe you can do it all yourself.

   d. Do not assume you can anticipate everything or that no game plan is needed.

   e. Do not believe the old adage "If it ain't broke, don't fix it!" Replace it with "If you care about it, improve it before it breaks!"

---

because supervisors had some authority and could get things done without having to wait around forever to get approval.

Now that management has seen that employee involvement and self-directed teams can work, and now that employees have seen that they really can get things done, we have a number of hourly employees facilitating teams. Another important factor is that the supervisors have seen that things can work using teams, so they have much less resistance.

We had quality circles here as early as 1980 or so, but the employee groups were not really working on the right things, (things) that had an impact on the bottom line. When we started to move to more focused JIT and TQ, what we call manufacturing resource issues, we just let the quality circles finish up their current projects, then phased them out and reconfigured the teams. The people we asked first if they would like to work on manufacturing resource teams were people from the old quality circles, because they had group involvement experiences already.

But what we did with these new teams was have employee groups work with the functional management of the area to decide on the processes and problems to be tackled on so that work was done on processes and problems that had an impact on quality and on the bottom line.

Real trust was built, so that if the employee group went in and worked, then came back and said to functional management, "What we identified as a problem is not really a problem, or not really the problem. The real problem is X," they were very much supported by management in going after that new-found problem.

Jim Litts, Johnson and Johnson

Employee involvement is the key to the whole thing. If people come to work and understand why they're doing what they're doing, it can't help but make a difference. Management has to go in to the employee base and convince people that they are valuable, that their ideas are valuable, and that management will listen to their ideas.

People have to be convinced that management will provide them with the resources to get their ideas implemented. Management has to provide an atmosphere where people can be supported by each other, where they feel supported, and where they are recognized when they accomplish things.

Paul Kikta, TRW

I prefer to look at employee empowerment rather than employee involvement. And I can distinguish between the two.

The old employee involvement was really one ratchet above quality circles, which focused on quality of work life. We got a bunch of people together and we felt good and we did our thing.

Employee empowerment is looking at a whole new way of utilizing and working with employees. The empowerment says not only is the company as a whole interested in you working on a particular issue, but that you will have the "stock-to-dock" responsibility for it, and the authority. Total Quality also offers the chance to increase employee empowerment in the office and staff areas—with knowledge workers—as well as in the plant.

When I look at employee empowerment concepts at the corporate staff, I think it's very workable. I think the work-cell concept that is used in a manufacturing setting is even more important in a corporate office setting, in order to break down the traditional functional silos that exist.

References

1. See bibliography section on EI.

2. Several of the examples and lessons in this chapter come from empirical research conducted by Gale Connell, who has also contributed text and ideas on this topic from which I have borrowed liberally.

3. E. Nevins, *Real Bosses Don't Say Thank You* (Somerville, NJ: Nevings Publishing Co., 1983).

4. M. Maccoby, *The Leader* (New York: Balantine Books, 1982.

5. Of the leaders of the quality movement, J. Juran has been most associated with the strategy of identifying problems and forming problem solving projects to solve one at a time. See bibliography for more on Juran and his philosophy.

6. J. E. Richard, "A President's Experience with Democratic Management," a paper presented at the Program of Conferences, the Industrial Relations Center, University of Chicago, 1959 (the entire paper is available from Rath & Strong, Lexington, MA 02173.)

7. AT&T Research is quoted in "Getting Emotional About Quality." J. Lader, Quality Progress, July 1988.

9

The Role of the Human Resource Department in Total Quality

While there has been a growing awareness among chief executive officers and other corporate top management of the role Total Quality can have in reinvigorating industrial companies, many TQ efforts do not reach their potential because the people aspects or culture aspects are not managed well. These efforts fail or get mediocre results because of lack of teamwork, insufficient employee involvement, inadequate motivation, people not feeling as though they can change current practices, or simply the wrong people being involved given the tasks that must be accomplished.

For help on these issues, top managers should be able to turn to their Human Resource departments. But many feel, and rightly so, I am afraid, that they cannot; that their Human Resource departments are not well-enough prepared to help them make these momentous changes.

I recently attended a conference of about 15 CEOs who were discussing Total Quality. They almost uniformly felt a need to make drastic changes in their company's way of doing business—in such areas as engineering, manufacturing, marketing, and office processes. They were articulate concerning changes in plant layout (going from straight line to work cells), in lead time (response to customers had to be faster), in inventory policy (inventory protects problems from being solved and has to be minimized), and in quality (do it right the first time). But they seemed at a loss on how to crystallize their gut feelings and communicate their perceptions of how to handle employee involvement.

I asked what their HR people were doing to help. One CEO responded, "My vice president of HR knows less about this than I do." Another said, "I don't even know what questions to ask the HR people because they've never really shown much interest in this organization culture area."

These two answers say that Human Resource professionals are missing a golden opportunity to be catalysts for change. At the same time corporate leaders have gone up the learning curve of what used to be considered the purview of applied behavioral science or Organization Development, HR professionals have dropped the ball they should be most well equipped to carry. In all too many cases, the HR function has been increasingly pushed into a role of administrator of existing corporate policies and procedures, a conservative influence rather than one that advocates change. Human Resources has become a function that merely uses policies and procedures to referee between employees and managers, rather than a facilitator to get employees and managers closer together.

Also, too many Human Resource professionals see Total Quality as a technical issue that they feel ill-equipped to handle or be a part of. But if HR professionals looked more carefully into Total Quality, they would see rich opportunities to have a positive influence over the radical changes this philosophy will bring to the workplace.

The lack of HR involvement in many Total Quality efforts not only causes the human resources profession to miss an opportunity, it also opens the door for people with less grounding in behavioral change to drive the climate change efforts. And that can be dangerous.

Today, the vast majority of people who are driving their companies' Total Quality efforts have backgrounds in non-HR staff jobs or technical backgrounds in Quality Assurance. While they may be well-meaning, they are simply not equipped with the years of knowledge and experience in management and small group training, and EI experiments that many HR professionals have, especially those who have practiced organization development. There are some notable exceptions. One of the more innovative is at Bull HN, the large, global computer and information network company. David Dotlich heads the corporation's HR function, its public relations function (so that one person is responsible for internal as well as external communication), and is also the Total Quality head.

Human Resource professionals need to get on board the Total Quality train, or the engine of manufacturing change in this country will leave without them; and without them, manufacturers may end up on the wrong track.

In one case, a Fortune 100 company had a corporate HR department that had become an administrative unit rather than an agent of climate and behavior change. While in years past, it was known in the Organization Development and applied behavioral science community as a state-of-the-art unit, the skilled trainers and OD people had left, some forced out after losing political battles and others giving up convinced that fundamental change in this company was unlikely to take place as quickly as they wanted. They were not replaced, and the department became dominated by personnel administrators with valuable and needed expertise in compensation, hiring, and labor relations. Cross-department teamwork slowly diminished because it was no longer being stressed and supported by training programs that the departed OD people had offered.

This transition took place gradually over the years from the late 1970s through the mid 1980s. The corporate leadership changed in 1985 and a new emphasis emerged, built on the conviction that customer satisfaction and a new organization climate were essential to regain market share lost over the previous decade and to compete effectively with ever-tougher competitors. A TQ effort was launched with high hopes and much fanfare.

Because of the roles that had been assumed by the personnel department, it never occurred to the corporate leaders to include HR in planning for Total Quality tasks such as small-group and interpersonal training, and measuring the organization climate. The decision was made to form a Total Quality department, and a person was hired from another company to head it. He came in and quickly started to build a staff of people, again bringing them in from the outside.

The three new people he brought in came from Total Quality units in other companies, and were engineers who had been part of Quality Control or Quality Assurance departments before the advent of Total Quality.

The new corporate leaders had determined that more teamwork was crucial to moving to the sort of climate that was essential to creating a Total Quality character in their company, and correctly linked teamwork and climate development goals with the TQ efforts; the Total Quality department was assigned the task of bringing them about. The group decided to tackle the teamwork issue in the same way that it sought to educate employees on the particulars of quality problem solving; it bought a packaged teamwork-training program from a large education/publishing concern.

There were videotapes, a workbook, and audiotapes, all packaged in attractive molded plastic containers. They were introduced and given to employees in one-day team orientation sessions where the basics of teamwork were discussed.

This approach has been the most expedient way for many companies to get the message across about the basic ingredients of teamwork, but hardly the way to forge bonds and increase communication between departments. Not surprisingly, in this company teamwork continued to deteriorate, despite the company having spent hundreds of thousands of dollars to improve how people worked together.

It is often the case that an activist, change-the-character-of-the-company role is foreign to many HR people and simply different from the roles they have assumed and been encouraged to play. In one case a corporate HR group of a large, diversified corporation began to investigate Total Quality because the various sectors and divisions had made commitments to TQ efforts. Here was another case of the operating divisions leading the way toward cultural change and the HR group at corporate trying to catch up. This particular group is one responsible for overall corporate policy and strategy on compensation, pensions, benefits, labor relations, and management development. It became clear that HR people in the operating units were involved to varying degrees in local TQ efforts but that the chief functional and strategic unit at headquarters, which set the tone and long-term direction for HR policy, was not up to speed on Total Quality and did not understand its short-term or long-term impact on the corporation's people.

When this corporate group had a one-day Total Quality awareness session, some from the department were enthusiastic and quickly saw the overall potential of TQ and some of the ways that it would affect HR policy and strategy. Others were more unsure and cautious. Others were threatened. One of the biggest challenges for this department and others like it from other corporations will be to treat the employees they are meant to serve the way the operating units are learning to treat their customers—to understand and then to meet their needs and exceed their expectations.

One problem in this regard with this particular corporate HR group is that all but one or two of them had never worked in an operating division; their whole careers had been spent at corporate headquarters and they had been encouraged and rewarded to become deeply competent in one, narrow, technical discipline. The person in charge of one of the departments in corporate HR is a widely recognized expert at designing cost-effective programs in one of those narrow areas. He is a senior person in that topic and has been encouraged by the corporation to specialize through his years of employment. His view of his mission is to design programs for employees in a way that saves the corporation money, rather than to construct the programs that best meet the needs of employees, doing so in a cost-conscious way. Needs of employees and their wants and desires are not sought as input into these programs, but cost reduction targets are the goals that drive development activity. He was one of the most confused and threatened persons in the group during the awareness session.

A second problem with this tradition-bound staff orientation is that measures are often created that do not support the TQ principle of treating fellow employees as partners in ensuring the company improves how it treats its customers. In one company, the corporate training and development department was measured on the number of the corporation's employees who attended company-sponsored training programs. There was no incentive for this department to provide the training programs that were most necessary for the company to become flexible, customer-oriented, or satisfying to employees. A metric on volume does not quickly cause someone to survey employees to find out what they believe they need in order to do an excellent job. It also doesn't encourage attention to the evaluation of participants as to how relevant and satisfying they have found training programs that they attend. Just as with a company that does not put high priority on customer satisfaction, any training and development department not driven by satisfaction of the employees who attend their programs is one that inevitably will not stay sharp and contemporary and will not help the company as a whole to excel.

Executive, Not Administrator

The question, then, is how Human Resource professionals prepare themselves—and the HR function—to assume the responsibilities necessary for Total Quality. Below are some possible answers.

First, the Human Resources leader must assert his or her role as a part of the executive team. Too often over the past 20 years, corporate leaders have pushed the Human Resource department into the role of traffic cop for all of the paperwork that must be done to keep the government happy, to keep labor unions either happy or at bay, and to satisfy the physical or economic needs of the work force.

The corporate president who feels the intellectual and emotional need for change and has an Organization Development-oriented Human Resource professional as part of the top-management team can turn to that person and ask, "What are the people consequences?" But if the president sees that top HR person as merely an administrator, he or she is more likely to seek answers elsewhere and then merely require that the HR person take care of the administrative changes that are decided on.

Becoming a member of the corporate team means understanding the business. There is a tacit assumption in many companies that even if one is a specialist in marketing, manufacturing, engineering, or finance, one has an understanding of basic business concepts, of what it takes to make the business successful and of the role his or her department plays in doing so. That same assumption is often not made of Human Resource specialists. HR specialists must get up to speed on the new business basics and must make other members of the senior management team understand that Human Resources is an important part of implementing them.

Those new business basics—providing flawless quality for the customer, Just-In-Time delivery, and exceptional service based on an attitude of meeting the customers' needs and exceeding expectations and of doing the right things for the right reasons in the right way the first time they are attempted—are what a company must do to compete effectively in today's marketplace. These business basics must be melded with the company's particular business imperatives.

Knowledge of the new basics and the company's particular business imperatives is one need. Another is for the HR people to assume a position for the HR function at the forefront of implementing change. They can take advantage of the window of opportunity that exists today for truly meaningful workplace change under the rubric of Total Quality. HR professionals must be involved because the long-term success of these TQ tools and techniques depends on the organization climate, teamwork, and the right people in the right jobs as much as it does on anything else.

Begin a Human Resource Strategy Early

At the same time the Human Resource department is asserting its role in implementing change, the HR leader must be developing a coherent plan for answering the questions the corporate leader will ask about TQ's effects on people. There are a number of ways the Human Resource department can help in the Total Quality effort, and a strategy must be developed that encompasses each.

The HR strategy must do the following:

- Define a role for the HR head and the department (or a part of the department) as an internal corporate consultant, a resource that can be called on to help solve people problems during the Total Quality implementation.

- Define some ways to measure the organizational climate and pinpoint the barriers that currently exist that keep people from feeling involved and wanting to work as a team.

- Identify the qualities the company needs from its next generation of management, hourly, and technical employees; then figure out how to go about recruiting and hiring those people and how to ensure they join up in the most effective way.

- Determine the kind of training of managers that is necessary to help people behave differently since different behavior is essential to realizing both the new business basics and the business imperatives of most companies. Such training includes team building, problem solving and decision making in times of rapid change, influencing in a positive way, and negotiating so that both parties' needs are met.

- Include ways to train HR people to be internal consultants, able and available to help other employees make the sorts of organizational and behavioral changes necessary.

- Determine the best way to train nonmanagement people. There is substantial reorientation and retraining needed in a Total Quality effort on different work practices and techniques.

- Come up with new and different reward systems. Total Quality puts different demands on the ways people are rewarded, and its precepts do not mesh with traditional reward systems such as individual incentives that encourage high output without regard to quality or meeting the needs of other departments. Gain sharing may provide an acceptable option, but even it must be tailored and implemented in a certain way to be successful; the HR department must join with industrial engineers to ensure such tailoring is complete.

- Develop a plan to manage the education effort that is such a big part of Total Quality. Education cannot be left to people who are specialists in functional areas but have little understanding of how adults learn.

- Finally, prepare to be an advocate and a role model for the Total Quality effort. Although everyone in the organization needs to model TQ behaviors, it is especially important for members of the HR department to be models. It is important that they exhibit collaborative behavior and push decision making down to lower levels in their own department and also use within the HR department the TQ techniques that are recommended for others.

Two things can come of this sort of activism. First, to the extent that the head of HR advocates the use of these programs and behavioral tools and techniques, he or she is seen by others as someone who is willing and able to practice in a business sense what is preached in an intellectual way. Second, if the head of Human Resources uses in the HR department such Total Quality tools as value-added analysis or internal client surveys, HR will be seen as a more integral part of the business, by those both inside and those outside the HR department.

Match and Develop Skills

The HR leader may not have all of the necessary skills but should find people with them or find places where the people in the HR organization can be trained to develop these skills. They include the following areas of competence.

- An ability to use a variety of different influence techniques and to determine from the circumstances of the situation the best technique to use.
- An ability to envision and figure out things that are not easily visible, such as the subtleties of an organization's climate and the underlying issues in a company's culture. This includes the ability to answer clearly such questions as, "Why do people act the way they do?"
- The collateral willingness and courage to challenge current assumptions of compensation, rewards, and incentives. People's behavior is often reinforced because of the messages they receive from the reward system. If teamwork, challenging the status quo, going out of the way to solve customer problems, and doing a task right the first time are necessary for Total Quality, the human resource people must come up with reward systems that reinforce such behavior.
- Strong training skills. These skills include a firm understanding of the principles of adult education, the ability to facilitate at meetings where emotions are often high, the ability to speak in public and make sense of complex subjects, the ability to conduct team-training and team-building workshops, and experience in training others in creative problem solving, decision making, influencing, and negotiation.

- A knowledge of the characteristics of excellent performers and the ability to identify those people and get them involved in Total Quality efforts.

Let's hear from a couple of HR professionals who are leading the TQ efforts in their particular organizations. One is David Dotlich from Bull HN and the other is Paul Kikta of TRW.

David Dotlich, Bull HN

David Dotlich is senior vice president for Human Resources and Corporate Communications for Bull HN Information Systems. In 1990 Dotlich had the Total Quality effort placed on his agenda. Bull HN is the company formed when Groupe Bull, the large French computer and systems company bought Honeywell's computer and systems business. Japan's NEC purchased a minority stake in the new company (the H in Bull HN stands for Honeywell and the N for NEC). Bull HN is based in Boston and develops, produces, sells, and/or services hardware and systems products in North America, the United Kingdom, Italy, and Australia. It also must coordinate closely with Groupe Bull headquartered in Paris, which aims at the rest of the countries in the world with a similar organization structure.

Bull's decision in 1988 to make Dotlich, a former University of Minnesota professor of Organization Development and consultant to Honeywell, not only vice president of HR but also of communications, was an innovative stroke yet a logical one for a multicultural, high-tech company. As Dotlich explains it, especially in a global company, the internal message given to employees and the external message sent to customers, potential customers, and the public at large from such a high-profile company as one in the computer industry, must be consistent.

In an interview for this book, Dotlich discusses not only the importance of a strong human resource position in the creation of a TQ effort, but the difficulties of trying to forge a consensus in a multicultural business of just what TQ is.

Basically, there are six components to our TQ effort.

First is training. There's a lot of training that goes on in France and some in this country.

The second thing is regular quality reviews conducted by the CEO on product and process issues, customer complaints, customer satisfaction surveys, and things like that.

Third is recognition and rewards for people who have done a good job; sanctions for people who haven't; pointing out and celebrating people and successes for particular jobs well done in order to create motivation for everyone else and particularly to create symbols in the organization of what it is that we intend to do.

The fourth thing would probably be some degree of measurement. We do a lot of customer-satisfaction surveys.

The fifth thing is a designated spiritual leader for quality, someone that's high up in the organization who has the task of making sure attention is paid to quality.

And the sixth is a quality network of people throughout the world who are in touch with each other to share ideas and applications and insights. This network is monitored and sort of facilitated by the person who has been the head of quality.

In this effort the leader is, of course, important. He has to invest symbolically in the effort. In a hierarchy, people tend to look to the leader for figuring out what's important. He has to spend time and effort in this to let other people know that quality is important.

The leader also needs to define what the values of the company are in relation to quality and to really, consistently hold people to those values. Some of those values are:

- *A satisfied customer is key to our success and survival. In a technology company, there's a real focus on producing exotic and elegant technology products. A TQ effort means a substantial shift to recognizing that quality is perceived from the customer's standpoint.*

- *A focus on process quality. A lot of people believe quality is only those things you can touch and hold; we've made a shift to focusing on interactions in such things as product development, lateral integration, all those things that make up the process of the organization.*

There are also the values in human interactions.

There are a few major reasons why the effort here was focused through the Human Resources area. Probably the most important is that the Human Resources organization really is, if anybody is, responsible for defining, communicating, and upholding the company's values. So if quality—or any other major change in a company—is done primarily through the value system it logically falls to the Human Resource organization to push that.

Also, the levers that Human Resources has responsibility for—training, rewards and recognition, and communications—are also the principal ways in which quality is imbued in a company.

In addition, a lot of quality problems are really boundary problems. Human Resources people work the boundary issues quite a bit; we work to link people together, define what there is in common, help people find a common agenda, facilitate interaction, and manage conflict. These are all process issues that assist the overall quality effort.

Our company's vision is to be an information supplier on a global basis, to help customers find solutions to information problems. There hasn't really been a specific infusion of quality into the corporate vision. Our quality efforts to date have been pretty much mechanistic. We're working to integrate our strategic vision with our focus on quality by spending a lot of time thinking and talking about these issues at the senior management level. This is necessary because to turn a quality vision into a day-to-day reality everyone has to recognize and understand the strategic directions of the company, what's important for our success and survival.

We are building this understanding through intensive communication, a lot of speeches from the key leaders, a lot of newspaper articles, videos, things like that, to inundate people with information about where we are going and why. At the same time we are asking people to develop, within their functions, quality measurements and goals that make sense for what it is they're trying to do. Obviously, if people are going to be measured, they're going to make more day-to-day effort to try to accomplish the things consistent with what they have committed to do.

We have tried to bring about much more awareness than ever before at all levels of the company about the cus-

tomer; who the customer is, what the customer needs, what he wants, how he buys, what he's looking for.

Probably the most important translation of a quality vision to day-to-day activities is the formation of cross-functional work groups. People are just beginning to see each other, and other functions, as part of the solution rather than part of the problem.

This is a very complex process for us because so much of our product development is done in different sites around the world. We're a vertical company, but everything we produce is lateral. This is the point at which globalism and quality begin to interact.

In a global business, people are no longer just looking at or talking to people in their own countries for ideas, for applications, and for useful approaches. The globe is not only the playing field for customers, but within the company. In our global company, people are networked together, which makes process quality so important. It takes a lot of time to get something done because of all the nodes that people have to communicate with, so good communications and process quality are vital.

Because of globalism, there's much more diffusion of accountability and responsibility. Obviously, in a quality effort, people have to be accountable. The organization is much more flexible, but it's much more difficult to measure and account for who's responsible for what.

Because of all of this, people have got to give their word and keep their word. There's almost a case of information overload, and people have got to understand that one of the most important things is not to drown each other out, or under, all of this information we generate.

In addition, we're working with three very distinct cultures. Every aspect of quality differs across the three cultures—time, for instance, and organizational values like power, the way you do things, and who is ultimately responsible. The Japanese tend to be much more of a homogenized culture and, as a result, everybody has a piece of the action. Everyone has accountability for making something happen. American companies tend to see power much more at the top, and so they tend to see quality as an *issue and a responsibility for those at the top (in a strategic sense) and those close to the bottom (making a correct piece).*

To understand the French vision of quality, it's really necessary to understand the French person and the French view of an organization. To the French, doing a quality job is important to life. Having quality in your life is also important—quality food, quality fashions, quality interactions, quality friends.

In [American] culture, we've compartmentalized organizations so that no one has real responsibility, and so that an individual's life is not part of his organizational life. So the French understand quality as a part of life and living, while Americans see quality as a part of working. A lot of times the American approach to quality is very confusing to French people—things like confrontational meetings and organization development sessions—and fly in the face of the way things are done in French companies. Because of this confusion, the French often refuse these American techniques, but they cannot be accused of refusing to commit to quality.

The French are also confused by Japanese notions of quality, and threatened by it more than by American notions. The Japanese and the French cultures don't work very easily together, because the Japanese culture downplays the individual while the French culture celebrates the individual. The Japanese believe in working diligently for the best agreement, then sticking to it once it's made; the French believe agreements should constantly be modified based on new information and new circumstances.

What the French bring to the quality party is a real capacity for organization—the French actually invented the notion of organization in some ways. They also have a terrific understanding of symbols and how symbols work. In our organization, the French organize terrific training events, with symbolic rewards and external events like climbing a mountain and things like that to symbolize teamwork. The French also have a tremendous ability to integrate new information and constantly redirect themselves, which is important to making quality happen. And they have a real capacity to use the hierarchy to get things done in a way that Americans don't.

In our multicultural company, we're also wrestling with the notion of customers. The Japanese are quite subservient to the notion of customer. They literally worship the customer and what the customer needs and wants. The French do not view the customer as kind, but as a partner on an equal footing. They are very much more likely to work problems through and negotiate and deal with the customer requirements. Americans, who are only now beginning to understand the importance of customers, fit somewhere in the middle.

Paul Kikta, TRW

Paul Kikta is an organization development specialist at TRW's corporate offices. He has a broad-based HR background as a manager, internal consultant, and trainer. He was recently given responsibility to help shape the TQ effort at the corporate office of TRW.

There are probably six or seven TQ efforts going on here at TRW. We are a highly decentralized corporation, and divisional leaders have a high degree of autonomy. The effort over which I have direct responsibility is at the corporate staff of the senior executives. I also have some influence and responsibility over other efforts.

Some items are transferable between the more operation-oriented divisions and the more service-oriented corporate staff. Other things are not transferable at all. The element that is most clearly transferable is the concept of process improvement, identification of processes and elimination of waste. But the concept of customer, for instance, is different at the corporate level than at the operational division, so the idea of customer satisfaction will be different. Rightly or wrongly, corporate staffs often see their customers as different from the "external" customer, the buying customer. Corporate staffs feel they have many masters to serve.

Because of this, there is a major difference between the operational leader and the staff or support-function leader.

The leader of the corporate effort has two roles; one is of support and the other is of leadership. In fact, the entire corporate staff has these two functions. The support side of the equation comes in assisting the people in the field in their meeting customer needs, providing for the satisfaction of the external customer. If your job is not directly involved with the external customer, then it is in assisting the next person in line to deal with the external customer.

This is different from saying that if you don't deal with the external customer then it is your responsibility to satisfy your internal customer. If you are only concerned with satisfying the internal customer, you can be lulled into a false sense of security, a feeling that "as long as I'm satisfying all those people internally, I'm doing a good job, and that good job translates into great customer satisfaction all along the line." In reality, you may very well satisfy an internal customer, but that may not help the internal customer to focus on or satisfy the external customer.

Now, the element of leadership by corporate staff comes in raising the level of expectation with customer satisfaction. If you look at support only, at customer satisfaction as having met customer expectations, you can do that okay if the customer maintains a pretty low expectation. But as a leader, the corporate staff can raise the expectation of the customer, by having an appropriate vision, sharing that vision with employees and customers, and being doggedly consistent in doing what needs to be done to live up to that vision.

And if the [corporate] staff really does lead well, it has to do more and more support. The toughest part is getting all of those middle managers on board, to get them to not just meet their internal customers' expectations, but to lead.

This effort [at TRW] has only been going on for a few months, and I'm now searching for some measurements and metrics to use to figure out how good a job is being done. I haven't found anyone who really does this well, inside my company or at other companies, so it's hard to do any benchmarking on this.

One set of metrics is, of course, to look at processes and see if we can increase speed of actions, and decrease time, cycle, and steps. Then we need to begin measuring the leadership, work the vision and see if the message is getting there. Then we need to get people in the field to help us determine if the processes attributable to a particular corporate support function enhance or inhibit their ability to create external customer satisfaction, and whether those processes enhance or inhibit the field's journey along the path of Total Quality.

We need to even measure behaviors. We need to find out from the field what behaviors the senior area officers are exhibiting that enhance or inhibit their ability to create customer satisfaction and get down the path of Total Quality. We hope to get that down into some, if not measurable, certainly definable criteria.

This kind of thinking is a far cry from the kind of quality efforts TRW has undertaken. In the 1980–1985 period, two centers were established, one called "quality college" and the other called "productivity college." These were centralized efforts of the corporate staff to raise the level of awareness on quality and productivity issues. Productivity college focused on some employee involvement and employee empowerment issues, while quality college focused on understanding design of experiments, statistical process control, and other technical quality-enhancement tools.

In about 1985 or 1986, these efforts were turned over to each operating division, so they could implement them consistent with their own cultures and their own management styles, a decision that was perfectly consistent with our corporate decentralized style. This new effort at corporate staff is not an effort to recentralize, but an effort to build some bridges and create some commonalities. By creating this kind of an effort I think there will become some core principles and values around Total Quality throughout the corporation.

But even at the executive staff level, the process is decentralized. I'm working with each executive vice president and his or her function to design the function's systems in Total Quality. There's probably 90% commonality among them, but with our effort there is still the ability to have some uniqueness to each approach that makes each executive vice president be able to say, "This is truly mine."

At the divisional level, there is a commonality of values, drivers, and customers that everyone can agree on. But at corporate staff, there are variables, there are differences of perspective. In some corporate functions, the leadership issue I discussed earlier is stronger, while in other corporate functions support is paramount. If you try to go at it in lockstep, I think, there is more resistance, more of a tendency for an executive to say: "that's okay for planning, or operations, but it doesn't work for me at law, or finance, or human resources."

The approach we use here necessitates that each functional executive in effect create a separate vision. But those visions have to play off the CEO's overriding corporate vision. The CEO is the person who has to say, "I've been to the mountain and here's what I saw." At present, the CEO is still climbing the mountain, but he's committed to the climb and he's putting out some midclimb pronouncements—which he calls missions and goals—that are not fully realized visions. At the same time, the functional executives working off those missions and goals to do the nuts-and-bolts work putting in place their systems. I've also seen a couple of functional executives come out with pretty good visions for their functions, although others are really struggling and some don't even understand what a vision might be.

Let me use this idea of vision to segue into why I think it's so important that human resources be involved in this process.

A number of things have to happen on an organizational level for Total Quality to become a reality. One is the creation of a vision. Another is developing a commonality of language, process. Where most organizations fail—and where there is a danger we might fail—is to look at the processes as technological improvements. Total quality is a behavioral change, a philosophical change.

The technical aspects are only actions along the way that reinforce the behavioral side. But it's behaviors that speak—"I hear what you say but I see what you do."

That lesson was clearly demonstrated by the Baldrige Award winners I have visited. They all admitted that along the way they made mistakes in relying on the techni-

cal side of quality. I'm not even just talking about machine technology; I'm talking about using the language of technology—"Let's do some problem solving in process"—and ideas like that. You can't think technology is going to create quality, only behavior will.

Changing behavior can't be done through massive education. Although I've had some resistance from traditionalists here, we're not going to do massive training and education. There is a massive awareness campaign going on. But what education and training does go on will be based on problems, issues, and process. This training will come in increments: get awareness of Total Quality, understand the concept of process, identify the process, identify the customer, then learn how to meet with the customer and analyze the customer's needs, desires, and what will satisfy that customer.

One way to get an idea of the importance of behavior is to look at the Baldrige Award. The number one criteria is leadership. Leadership is the driver. The next four elements involve the system, the sixth element is measurement of the system, and the seventh element is the goal: customer satisfaction. But you go back to the driver and its leadership, and if you look at the elements of leadership it's really behaviors.

But you can't just change behaviors for the sake of changing behaviors; that doesn't do any good. You have to change behaviors with the ultimate goal in mind—customer satisfaction.

What I see—I would hope to see it a year down the road—is an organization where when there are problems to be solved interdepartmentally, there are some very specific processes, there are some things that always happen and there are some things that never happen. Flow charts are done, analysis is done, decisions are made based on fact and data. Meetings are much shorter, because they're more focused. At the beginning of a meeting, the customer's requirements are spelled out and what the problem is is spelled out, the alternatives are spelled out, the goals for what the meeting will accomplish are spelled out. These are cultural things. These behaviors, and the whole Total Quality effort, are an extension of some very old values of our corporation. If you look at the 75-year history of TRW, we had some very early values from the founders that were very much ahead of their time in the human-resource value system. Some of what we're doing with today's Total Quality effort is really a reaffirmation of those values, bringing back some things that have been lost to where they were.

My role in all of this is kind of unique. I have a some-what unusual background, having worked the last eight years essentially as an internal consultant for TRW on Total Quality, Organization Development, and training issues, focused in the divisions and on a worldwide basis.

A danger I see in all of this, and something I will not allow, is for this broad behavioral and cultural change to become my responsibility—the responsibility of the Organization Development specialist. If indeed the vision and the behavioral change at the senior management level don't come about, this could become just another "program of the year." All of the efforts throughout the organization, no matter how valiant they are, will be only that—efforts. The culture will collapse and the system will collapse under it.

There are some things that can be done from the bottom up. But only the leadership can institutionalize a TQ effort, and if after two or three years it is not institutional-ized—to the point where reward systems and measurement systems don't reinforce it—it will collapse.

An Easy Sale

If Human Resource leaders and Human Resource departments can assess their competencies, improve where they are weak, and "market" within the company their expertise in the people issues of Total Quality, then they will become important players in the major changes that are taking place in American compa-nies and will continue to take place through the end of this cen-tury.

Today, getting leaders to recognize the need for assessing and changing the climates in their organizations in order to suc-cessfully implement Total Quality is an easy sale—a sale that in many cases already has a buyer who is willing to buy. Human

Resource professionals must prove to corporate leaders that they can and will be active players in carrying out these changes. They must be ready and able to guide corporate leadership, to provide better ways to ensure employee involvement, and to be a catalyst for change. Doing so will increase the stature and influence of HR and will also better ensure that the skills necessary for TQ success are in place.

Part IV
Where Do We Go from Here?

10

What Comes Next?

If Total Quality is the most current and comprehensive of a long line of approaches to achieve organizational excellence, what will follow it? Will there be a "son of TQ?" Something even more comprehensive, more complex, more complicated, and more difficult to implement? Just as Total Quality could not be predicted in 1975, the development paradigm that will succeed it cannot be predicted now, either. I will leave speculation to futurists, academics, and other theoreticians.

What may be anticipated, however, is how TQ itself might evolve over the next five or so years. Certainly, there is too much activity and experimentation going on under the TQ banner for it not to mutate into something other than what it is at present. Below is some speculation on several directions in which this development could go. First is a connection with Computer Integrated Manufacturing. Second is extension of TQ into parts of the business and into industries it has only begun to enter. Third is a prediction of an added element, a new and logical extension that will be added to TQ that has to date been conspicuously absent from the Total Quality paradigm.

Computer Integrated Manufacturing

Perhaps TQ will form a liaison with Computer Integrated Manufacturing (CIM). As was suggested in Chapter 2, CIM showed great promise in the early 1980s. But its potential has yet to materialize for a few reasons.

First, the systems that CIM requires to be linked and merged were never developed with the intention that they would work together in concert. Production Control software was not intended to be linked with a general ledger package, which wasn't designed with the needs of Computer Aided Design software in mind, which is based on a different logic than most sales forecasting systems. Proprietary software is giving way to open systems architecture with its common, or at least complementary, formats.

The second reason that CIM has yet to realize its potential is that most manufacturers of automated equipment were not able to reduce their costs enough to price their equipment at a level so that they could sell enough volume. Multibillion dollar corporations could afford large, complex equipment but they alone could not carry an entire industry. It's ironic that over the past several years some of the equipment manufacturers who have survived have used Just-In-Time, which eschews automation, as a way to reduce costs so that they could sell their equipment.

The third reason is that CIM required enormous reorientation and training. It required that the work force develop sophisticated knowledge and skills. We might have a skilled CIM-literate work force by now if CIM proponents had laid the groundwork early on and established education and training centers at vocational education schools across developed countries that have educational infrastructures such as countries in North America and Europe. Federal governments or consortia of governments such as the European Common Market might also have established long-term manufacturing or, better, technology strategies that provided for education and training.

Certainly the activities in manufacturing companies over the last 10 years have provided an environment for CIM that is much more likely to produce the spectacular results of which it is capable. Those businesses that have merged the JIT manufacturing strategy with Total Quality have improved flexibility, reduced costs, improved the predictability of their production processes, and created a work force more accepting of change and increased responsibility. The environment may be more amenable than it was in the early 1980s.

Extending TQ

Total Quality was originally aimed at and intended for those parts of the organization that made and distributed the product.

It was a better, more comprehensive way to ensure product quality and reliability. It moved to engineering and product development as manufacturing's first cousin, still having to do with the performance of the product. It appealed to many executives because of its cost-saving potential (especially when JIT was included) which was particularly seductive since our measurement systems are geared to track visible costs through metrics such as direct labor variances and return on assets employed, rather than less visible, but larger, costs such as indirect labor or the cost of poor forecasting or bad managerial decisions. But, as this book has tried to point out (as has much of what has been written recently about TQ) TQ is much more than a vehicle for enhancing manufacturing or, for that matter, products. In fact, it could be argued that it can't truly be *Total* Quality without including the total organization. It is a way to raise the capability of the entire organization. It has only been in the last few years, though, that Total Quality has found its way into nonproduction departments, and that is, by and large, in but a handful of organizations. There are, obviously, exceptions such as Motorola, Ford, and Milliken, but by and large, Total Quality outside of manufacturing has been at the experimental stage in most businesses. One other notable exception is a company in Hutchinson, Minnesota, called Hutchinson Technology Inc. (HTI).

HTI began its Total Quality effort in early 1980s as a way to reduce time and costs, enhance production and design flexibility, and gain greater control of its production processes. The effort was so successful that HTI became a showplace for some of its customers such as IBM. Building on success in manufacturing, HTI's president, Wayne Fortun, spearheaded the effort to bring Total Quality into every area of the company. What has resulted over the past several years can provide both lessons and inspiration for any company anxious to extend Total Quality throughout the organization.

Basically, this approach contends that every department produces products of some kind that other departments in the company use and depend upon. The effort is divided into two phases. In phase I the department defines its products, identifies those other departments or units to whom those products go (these users are called clients), and maps out and measures the processes that produce the products. Phase II involves solving problems to improve processes as well as negotiating with clients to set and track improvement goals. Quality improvement, Just-In-Time, and Organization Development tools are employed as needed to solve problems. It has proven to be a very effective process that while simple in its structure enables large numbers of people from administrative departments to become involved in continuous improvement of work processes.

In addition to manufacturing companies using Total Quality in each department throughout their organization, TQ is on the verge of being applied to other industries. Banks and insurance companies are fertile ground for the customer-oriented, respond-fast, high-employee-involvement, and cost-reduction benefits of Total Quality. Few have experimented to date, perhaps because leaders of those companies see TQ as something for a manufacturing firm that has little application to their industry, perhaps because of a tunnel-vision, not-invented-here attitude.

That will change. The financial institutions in the United States are entering, are in, an era of crisis. The failures of savings and loan associations of the late 1980s as well as the failure of larger institutions such as Bank of New England in 1991 certainly had complicated causes, many structural in the industry itself and its relationship with the government regulatory arms that control it. But, at the same time, equally at fault were the decision-making processes of those institutions, the degree to which dissent and collaboration were encouraged, their ability to innovate and bring new financial products to market, the degree to which they were able to stay flexible and respond in a changing environment, and the ability of various factions and departments to collaborative as a team. While TQ will not be a panacea, it can be applied with benefit to any company in any industry that must become more visible and more customer oriented.

The Missing Element

A third change we will see in the next several years is that Total Quality will include, not merely be for, the customer. A comment was made in Chapter 2 that one thing that separated Total Quality from other, previous organization excellence models was that the customer was added to the equation. Previous efforts were internally focused to the degree that the customer wasn't considered. Total Quality is focused on the customer—in fact, has elevated the customer to the position of preeminent importance. But, even with the necessary addition, the customer remains an object, someone outside of the spotlight, the audience for whom the supplier company is the acting troupe.

A logical extension of Total Quality includes a paradigm that has the customer on the playing field, or to continue the analogy, on the stage. Many companies that have had the most success with TQ are on the verge of developing long-term relationships with their most important customers. Why not build into TQ the phase where the customer takes on some of the characteristics of the partner, the "significant other," who is part of product development strategy sessions, part of strategic planning, or has a role to play in assessing and improving the capabilities of the companies who are its suppliers? Perhaps such a phase could include the supplier working with the customer on how to be more effective at being a customer.

Is such a relationship utopian? Is it unrealistic? Perhaps it is, given our current organizational attitudes and assumptions. At this writing, however, there are examples of customers and their suppliers moving in that direction. If both sides work hard at perfecting the relationship, negotiating in good faith, and if financial results improve as a result, for both parties what are now experiments could become a trend. With the addition of the customer on center stage, we may be ready to move from Total Quality to Total Customer Value. Stay tuned.

Appendixes

Appendix A

Standards for Quality

As a reflection of the growth of the TQ movement and the maturing of development activities, standards are beginning to be refined and accepted. This Appendix summarizes four sets of standards. The Malcolm C. Baldrige National Quality Award, Sematech, the International Standards Organization (ISO), and the Deming Prize.

Baldrige National Quality Award

The Malcolm C. Baldrige National Quality Award was established in 1987 in honor of Malcolm Baldrige, who was the Secretary of Commerce under President Ronald Reagan and died after falling from a horse. The award was generally well thought through and, in particular, well marketed. Large, well-known, well-managed companies were challenged to apply for it and gain from the publicity that would result. It also met the need for simple, easily understandable criteria that helped to take quality out of its statistical, arcane corner. Last, it was geared to top managers; the presidents of the companies that have won the award such as Motorola, Xerox, and Milliken have used the opportunity to establish a visionary platform from which to communicate to both employees and to customers.

There are seven categories by which applicants are judged. Below is a summary of each and the weight it has for the total award.

Leadership (100 points) Examines the senior executives' leadership in creating quality values and incorporating those values into the way their company conducts business. It also examines how the company projects the quality values to the marketplace. Whether or not the company has a Quality department or regulatory affairs office is not considered as part of the evaluation.

This category is divided into four sections:

1. *Senior Executive Leadership* Describes leadership style, personal involvement, and visibility in maintaining an environment for quality excellence.
2. *Quality Values* Summarizes the company's quality values, how they are communicated throughout the company, and how well those values have been adopted and reinforced in the way the company operates.
3. *Management for Quality* Describes how quality values are integrated into day-to-day leadership, management, and supervision of all company units.
4. *Public Responsibility* Describes how the company extends itself to the external community, and includes responsibility for public health, safety, and environmental protection, and also ethical business practices.

Information and Analysis (70 points) Examines the scope, validity, use, and management of data and information that underlie the company's overall quality improvement program. Data, information, and analysis are examined for their adequacy to support a prevention-based approach to quality and customer satisfaction built upon "management by fact."

Strategic Quality Planning (60 points) Examines the company's planning process in achieving or retaining quality leadership and how quality improvement planning is integrated into overall business planning. Short-term or longer-term plans to achieve a quality leadership position are also looked at.

Human Resource Utilization (150 points) Examines the company's effectiveness at developing and utilizing the full potential of its work force, including management, and to maintain an environment that is conducive to full participation, continuous improvement, and personal and organizational growth.

Quality Assurance of Products and Services (140 points)   Examines the statistical and procedural approaches used for designing and producing goods and services based, primarily, upon process design and control. Included here are materials and services purchased from suppliers.

Quality Results (180 points)   Examines the levels of quality improvement based upon objective measures derived from analysis of customers' requirements and expectations and from analysis of business operation.

Customer Satisfaction (300 points)   Examines the company's knowledge of its customers, overall customer service systems, responsiveness, and ability to meet customers' requirements and expectations.

ISO 9000

As Europe moves closer to more interdependence and cooperation among countries, common product standards are being established. Perhaps the most comprehensive is the set of quality standards offered by the International Standards Organization known as the ISO 9000 series (it was also adopted by the European Committee for Standardization and is also known as Euro Norm 29000).

Some Background

The International Organization for Standards is actually an agency made up of the standards groups of 91 countries, and is comprised of about 180 standing technical committees. ISO Technical Committee 176 was formed in 1979 to harmonize increasing international activity and the need for producing products and services of high quality. Two subcommittees were formed, one to agree on common terminology and the second to establish international standards. The standards come under ISO 9000 and were finalized and published in 1987.

The Standards

The set of standards is divided into five subsets.

ISO 9000	The general guidelines for use of the set of standards
ISO 9001	A model for assuring quality in design, development, production, installation, and service of the product
ISO 9002	A complementary model for production and installation
ISO 9003	Specifications for final inspection and testing
ISO 9004	Principal concepts and a guide for overall quality management

The standards also cover how to establish a Total Quality environment by suggesting standards for quality management, for establishing quality policies, and for setting up a quality system. ISO 9000 offers a 10-step process for accreditation.

1. Management education

2. Writing a quality policy
3. Nominating a quality representative
4. Identifying responsibilities
5. Identifying business processes
6. Writing a quality manual
7. Writing procedures
8. Writing work instructions
9. Training in how to use the system
10. Implementation

The European Economic Community is requiring that products be made to ISO 9000 standards and that companies selling products in Europe after January 1, 1993, be accredited according to these standards. There is no law that will force companies to conform in this way, but the expectation is that European customers will require such certification from their suppliers.

Many questions are yet to be answered regarding ISO 9000 and much remains uncertain. A Conference Board briefing on the subject contends that "there are limitations to the standard. It does not define world-class performance in key areas. It has poor focus on the removal of non-value-added activities, and it requires independent personnel for verification. Although applicable to any organization (service and noncommercial included) it was written . . . with manufacturing in mind, and its terminology reflects this bias."[1] It is also not specific on the organizational character changes and leadership requirements necessary to sustain conformance to ISO specifications.

While it may not be complete (work continues on sharpening the set of standards), ISO 9000 is something to be reckoned with for any company wishing to do business in Europe. It also offers yet another set of guidelines and road map for improving customer satisfaction.

Sematech

Sematech is a consortium of American companies, both semiconductor manufacturers and companies that supply them, some 140 companies in all. Its purpose is to revitalize the American semiconductor industry by developing partnering and cooperation between customers and suppliers of the industry as well as enhancing the degree to which the industry can benefit from various resources in research universities (Sematech has funded research programs in universities in 11 states across the United States), and the federal government (namely the Department of Defense).

Sematech was founded in 1987 and by 1989 had decided that Total Quality was an essential vehicle for the resuscitation of the semiconductor industry. It has laid out the journey toward a TQ character as a five-stage trip. Table A.1 lists these stages and criteria for each. Sematech believes these five stages characterize the evolution of quality maturity in an organization. It points out that "organizations often place considerable emphasis on stages 1 to 3 with the mistaken belief that enough pressure on output will bring about desired quality results. However, a focus on continuous improvement . . . is the only path to Total Quality. Generally, movement from stage 3 to stage 4 is the most difficult. . . . (at) stage 5 a company excels and is a significant industry leader."[2]

Table A.1
Five Stages

Stage 1. Short-term Focus
Revenues and budgets are a higher priority than quality.
No mission statement about quality exists.
Little or no quality data are available or used.
Organization does not have a strategic plan or planning process.
Only skill-related, on-the-job training is provided for employees.
Quality of incoming materials is not controlled.
Intuitive design practices are used.
High incidence of scrap and rework exists.
Organizational focus is on meeting acceptable quality levels.
Customer complaints are frequent.

Sales department is the only customer contact.
Repeat business is relatively low.

State 2. Product Focus
Quality is viewed as "meeting specifications."
Quality mission is pass/fail based.
Moderate-to-high scrap and rework.
Organization tracks scrap and rework.
Statistical analysis is used very little or not at all.
Strategic quality plan is short term (<2 years).
Employee involvement in quality activities is selective.
Training is limited to skills.
Incoming inspection and final product inspection occur.
Consistent design methods are lacking.
Quality indicators for products are tracked.
Some customer complaints still exist.
Senior executives meet only key customers.
Organization equates customer satisfaction with meeting
   product quality.

Stage 3. Product and Service Focus
Quality mission is product focused and is an executive priority.
A broad-based internal data-collection activity is in place and
   functioning.
Some statistical analysis is performed.
Financial, product, and product quality plans are long term.
Some quality teams exist.
Job-related and basic-quality training is available for all
   employees.
Supplier qualification and certification programs exist.
Production processes are statistically controlled.
Consistent design practices are used for products.
Low scrap and rework occurs.
Product and service quality indicators are tracked.
Periodic customer surveys determine expectations.
Customer complaints are rare.
Senior executives meet many customers, but sporadically.

Stage 4. Process or System Focus
A senior executive owns Quality, which itself has a high-priority,
   comprehensive mission.

Widespread internal and some external quality data exist.

Consistent statistical analysis and validity procedures are in use.

Effective long and short-term quality plans are based on benchmarking.

Cross-functional quality teams are functioning.

Considerable quality training is available for all employees.

Basic supplier partnering is in place, some expanded partnering exists.

In-line, real-time process control systems are in use.

Analytical design tools are used consistently.

Quality indicators are driven by customer requirements.

Quality improvement trends are clearly visible.

Senior executives drive customer partnering.

Continual, real-time customer input is sought.

An internal and external customer focus is in place.

Stage 5. Continuous Improvement Focus

Employees are completely empowered to fulfill the organization's quality mission.

The organization's quality mission is totally customer driven.

Real-time, statistically valid internal and external data are used.

Quality and business plans are completely integrated and benchmarked to world-class standards.

All employees are members of quality teams.

Positive impact of training programs has been proven.

Expanded partnering exists with all key suppliers.

Continuous improvement and optimization of all processes is occurring.

The total organization is experiencing world-class Total Quality results.

Supply-chain focus supports continuous quality improvement.

Customer needs and services are anticipated.

Products and services are benchmarked against the best competitors.

Deming Award

Edwards Deming, along with Joseph Juran, was instrumental in teaching the Japanese how to manufacture high-quality products. They both began teaching statistical techniques in Japan in the years immediately following World War II. The Deming Award was established in 1951 by the Japanese Union of Scientists and Engineers. 1986 was the first year it allowed companies from other countries to apply. In 1989, Florida Power & Light became the first non-Japanese company to win the prize.

The award places particular emphasis on how the management and control processes support the manufacture of quality products or delivery of services.

The questions examiners ask in making the award are listed below.

- Are all parts of the management system working together to satisfy customer needs?
- Do employees understand how and why the quality-improvement program works?
- Are managers enthusiastic about the quality-improvement program?
- Is the company constantly growing?
- Are employees learning to use Quality Control techniques and participating in the Quality Control teams?
- Do employees support management through the use of quality in daily work?
- Do employees know what policies are important to their department to help achieve planned targets?
- Are the results achieved because of planning—or luck?

Companies that compete for the Deming Prize are asked to prove that they have found a way to institutionalize improvement efforts on a companywide basis. Many Deming Prize winners have permanently adopted rigorous management reviews that are part of the contest-evaluation process.

References

1. Trevor Davis, "European and International Standards for Quality," *Global Perspectives of Total Quality,* Report 958 (New York: The Conference Board, 1991).

2. From "Partnering for Total Quality—A Total Quality Overview," a booklet prepared by Sematech, Austin, Texas, 1990.

Appendix B

Elements of Total Quality Efforts

Quality Technical Tools

Below are summaries of technical tools and techniques largely from Quality Engineering:

Design of Experiments A procedure to discover the conditions which cause variability. Genichi Taguchi tried to take it a step farther by figuring out a way ("orthogonal arrays") to handle many variables all at once and get quickly to the point of establishing correct tolerances for design production.[*]

Flow Charts Charts that depict the flow of the product or piece of information through its various steps and phases.

Pareto Analysis Borrowed from the distribution of wealth theory of the Italian economist of the same name who pointed out that 20% of the population controlled 80% of the wealth in Italy. As it is used in quality engineering, it is a method to analyze data so that the vital few causes (usually 20%) are identified which bring about 80% of the effect. Pareto charts use bar diagrams to depict those causes by listing causes on the X-axis and number of or percentage of occurrences on the Y-axis.

---

[*]There are, though, some disagreements as to the full validity of Taguchi's method; see "An Interview with Dorian Shanin" in *Quality Digest,* July 1990 and K. Bhote, *World Class Quality* (New York: American Management Association, 1988).

Cause and Effect Diagrams Also called a fishbone or an Ishikawa Diagram, it is a way to distinguish effects from their causes and to narrow the range of possible root causes; once this range of possible root causes is determined, problem solving can begin. The element producing most of the problem (discovered from Pareto analysis) is made the "backbone" of a fishbone chart. Then, one determines the vital few contributing causes and connects to the "backbone" the secondary causes producing the element representing the backbone. The sources of each of these secondary causes are determined and they are listed as third-level "bones." The bones are then prioritized and experiments are conducted to reduce or eliminate them.

Histograms/Frequency Distributions A histogram is a bar graph to translate information from such procedures as Pareto analysis to show variability. Frequency distributions are line diagrams helpful in clarifying large amounts of data.

Control Charts These charts determine whether any particular process is in control once variation has been reduced through design of experiments. Also called "X-bar and R" charts ($\bar{X}$ standing for average and R for range), they merely tell if the process is within certain limits of tolerance. They are more precise than frequency distributions because they show trends over time and can distinguish the kinds of variations of the process. They can be cumbersome and, often, precontrol will produce the same results in a much shorter time.

Precontrol A procedure for a line operator to determine when to sample, precontrol allows much less sampling and involves fewer steps than control charts while maintaining statistical validity. Like control charts, it merely indicates when a process is outside tolerable limits, thereby triggering action such as design of experiments and problem solving.

Quality Function Deployment A relatively new procedure for product development that starts with asking the customer what is desired in a product. Those replies are recorded and matched with product characteristics in a matrix form. It also reflects the priority customers give to certain product features. QFD, as it is commonly known, is one of a handful of tools now being applied to enhance design and improve manufacturability since it forces design engineers and production managers to work together to think through what the product will look like and how it will perform.

Process Capability Analysis   A procedure that graphically displays the degree to which the process used to make a product is in control. It is a way to measure variability and typically shows the limits of what is expected (the specification limits) compared to how the process actually behaves. If the process behaves in a way that it exceeds the specification limits, variability is too great and the process is considered to be out of control.

SPC/SQC Education

The pages that follow outline a basic Statistical Process Control education course. This is not intended to be a recommended design for every situation. It is a program delivered by specially trained professionals and is presented here to offer an idea of the content of such a program.

Terms used may not be entirely familiar but many are explained briefly in the Appendix on quality technical tools. The bibliography also offers other sources of information. It is not the purpose of this book to educate readers in the use of statistics to solve problems, that has been done admirably by others better equipped than I for the task. The point of offering this course synopsis is merely to give the reader an idea of the structure, the flow, and the content of such an educational event. Ten "units" are summarized in this outline. It is typical for the design of the course to be tailored to meet the educational and time demands of those who are to participate, perhaps in four-hour segments conducted once per week or in segments of one full day, several shorter segments, then another full day.

Statistical Quality Control Seminar
Unit 1

At the conclusion of this unit, participants will be able to fulfill the following objectives:

1. Explain the concept of Statistical Process Control (SPC) and its purpose (what it does and doesn't do).
2. Explain why there is a requirement to implement SPC, especially at manufacturing locations.
3. Explain that SPC is a collection of tools that can help bring about quality improvement in manufacturing processes and list some of those tools.
4. State the course objectives.
5. Cite the basic course outline and schedule and refer to the Table of Contents in the course participant's manual for detailed guidance.
6. Explain how SQC/SPC techniques help achieve the objectives.

Unit 2

At the conclusion of this unit, participants will be able to:

1. Define random variation and recognize, in a classroom example, the difference between common cause and special causes.

2. List the six primary categories of variation in processes.

3. List the three major types of processes that are utilized in manufacturing and state the differences in sampling frequencies required by these three types of processes.

4. State the fundamental principles and list the basic elements of control charts.

5. List the purposes, risks, and associated costs of using control charts.

6. Give three examples of common and special causes variation related to your job.

Unit 3

At the conclusion of this unit, participants will be able to:

1. State the primary purpose of an X-chart.

2. Describe X and MR (moving range) charts, the nature and purpose of their center line and control limits, and define moving range.

3. State the reason for using the two charts together and list the assumptions made when using these charts.

4. Construct an X chart and MR chart, calculate and enter control chart limits and center line using data provided by the instructor.

5. Correctly interpret observations in relation to control limits.

Unit 4

At the conclusion of this unit, participants will be able to:

1. Explain how Pareto analysis can be used as a process variable selection tool.

2. Perform a Pareto analysis based on data provided by the instructor.

3. Use a "fishbone diagram" to relate sources and sub-sources of variation that are present in a process to their influence on process outputs.

4. Use the input/output model and flow charting to identify process variables that may require additional control.

5. Use a case study to select variables which would be candidates for the use of X and MR control charts.

Unit 5

At the conclusion of this unit, participants will be able to:

1. State the purpose of the X-bar and s control charts and the difference in purpose from the X and MR charts.

2. List the nature and purpose of the center line and control limits of the X-Bar and s control charts.

3. Explain the reason for using the X-bar and s control charts together.

4. Describe the range (R) chart method and its suitability for controlling process variation.

5. Calculate control limits for X-bar and s charts.

6. Correctly interpret observations in relation to control limits using the charted X-bar and s charts.

Unit 6

At the conclusion of this unit, participants will be able to:

1. State that the CUSUM control chart is more sensitive than the X-bar or the Individual X chart for detecting mean shifts when a special cause may have occurred.

2. List and discuss CUSUM chart applications to your job or company processes in general.

3. Explain why a moving range chart is used with the CUSUM control chart.

4. Calculate the limits for the "V-mask" (template) used for the detection of the process shifts and create a V-mask for a CUSUM chart.

5. Draw and interpret CUSUM charts using individual (X) measurements from a given set of data.

6. State that CUSUM methods can be applied to sample means (*X*-bar).

7. Identify processes and process variables where CUSUM methods are appropriate to the participant's job function.

8. Be aware that there are modifications and enhancements to CUSUM methods and their sources, particularly decision interval and fast initial response methods.

9. Be aware that CUSUM methods are useful for monitoring processes where the target is changing.

Unit 7
At the conclusion of this unit, participants will be able to:

1. State the primary purpose of discrete distribution charts.

2. State the purpose of each type of discrete distribution chart.

3. Establish center lines and control limits for a "*p*" distribution chart.

4. Identify types of processes and situations where these control methods may be applicable to the participant's job function and to company operations generally.

5. State the assumptions upon which discrete distribution charts are based.

6. Be aware of the formulas for center lines and control limits for *np*, *c*, and *u* charts.

Unit 8
At the conclusion of this unit, participants will be able to:

1. Explain the meaning of Process Capability and calculate the Process Capability Number.

2. Calculate the C_p, C_{pk}, and C_r, capability indexes.

3. Explain why different indexes are used and the conditions which must exist in order to use them.

4. Quantify the capability of processes for multiple independent product variables.

5. Correctly interpret the indices.

6. Calculate the fraction off-specifications, given C_p, or C_{pk}.

7. Calculate C_{pk} given a fraction off-specifications.

Unit 9

At the conclusion of this unit, participants will be able to:

1. Identify potential outliers.

2. Use existing data to test for normality and state some possible transformations for treating nonnormal distributions of process measurements.

3. Use existing data to perform tests for independence.

4. Estimate necessary statistical parameters of the process variables, identify when reestimation is necessary and ensure a capability for statistical estimation.

5. Cite examples of how techniques in this UNIT apply to your job function.

Unit 10

At the conclusion of this unit, participants will be able to:

1. List the basic steps in implementing an SPC system.

2. Explain how the tools and skills presented in this course relate to these basic steps.

3. Prepare and present a plan for implementing an SPC system in your current job function that includes responsibilities, schedule, training, and software and hardware requirements.

A Typical TQ Awareness Session

1 DAY

8:00 A.M.   **Introduction**
- Objectives and Expectations
- Agenda

8:20 A.M.   **TQ Overview**
- History of TQ
- How It Has Been Developed
- Typical Results

10:00 A.M.   **Break**

10:15 A.M.   **The Customer**
- The Essential Reason
- Customer Values and Expectations
- The Employee as Customer

12:00 P.M.   **Break**

1:30 P.M.   **TQ Tools and Techniques**
- Quality Engineering
- Just-In-Time
- Organization Development
- Training and Education Programs

3:30 P.M.   **Break**

3:45 P.M.   **Implementing Total Quality**
- Steps in the Implementation Process
- Do's and Don't's
- Roles and Responsibilities

5:30 P.M.   **Wrap-up**

6:00 P.M.   **End**

Just-In-Time Technical Tools

Below is a brief description of Just-In-Time and then of some of the more common JIT techniques.

Just-In-Time (JIT)

JIT is both a philosophy and a strategy. The philosophy emphasizes several principles that are fundamentally different from traditional practice and conventional wisdom. Among them is the relentless elimination of waste in all aspects of the enterprise. Waste is defined as anything that does not add value to the product (a definition first offered by Ed Hay who at the time was at Bendix Corporation). Storing something, for example, does not add value, which is the primary reason that JIT attacks inventory.

The Japanese were the first to combine the various elements we now refer to as Just-In-Time. Its elements were first applied in manufacturing and achieved truly astounding gains when implemented in the appropriate way: 89% reduction in work in process inventory, 90% in finished goods, 75% to 94% reduction in setup time, 50% improvement in direct labor productivity, and 60% improvement for indirect labor. When applied to purchasing, gains have been achieved of 50% reduction in purchased price.

As some pioneers learned to implement JIT in the United States in the early 1980s, it became apparent that while JIT could achieve improvements in most any situation, its gains were the most impressive and lasting when the process by which the product was made was predictable and when the organization climate supports teamwork.

Pull Systems A scheduling and planning technique that links production processes to customer demand. It does so as simply as possible, often through the use of cards or some other signal which shows that the department, station, or work center has completed its part of the production process and is ready for another part or subassembly from its supplier. When done throughout the entire operation, the product should be made in one-at-a-time fashion, thereby better ensuring both synchronization throughout and also better quality since each part can be seen clearly and mistakes are not hidden by producing and storing the product in batches.

Pull systems must be used in combination with other elements of the JIT strategy—setup reduction, establishment of work centers, and process improvement, in particular.

Work Centers A layout technique that groups operations and/or machines so that a family of parts can be produced and/or assembled in the same physical location. Essential to the creation of so-called focused factories, this technique is often referred to as group technology. Long before the advent of JIT, though, group technology meant the grouping of part numbers in a particular way to facilitate costing, production, and inventory control.

Setup Reduction A methodology to dramatically reduce the time it takes to replace a die or otherwise change over a machine when it is required to make a different (or a different size) product. When done well, time savings of at least 75% should be realized without spending money for new parts or machines; and these results can often be achieved relatively quickly. The sorts of changes that can produce these dramatic results are largely mechanical and procedural and require that people change habits that have developed and been passed down over time. The key to unlock this potential is that the people who are most involved in the setup activity must be involved in analyzing current practices and in discovering new ways to accomplish this common task in a fraction of the current time; then they must be empowered to experiment and make the changes they deem necessary.

Setups (also called changeovers) are one major cause of high work-in-process inventory and excessive lead times in manufacturing plants. A setup provides a perfect opportunity for pilot projects as part of a TQ effort since it meets the criteria for pilots—an opportunity for employees to be involved in attaining dramatic results quickly by using new techniques.

Value-Added Flow Analysis An analytical technique that separates steps in any process that add value from those that do not. Among the JIT rules Rath & Strong developed in the mid 1980s were the "3% to 20% rule" and the "1/2 of 1% rule." The former said that in any process, whether production in a factory or information in an office, from 3% to 20% of the steps in the process will add value. The second rule says that those 3% to 20% of the steps will happen less than 1/2 of 1% of the time.

Value-added flow analysis is the diagnostic protocol that pinpoints both the percentage of value-added steps as well as the time taken up by both the value-added and, in particular, the non-value-added steps. To reduce time as part of a strategy of becoming more competitive, reduce or eliminate non-value-added steps.

Drumbeat Also referred to as uniform plant loading in some manufacturing applications of JIT, Drumbeat is the set of techniques to ensure uniform scheduling of the product through the process of making it. An analogy used in JIT's early days was a convoy of trucks racing down a highway, only a few feet apart. Drumbeat is independent of whether the sales forecast is accurate because it seeks to reduce the time horizon for scheduling. It does not require a complicated production schedule but does require communication and coordination as plans are set for what to make and when to make it.

Opportunity Analysis A diagnostic technique pinpointing physical, technical, and financial opportunities can realistically be achieved through a TQ effort. It is from opportunity analysis that quantitative measures of success should come. Usually included in an opportunity analysis is a value-added flow analysis (VAFA) to assess the degree to which each step in any process adds value for the customer who is supposed to benefit from the processes' output.

Just-In-Time Purchasing In the average company in the West, 70% of its costs are purchased material and components. Because of this the company serious about TQ must ensure that its suppliers are as flexible, responsive, customer oriented, and as much a part of the team as possible. That's where JIT purchasing comes in. Originally called "Systems Contracting," developed by Ernie Anderson[1] in 1957, JIT purchasing seeks to establish a different relationship between the supplier and the company to whom it is supplying something, one that is long term and of mutual benefit. It typically involves dramatically reducing the number of suppliers (contrary to the traditional notion that having more suppliers offers better nego-tiating leverage on price and safety in case one supplier shuts down) to only one or a few of the best companies who are judged to be best able to ship parts or supplies "just-in-time" and of flawless quality. The supplier and the company to whom it sells goods or services then work together to help ensure the supplier is operating in the best possible way, largely by solving problems inside the supplier company to eliminate waste and maximize flexibility.[2]

Management and Leadership Tools

Listed below are management and leadership tools useful in various phases of the TQ effort. These have been shown through experience to be useful mechanisms by which the TQ effort can have positive impact on the organization's culture.

Climate Survey A survey of employees that is analyzed particularly to determine the impact of the work environment on the motivation and satisfaction of employees. The survey can be done through a questionnaire, focus group interviews, or a combination.

Task Team Training Ad hoc groups of employees are formed to work on a pilot or other problem-solving or data-gathering task. Groups disband when the tasks assigned to them have been completed. Typically, group size ranges from 5 to 10 people. The training should cover such topics as individual learning styles and their impact on group problem solving, principles of small group decision making, interpersonal skills such as listening with understanding, principles of individual motivation, and change management. It should also include planning tasks such as the charter of the group and the path by which it will achieve the tasks it has been assigned.

Common Vision Workshop A workshop for leaders where a vision is clarified of the sort of company they wish to create through Total Quality. It typically lasts for two to three days and depending on the situation may include a second off-site meeting. Part of the workshop should include the clarification of the group's values, the basic beliefs on which they wish to build a stronger, better company. These should be reflected in "stakes-in-the-ground," or the principles that will form the basis for the TQ effort. The essence of the workshop should be a set of descriptive statements that describe what will be seen and heard, and how it will feel to work in the best possible TQ environment for that particular company or unit. This format is equally applicable for the leadership team of a company or for a department management team faced with the task of creating a radically different place.

Gainsharing   A form of bonus or incentive that distributes gains made (usually productivity gains) equally among workers and management, gain sharing provides the feature of enabling all employees to participate. It has been used successfully to replace individual or group incentive systems, which are somewhat antithetical to TQ because they encourage individual competition and typically reward speed of output at the expense of quality.

Steering Committee Training   The training program for the group assigned the charge of leading the TQ effort or a significant portion of it should cover both the interpersonal and small group aspects of teamwork since a major ingredient in its success will be the ability of this group to work together as a team. It should also include ways to help the group devise a specific, realistic, measurable, and time-phased plan for carrying out the effort. Unlike a task team, the steering committee will exist through several phases of the TQ effort (which could span two to four years) until the line organization assumes full responsibility.

Awareness Sessions   Brief (usually half-day to one-and-one-half-day), focused sessions for various employee populations that outline what TQ is and the principles of making it successful. Rather than a detailed education session, the awareness session should describe the basics of the TQ movement, where it came from, what it seeks to achieve, the principles on which it is based and the general ingredients of an effort to implement it. It should be tailored to the needs of each group by including examples with which participants are familiar.

Team-Building Training   Off-site workshops, usually conducted for natural work groups (a boss and direct reports) to build strong interpersonal bonds and improve their ability to work as a team. Typically included are ways for each person to learn more about his or her interpersonal style and its impact on others, ways to clarify roles that each team member must play, ways to facilitate feedback and open communication within the team, and ways to clarify a model of teamwork toward which the group can move. Unlike some other forms of training, team building works best when it is done regularly; some of the best teams will meet off site several times a year to concentrate on and try to sharpen teamwork.

Problem-Solving/Decision-Making Skills Training
The major benefit of training in the methods and methodology of problem solving and decision making is often the establishment of a common language. This facilitates communication in task teams made up of people from different disciplines who have been trained differently (people from Engineering, Sales, Human Resources, Finance, and so forth) and enables them to achieve results more easily. Usually included is a general model for problem solving in any situation, along with exercises, cases, and similar ways to practice problem-solving and decision-making skills.

Facilitator Training A two- to three-day session prepares employees to facilitate task team and other ad hoc or standing committee meetings. Included typically are segments on meeting management, small group decision making, and interpersonal and influence skills. Because TQ leads to more meetings, facilitators can often make meetings productive rather than a waste of time.

Internal Consultant Training and Trainer Training
In addition to facilitation at meetings, there will be a need for two other types of helpers as a TQ effort matures: trainers and consultants. Internal trainers are employees who have been trained to deliver certain programs such as task team training. Internal consultants are employees who have been trained to counsel, to analyze, to help plan, and to troubleshoot. A hierarchy of skills and complexity would show facilitating, then training, then, at the most complex level, consulting. Trainer training usually requires that the employee attend a session of the type he or she will be learning to deliver, then to go through 7 to 10 days of special preparation on the theory and practice of adult learning, and finally to co-train that program before being certified. Consultant training is more complex and takes longer, often two or three workshops, attending an outside workshop, and regular counsel from an external consultant.

Often, trainer training and consultant training are excellent preparation for employees to take on greater management responsibility.

Era Management   An era (in business terms) is a period of time when the conditions under which the business operates stay more or less the same. Changes in eras can be marked by a top management change, a significant market change, the introduction of a blockbuster new product, or similar event that could alter the fortunes of the enterprise. After specifying the appropriate time frame for the emerging era (usually 18 to 36 months), this methodology helps the leader design a personal road map through which he or she will alter the organization's character through TQ. It defines major themes, identifies A-items, or superordinate priorities to be achieved over that time frame, and defines the events that can achieve them in the appropriate sequence.[3]

References

1. See E. Hay, *The Just-In-Time Breakthrough* (New York: Wiley, 1988).

2. An excellent case study is available from *Purchasing* magazine, which in 1985 awarded Xerox its Medal of Professional Excellence.

3. See D. Ciampa, *Manufacturing's New Mandate* (New York: Wiley, 1989).

Bibliography

The lists that follow offer works that will provide useful addendums as well as additional and/or different thoughts on the various important categories of the basis of Total Quality. It is not intended to be exhaustive.

Just-In-Time

Blackburn, J. *Time Based Competition* (Homewood, IL: R. D. Irwin, 1991).

Fukuda, R. *Managerial Engineering* (Stamford, CT: Productivity, 1983).

Hall, R. *Attaining Manufacturing Excellence* (Homewood, IL: Dow Jones Irwin, 1987).

Hay, E. *The Just-In-Time Breakthrough* (New York: Wiley & Sons, 1988).

Moody, P. *Strategic Manufacturing* (Homewood, IL: Dow Jones Irwin, 1990).

Schonberger, R. *Japanese Manufacturing Techniques* (New York: Free Press, 1982).

—— *World Class Manufacturing* (New York: Free Press, 1986).

Shingo, S. *Study of Toyota Production Systems* (Tokyo: Japan Management ASC, 1981).

Leadership

Bennis, W., and B. Nanns. *Leaders* (New York: Harper & Row, 1985).

Ciampa, D. *Manufacturing's New Mandate* (New York: Wiley & Sons, 1988).

Gardner, J. *Leadership Papers 1–4* (Washington, DC: Independent Sector, 1986).

George, A. *Presidential Decision Making in Foreign Policy* (Boulder, CO: Westview Press, 1980).

Kotter, J. *The Leadership Factor* (New York: Free Press, 1988).

Kouzes J., and P. Posner. *The Leadership Challenge* (San Francisco: Jossey-Bass, 1987).

Maccoby, M. *The Leader* (New York: Ballantine Books, 1981).

Marrow, A. *Behind the Executive Mask* (New York: American Management Association, 1964).

Schein, E. *Organizational Culture and Leadership* (San Francisco: Jossey-Bass, 1985).

Senge, P. *The Fifth Discipline* (New York: Doubleday, 1990).

Quinn, J. *Strategic Change* (Homewood, IL: R. D. Irwin 1980).

Zaleznick, A. *The Managerial Mistique* (New York: Harper & Row, 1989).

Manufacturing

Bluestone, B., and B. Harrison. *The DeIndustrialization of America* (New York: Basic Books, 1982).

Dertouzos, R., R. Lester, and R. Solow. *Made in America* (Cambridge, MA: MIT Press, 1989).

Harrington, J. *Understanding the Manufacturing Process* (New York: M. Dekker, 1984).

Hayes, R., et al. *Dynamic Manufacturing* (New York: Free Press, 1988).

Johnson, H., and R. Kaplan. *Relevance Lost—the Rise and Fall of Management Accounting* (Boston: Harvard Business School Press, 1987).

National ASC of Accountants. *Meeting the Technology Challenge: Cost Accounting in a JIT Environment* (Montvale, NJ: NAA, 1988).

National Center for Manufacturing Sciences. *Competing in World Class Manufacturing* (Homewood, IL: R. D. Irwin, 1990).

Stalk, G., and T. Hout. *Competing Against Time* (New York: Free Press, 1990).

General

Davis, S. *Future Perfect* (Reading, MA: Addison-Wesley, 1987).

Mokyr, J. *The Lever of Riches* (Oxford University Press, 1990).

Nayak, P., and J. Ketteringham. *Breakthroughs* (Cambridge, MA: A. D. Little, 1986).

Ohmae, K. *The Mind of the Strategist* (New York: McGraw-Hill, 1982).

Von Bertalanffy, L. *General Systems Theory* (New York: G. Braziller, 1968).

Quality

Bhote, K. *World Class Quality* (New York: American Management Association, 1988).

Deming, W. E. *Out of the Crisis* (Cambridge, MA: MIT Press, 1986).

Feigenbaum, A. *Total Quality Control* (New York: McGraw-Hill, 1983).

Garvin, D. *Managing Quality* (New York: Free Press, 1988).

Groocock, J. *The Chain of Quality* (New York: Wiley & Sons, 1986).

Guaspari, J. *I Know It When I See It* (New York: American Management Association, 1985).

—— *The Customer Connection* (New York: American Management Association, 1988).

Ishikawa, K. *Guide to Quality Control* (White Plains, NY: Asian Productivity Organization & Quality Resources, 1982).

Juran, J. *Juran on Planning for Quality* (New York: Free Press, 1988).

—— *Juran on Leadership for Quality* (New York: Free Press, 1989).

King, B. *Better Decisions in Half the Time: Implementing QFD* (Lawrence, MA: GOAL/QPC, 1987).

Tufte, E. *Envisioning Information* (Cheshire, CT: Graphics Press, 1990).

Walsh, L., et al. *Quality Management Handbook* (New York: Dekker, 1986).

Organization Development

Alinsky, S. *Rules for Radicals* (New York: Random House, 1971).

Beck, A., and E. Hillmar. *A Practical Approach to Organization Development Through MBO* (Reading, MA: Addison-Wesley, 1972).

Beckhard, R. *Organization Development: Strategies and Models* (Reading, MA: Addison-Wesley, 1969).

Bennis, W. *Organization Development: Nature and Origins* (Reading, MA: Addison-Wesley, 1969).

Bennis, W., W. Benne, and R. Chin. *The Planning of Change* (New York: Holt, Rinehart and Winston, 1970).

Bennis, W. G., et al. *Interpersonal Dynamics* (Homewood, IL: Dorsey Press, 1973).

Bennis, W., and J. Slater. *The Temporary Society* (New York: Harper & Row, 1968).

Blake, R., and J. Mouton. *The Managerial Grid* (New York: Gulf, 1964).

Bradford, L., J. Gibb, and K. Benne. *T Group Therapy and The Laboratory Method* (New York: Wiley, 1964).

Dalton, G., P. R. Lawrence, and J. N. Lorsch. *Organization Structure and Design* (Homewood, IL: Irwin Dorsey, 1970).

Deal, T., and A. Kennedy. *Corporate Cultures* (Reading, MA: Addison-Wesley, 1982).

Etzioni, A. *Modern Organizations* (Englewood Cliffs, NJ: Prentice-Hall, 1964).

Fitz-Enz, J. *Human Value Management* (San Francisco: Jossey-Bass, 1990).

Herzberg, F., B. Mausner, and B. Snyderman. *The Motivation to Work* (New York: Wiley, 1959).

Jay, A. *Management and Machiavelli* (New York: Holt, Rinehart and Winston, 1967).

Kepner, C., and B. Tregoe. *The Rational Manager* (New York: McGraw-Hill, 1965).

Knowles, M. *The Modern Practice of Adult Education* (New York: Association Press, 1970).

Lawrence, P. R., and J. N. Lorsch. *Organization and Environment* (Harvard Press, 1967).

―――― *Developing Organizations* (Reading, MA: Addison-Wesley, 1969).

Lynton, R., and U. Pareek. *Training for Development* (Homewood, IL: Irwin Dorsey, 1967).

Mahler, W. *Diagnostic Studies* (Reading, MA: Addison-Wesley, 1974).

Marrow, A. J. *Making Waves in Foggy Bottom* (Washington, DC: NTL Institute, 1974).

Maslow, A. *Motivation and Personality* (New York: Harper & Row, 1970).

McClelland, D. *The Achieving Society* (New York: Van Nostrand, 1961).

McGregor, D. *The Human Side of Enterprise* (New York: McGraw-Hill, 1960).

Nylen, Mitchell, and Stout. *Handbook of Staff Development and HR Training Materials Developed for Use in Africa* (Washington, DC: NTL Institute, 1967).

Prince, G. *The Practice of Creativity* (New York: Harper & Row, 1970).

Quinn, J. B. *Strategies for Change* (Homewood, IL: R. D. Irwin, 1980).

Rogers, C. *Client Centered Therapy* (Boston: Houghton Mifflin, 1951).

Russell, B. *Authority and the Individual* (Boston: Beacon Press, 1963).

Schein, E. *Organizational Culture and Leadership* (San Francisco: Jossey-Bass, 1985).

―――― *Process Consultation.* 2d ed. (Reading, MA: Addison-Wesley, 1988).

Seller, J. *Systems Analysis in Organization Behavior* (Homewood, IL: Irwin Dorsey, 1967).

Sloan, A. *My Years with General Motors* (Garden City: NY: Doubleday, 1963).

Tagiuri, R., and G. Litwin. *Organization Climate* (Harvard Press, 1968).

Employee Involvement

Apcar, M. "Middle Managers and Supervisors Resist Moves to More Participatory Management." *Wall Street Journal,* September 16, 1985.

Bean, A., C. Ordowich, and W. Westley. "Including the Supervisor in Employee Involvement Efforts." *National Productivity Review* (Winter 1985-86).

Carrington, J. "Does Management Owe the Supervisor Promotional Opportunity?" *Personnel Journal* (June 1969).

Drucker, P. "Twilight of the First-Line Supervisor?" *Wall Street Journal* (June 7, 1983).

Hackman, J., and G. Oldham. *Work Redesign* (Reading, MA: Addison-Wesley, 1980).

Klein, J. "First-Line Supervisory Reactions and Accommodations to Worker Involvement Programs." Unpublished Ph.D. dissertation, Massachusetts Institute of Technology, Sloan School of Management, Cambridge, MA, September 1983.

—— "Why Supervisors Resist Employee Involvement." *Harvard Business Review* (September-October 1984).

—— "First-Line Supervisor and Shop Floor Involvement." In T. Kochan and T. Burocci, eds., *Human Resource Management and Industrial Relations* (Boston: Little, Brown, 1985).

—— "The Development of Manufacturing Managers for the Future." Harvard Business School Case 0-686-048, 1985.

Klein, J., and P. Posey. "Traditional Versus New Work Systems Supervision: Is There a Difference?" Harvard Business School Working Paper 1-786-036, April 1986.

Levine, H. "The Squeeze on Middle Management." *Personnel* (January 1986).

Roethlisberger, F. "The Foreman: Master and Victim of Double Talk." *Harvard Business Review* (Spring 1945).

Schlesinger, L. *Quality of Worklife and the Supervisor* (New York: Praeger, 1982).

Schlesinger, L., and B. Oshry. "Quality of Work Life and the Manager: Muddle in the Middle." *Organizational Dynamics* (Summer 1984).

Walton, R., and L. Schlesinger. "Do Supervisors Thrive in Participative Work Systems?" *Organizational Dynamics* (Summer 1984).

Weir, M., and S. Mills. "The Supervisor as a Change Catalyst." *Industrial Relations Journal* 4, no. 4 (Winter 1973).

Zemke, Ron. "The Case of the Missing Managerial Malaise." *Training* (November 1985).